The Cardinals

*Thirteen Centuries of the Men
Behind the Papal Throne*

Michael Walsh

WILLIAM B. EERDMANS PUBLISHING COMPANY
GRAND RAPIDS, MICHIGAN / CAMBRIDGE, U.K.

First published 2010 in the U.K. by the Canterbury Press Norwich
Editorial office, 13–17 Long Lane, London, EC1A 9PN, UK
www.scm-canterburypress.co.uk

This edition published 2011 in the United States of America by
Wm. B. Eerdmans Publishing Co.
2140 Oak Industrial Drive N.E., Grand Rapids, Michigan 49505 /
P.O. Box 163, Cambridge CB3 9PU U.K.
www.eerdmans.com

Printed in the United States of America

15 14 13 12 11   7 6 5 4 3 2 1

Library of Congress Cataloging-in-Publication Data

Walsh, Michael J., 1937–
The cardinals: Thirteen centuries of the men behind the papal throne / Michael Walsh.
p.   cm.
"First published 2010 in the U.K. by the Canterbury Press Norwich."
Includes bibliographical references and index.
ISBN 978-0-8028-2941-2 (pbk.: alk. paper)
1. Cardinals — Biography. 2. Catholic Church — Clergy — Biography.
3. Catholic Church — History.
I. Title.
BX4664.3.W35 2011
270.092′2 — dc22
[B]
2010045207

Contents

A Note to the Reader

When I was approached to write this book I was, at almost the same time, asked to revise the *Oxford Dictionary of Popes*. I believed at the time that the *Dictionary* would help inform this collection of lives of the cardinals; I therefore undertook that one first. I have come to the conclusion that I was mistaken: the lives of the cardinals frequently illuminate the lives of the popes, much more so than vice versa. So my apologies to the publishers of this volume for keeping them waiting.

I have not footnoted the lives, though it should be clear from the bibliography which books have been used. On the other hand, I have chosen to footnote the introductory chapter. When I explained to those who asked what I was writing about, I realized that many knew very little about the office of cardinal, so in the first chapter I have attempted to supply a resource for enquirers as well as an introduction to this book.

The Cardinals was inspired by Trevor Beeson's *The Bishops*, published to considerable acclaim in 2002. I can only hope this volume does half as well, but as readers of both will swiftly discover, the lives of cardinals of the Roman Church do not have a great deal in common with the lives of bishops of the Church of England.

Introduction

The office of cardinal is a well-known function in the Roman Catholic Church. Many countries have a cardinal as the head, officially or unofficially, of the Church in that region. In some countries with large Catholic populations there may be several cardinals (in Brazil, for example, or the United States of America). In the Vatican they head most of the various 'ministries' – the accepted name is 'dicasteries' – through which the Catholic Church worldwide is governed. They come into their own most obviously when a pope dies and someone else has to be elected in his place: it is a long time, getting on for seven centuries, since the man chosen to be pope was not himself among the ranks of the cardinals. They are, in other words, a highly visible part of the ecclesiastical furniture, especially since twentieth-century popes have been creating rather a lot of them.

Given their numbers and their prominence, it is surprising how little has been written about cardinals, at least in English, in recent years. As John Broderick SJ commented three-quarters of a century ago, 'Despite the importance of the Sacred College, an adequate, modern, scholarly synthesis of its history remains as desideratum.'[1] On the other hand, quite a few books have been published on the cardinals' most significant function, the conclave in which a pope is elected,[2] and as the bibliography to this book bears witness, there is a plethora of biographies of individual cardinals. But of general histories in English I can find only one, *The Papal Princes* by Glenn D. Kittler,[3] a work of pious devotion to the Holy See rather than a critical discussion of the role of the 'papal

---

1 John F. Broderick, 'The Sacred College of Cardinals: Size and Geographical Composition', *Archivum Historiae Pontificiae* 25 (1987), pp. 7–71. The quotation is on p. 7.

2 For example, Frederic J. Baumgartner, *Behind Locked Doors* (New York: Palgrave Macmillan, 2003); John L. Allen, *Conclave* (New York: Doubleday, 2002); Francis A. Burkle-Young, *Passing the Keys* (Lanham MD: Madison Books, 1999); Michael J. Walsh, *The Conclave: A Sometimes Secret and Occasionally Bloody History* (London: Canterbury Press, 2003). One of the best modern studies is in Italian: Giancarlo Zizola, *Il Conclave: Storia e Segreti* (Rome: Newton Compton, 1993).

3 New York: Dell Publishing, 1961. It contains, however, a rare description of the archaic and arcane ceremony by which a cardinal acceded to his new office, pp. 323–7.

princes'. There is a highly fanciful, not to say romantic, account of the origins of the cardinalate, according to which in times of persecution

> The Christian community found itself relying increasingly on a group of men who knew their way around Rome, who knew which Romans would help them and which would not, which could be trusted and which could not. Their ability to open and close influential or threatening doors gave rise to a nickname: they were called hinge-men. The Roman word for 'hinge' was *cardo*.[4]

Kittler is right at least in this: it is generally agreed[5] that the origins of the term 'cardinal' is *cardo*, the Latin for hinge. In a much-quoted passage, Leo IX (1049–54), writing to the Patriarch of Constantinople, describes the pope himself as the hinge or pivot on which the Church turns, but goes on to say that his chief assistants are rightly called cardinals because they are linked to the hinge. Stephan Kuttner[6] has shown that the term was originally applied to clergy who were appointed to serve a church other than the one for which they were originally ordained. They were 'incardinated', presumably 'hinged on to', their new position – a term still used in the Catholic Church for a priest who permanently moves to a new diocese.

The term 'incardinatus' is first found in a letter of Pope Gelasius (492–6) to a bishop Celestine, where it seems to describe a bishop who is in charge of a church other than the one for which he had originally been consecrated. A bishop who has been incardinated has more authority than one who is just visiting. In other words, he has taken over the office of ordinary. It has to be remembered that at this period, and for a long time afterwards, it was not regarded as legitimate that a bishop should change his diocese. Even at the end of the ninth century it was one of the charges against Pope Formosus in the infamous 'synod of the cadaver' that he had violated the canons forbidding a bishop to transfer from one diocese to another. In the cases written about by Gelasius, Gregory the Great (590–604) and others, it seems that the bishop being 'incardinated' had been driven from his own diocese by invading armies of one sort or another. So common was this situation that model letters appointing bishops in these circumstances were included in the *Liber Diurnus*, a collection of formularies first compiled at the end of the eighth, or the beginning of the ninth, century but containing much older material. A

---

4 Op. cit., p. 19.

5 Michel Andrieu, 'L'origine du titre de cardinal dans l'église romaine', in *Miscellanea Giovanni Mercati* V (Città de Vaticano, 1946), p. 113.

6 Cf. Stephan Kuttner, '*Cardinalis*: The history of a canonical concept', *Traditio* 3 (1945), pp. 129–214. The reference is at p. 176.

person so incardinated was a 'cardinalis': 'The adjective *cardinalis* is therefore a synonym for *incardinatus* and means belonging, through incorporation, into a particular religious centre.'[7]

This interpretation has not gone unchallenged. According to an alternative version, *cardinalis* simply refers to a cleric who has offered his services to the chief church of a region, the cathedral. 'I regard this view as more plausible', says one historian,[8] on the grounds that 'cardinals' are to be found in a good number of dioceses around Europe, including in England. It is true that the early examples from Gelasius onwards do not refer to Rome, but to dioceses distant from Rome. The first time that cardinals are referred to in the papal city is in the life of Pope Stephen III (768–72), which is to be found in the *Liber Pontificalis*, or 'Book of the Popes'. This contains biographies of the bishops of Rome from St Peter onward, though it started to be composed only toward the end of the fifth century. Many of the later entries appear to have been written by eye-witnesses, and this is true for that on Stephen III. The first of the two mentions of cardinals refers to the canons of the 769 Lateran synod:

> No layman should ever presume to be promoted to the sacred honour of the pontificate, nor even anyone in orders, unless he had risen through the separate grades and had been made cardinal deacon or priest.[9]

It was of course the case that, apart from a layman usurping the process of election, only a deacon or priest would be elected, given the prohibition on bishops changing their sees. Indeed, it was very often a deacon who was elected, possibly because, thanks to his ministrations to the poor of his deaconry, he would be better known to the populace than the higher clergy.

In the second mention of cardinals, Pope Stephen is praised for maintaining the traditions of the Roman Church:

> He laid down that every Sunday the seven cardinal bishops in their weekly turns, who are on duty in the Saviour's church,[10] should celebrate the ceremonies of mass on St Peter's altar.[11]

---

7 Andrieu, 'L'origine', p. 123. Andrieu points out that it was also used by Pope Pelagius I (555–60) with reference to a priest (*ibid.*, p. 120).

8 A. Paravicini Bagliani in Jean-Marie Mayeur *et al.* (eds), *Histoire du Christianisme* V (Paris: Desclée, 1993), pp. 94–5.

9 Raymond Davis, *The Lives of the Eighth-Century Popes (Liber Pontificalis)*, 2nd edition (Liverpool: Liverpool University Press, 2007), p. 98.

10 St John Lateran (San Giovanni in Laterano), the cathedral church of Rome, originally dedicated to the Redeemer. The Lateran complex rather than the Vatican was the seat of papal government until the curia moved to Avignon at the beginning of the fourteenth century.

11 Davis, *Lives*, p. 101.

It is clear by the passing reference to the cardinal bishops that their status was not new, that the author of the biography expected his readers to know about cardinal bishops, and to know, too, that there were seven of them. The seven sees (the number was later reduced to six) were those surrounding Rome, known as the suburbicarian sees,[12] and their bishops clearly had a quite specific liturgical function in the most important of the basilicas, the pope's own cathedral. There were, however, four more important basilicas, those of St Peter's itself, St Mary Major (Santa Maria Maggiore), St Paul's Outside the Walls and St Lawrence Outside the Walls (San Paulo/San Lorenzo fuori le Mura). These were served by the cardinal priests and deacons.

The number of deacons is a bit of a puzzle. Pope Fabian (236–50) is credited with reorganizing the administration of the Roman See and appointing seven deacons. The number seven did not relate to any obvious division of Rome, civil or ecclesiastical, but possibly reflected the apostles' appointment of seven deacons to minister to the nascent Christian community in Jerusalem, as recorded in the Acts of the Apostles.[13] These deacons were organized from the centre of the diocese of Rome, the Lateran palace. Seven deacons, permanently attached to the liturgy in the Lateran basilica, were known as 'palatine' deacons. Later Rome was divided into twelve districts, and the number of deaconries (*diaconiae*) was therefore increased. By the end of the eleventh century it had been fixed at eighteen. They were almost all based upon ancient buildings of imperial Rome, warehouses and the like, and as well as providing storage space they might also be hospices for pilgrims and similar institutions. Though they came to be linked to the *tituli* (see below) they were all equipped with a chapel.[14] It is from these that the concept of cardinal deacons arose. There must, of course, have been a number of other deacons who were not immediately responsible for the welfare of the people in their district but were simply passing through the status of deacon on the way to the priesthood.

The number of cardinal priests is somewhat more straightforward. These were the priests attached to the 'titular' churches. As cardinals are still today allotted to titular churches so that, by this fiction, they become the parish clergy of Rome, it is necessary to explain how these 'titles' came about. The Latin *titulus* can be directly translated into English as a 'title' in the legal sense

---

12 Ostia, Porto, Santa Rufina (also known as Silva Candida), Albano, Sabina, Tusculum (i.e. the modern Frascati) and Praeneste, i.e. Palestrina. Porto and Santa Rufina were united in 1119, reducing the number to six. The bishops of Ostia, Porto and Albano were traditionally called upon to consecrate a new pope, if he were not already a bishop. The bishop of Ostia was, and still is, the senior cardinal.

13 Acts 6.1–6.

14 See Jean Gaudemet, 'Diaconia', in Philippe Levillain, *The Papacy: An Encyclopedia* (New York: Routledge, 1994), I, pp. 497–8.

of the term, namely implying ownership, the title to a property. It used to be thought that the oldest *tituli* were private houses where the earliest Christians in Rome met for worship, so, for instance, the *titulus Clementis* meant [the place of worship in] the house of Clement. Over time, it would seem to have been in the course of the sixth century, the name of the original owner came to be thought to have been that of a saint, so *titulus Clementis* became *titulus sancti Clementis*.[15] It is unlikely that even the earliest titular churches can be physically identified as having originally been private houses, but the Christian community in Rome would not, certainly in the first two or three centuries, have constituted a juridical entity which was able to own property.[16] The building used for worship, therefore, had to be owned by individuals, and some may of course have represented what were at first private houses. Peter Lampe has identified nine *tituli* which bear the name of people who can be identified in the first couple of centuries of the Christian community in Rome, though some of these may very well be mythical.[17] According to the *Liber Pontificalis*, Pope St Cletus, to whom the dates 85 to 95 AD are customarily assigned, on the instructions of St Peter ordained twenty-five priests for Rome[18] as, right at the beginning of the fourth century, did Pope Marcellus,[19] while Pope Urban I (222–30) donated to the churches twenty-five silver patens.[20] Although the *Liber Pontificalis* may, and probably does, incorporate early traditions, it would be unsafe to assume that these twenty-five *tituli* existed in the very early days of Christian Rome. Instead they represent the situation when the biographies were composed, in other words in the very late fifth and the sixth centuries.

The number was not fixed. By the tenth century there were twenty-eight of them. The *Liber Pontificalis* reports that it was Pope Simplicius (468–83) who made the first rudimentary organization of the Roman churches so that the clergy from the *tituli* took turns in providing the liturgical services at the basilicas of St Peter's, St Lawrence's and St Paul's: Santa Maria Maggiore, not long completed, does not get a mention.[21] By the time the total of *tituli* had risen to twenty-eight, each of the four major basilicas was served by the clergy

---

15 Carol M. Richardson, *Reclaiming Rome* (Leyden: Brill, 2009), pp. 185–8.

16 It should, perhaps, be remarked that persecution of the Christian community was spasmodic rather than continuous, despite the imaginative account given by Kittler (above, p. 2) and others.

17 Peter Lampe, *From Paul to Valentinus* (Minneapolis: Fortress Press, 2003), pp. 19–23. The nine *tituli* are associated with the names of Praxedes, Pudens (or Pudentiana), Prisca, Sabina, Balbina, Nicomedes, Clemens, Caecilia and Callistus.

18 Raymond Davis, *The Book of Pontiffs* (Liverpool: Liverpool University Press, 2000), p. 2.

19 *Ibid.*, p. 13.

20 *Ibid.*, p. 7.

21 *Ibid.*, p. 43.

of seven of them. There was, of course, more than one priest attached to each of these churches, but towards the end of the seventh century, argues Andrieu, one priest had emerged as the main, or cardinal, one, i.e. 'cardinal' in the sense of 'prime' or 'chief', and not directly as a derivative of *incardinatus*.[22]

By the mid eighth century, therefore, there were in Rome three ranks of cardinals, all with different roles: the cardinal bishops of the suburbicarian sees, the cardinal priests in charge of the *tituli*, effectively Rome's parish priests, and the cardinal deacons in charge of the *diaconiae* or welfare centres. The bishops were increasingly involved in the central administration of the Church of Rome, advising the pope, representing the pope of the day as legates, accompanying him on journeys and so on. The cardinal priests similarly took part in the Church administration, at least of the city of Rome. A constitution of the energetic Pope John VIII (872–82) instructed them to meet at least twice a month, in one *titulus* or another – or even in a *diaconia* – basically to sit in judgement over the discipline of the clergy, or act as arbiters in disputes between the clergy and the laity. They were, he says, to be like the seventy elders who served Moses[23] – the pope himself presumably being Moses. This particular constitution was effectively the reiteration of an earlier synod under Pope Leo IV in December 853, though that had laid down a weekly meeting rather than a fortnightly one.

At this period, synods were the means by which the pope of the day consulted the clergy. Membership of these synods, however, was not restricted to cardinals, and there was no process by which they could express a common voice. It was the reform movement of the eleventh century which definitively changed the status of cardinals. After the turmoil of the tenth century there had been many efforts at reforming the papacy, many of them led by appointees to the papacy of German Emperors. Leo IX (1049–54) was also an imperial appointment, but Bruno of Egisheim only accepted on condition that the Emperor's choice was ratified by the clergy and people of Rome. When he arrived there, dressed as a pilgrim, he was received with acclamation and crowned on 12 February.[24] There had been some non-Roman cardinals appointed before Leo's pontificate, but under him it became the policy to select men who were deeply committed to reform – many of them monks – from across Europe. This had the added benefit of making the aims of the reformers – the eradication of simony, the establishment of clerical celibacy as the norm, and the freedom for bishops, abbots and other prelates from subservience to

---

22 Andrieu, 'L'origine', p. 130–2.

23 P. Jaffé, *Regesta Pontificum Romanorum* (Leipzig: Veit, 1885), no. 3366.

24 For a short life of Leo, and of the other popes mentioned in the text, see J. N. D. Kelly and M. J. Walsh, *Oxford Dictionary of Popes*, 2nd edition (Oxford: Oxford University Press, 2010).

the civil authority (the 'investiture controversy') – better known throughout Europe. Leo's successor, Victor II, was also nominated by the Emperor, but Victor's successor, Stephen IX (X),[25] was nominated by leading members of the reform group in Rome and consecrated before anyone could propose an alternative. On the death of Stephen, however, what the reformers feared came to pass: the powerful Roman nobility, opposed to the reform which would deny them control of the papacy intervened and bribed the Roman populace to elect the Bishop of Velletri. The reform cardinals fled the city, and, gathered in Siena, elected the Burgundy-(or possibly Lorraine-)born Bishop of Florence, who took the name Nicholas II.

On 12 or 13 April 1059 Pope Nicholas held a synod in the Lateran. In an attempt finally to prevent the Roman nobility or the Roman militia ever again attempting to control elections to the papacy, the synod issued a decree on the method to be used in future elections. This decree was promulgated in a bull of Pope Nicholas entitled *In Nomine Domini* ('In the name of the Lord').[26] In future, said the bull, the Bishop of Rome is to be elected by the cardinal bishops, and by them alone. After he had been chosen by the bishops, the cardinal priests and deacons were to be asked to give their consent, and after them the rest of the clergy of Rome, and finally the people. Nicholas's successor, Alexander II, was chosen by this method, but the imperial court, furious at being ignored, and spurred on by the Roman nobility, chose an antipope. Alexander II was followed by the leading reformer Gregory VII, who was elected not according to the election decree but by popular acclaim. The antipope also had a successor, calling himself Clement III, who on the instructions of the German King Henry IV, was elected at Brixen in 1080 but then, just under four years later when Henry arrived in Rome, was re-elected by the clergy and people of the city. His pontificate – he died in September 1100 – was significant in the formation of the college of cardinals. Many of the cardinal priests went over to his side and became influential during his pontificate. In order to win them back, they were given a part with the cardinal bishops in the election of Pope Urban II in 1088, though only through a single representative, the Cluniac monk Rainiero, as were the cardinal deacons. On Urban's death in 1099, however, all cardinal priests and deacons took part in the election of Paschal II – the former Cardinal Priest Raniero.

In the development of the cardinatial office Urban's pontificate was important in a number of ways. First of all, he established the consistory. Hitherto major decisions had been made, as has been remarked, by a synod held in Rome. Now Pope Urban referred these to a consistory, a gathering of cardinals.

---

25 There is some confusion in the numbering of popes named Stephen.

26 Papal documents, it should be explained, are known by their opening few words, usually, though not always, in Latin.

Other officials of the Roman Church were very often also present, but insofar as he was seeking advice, the pope's principal advisors were now the cardinals in consistory. They were the most significant part of the papal curia, or court, 'court' in this case having the two meanings of an entourage surrounding a prince, and a place where judicial decisions were taken. Both these terms were taken from the structure surrounding the Emperor, and they signified Urban's determination to remodel his administration. From Leo IX's time popes had been determined to regain control over the finances of the Church – it was this desire that lay at the heart of the investiture controversy – and to do so had given financial responsibility to a member of the papal entourage who was reckoned to have particular expertise in this regard. Cluniac monks were thought, through their experience of the administration of what could be regarded as the first monastic 'order', to be especially skilled in finance, as well as wholly committed to reform, hence the recruitment of Cluniacs into the ranks of the cardinals.

Over the next five hundred years their power generally increased, quite apart from their own, generally accepted, right to elect a pope. From the pontificate of Callistus II (1119–24) they were involved in judicial decisions; from Honorius II (1124–30) their signatures were to be found on privileges granted by the pope. As the university system developed in Italy and across Europe, it became increasingly important to raise to the rank of cardinal clerics who had qualifications in law – as many of the lives in this collection bear witness – and in theology (cf., for example, the appointment of Robert Pullen, p. 31). Pullen was English, but in the second half of the twelfth century the proportion of non-Italians among cardinals was in decline, despite Alexander III's (1159–81) instruction to his legate in France to seek out learned men for promotion. Alexander III also launched a policy of creating cardinals from already consecrated bishops. Some were called into the curia, but others were left in charge of their dioceses in addition to having an advisory function to the papacy, thus increasing the central authority of the pope which reached its medieval apogee during the pontificate of Innocent III (1198–1216).

The sense of the cardinalate being a corporate body, or college,[27] was enhanced by the first canon of the third Council of the Lateran held in 1179 and regarded by the Catholic Church to have been an ecumenical council. The canon, *Licet de evitanda*,[28] lays down as a rule for papal elections that the

---

27 As far as is recorded, the cardinals were first referred to as a college at the Council of Rheims in 1148. Cf. Broderick, 'Sacred College', p. 9.

28 Norman P. Tanner (ed.), *Decrees of the Ecumenical Councils* (London: Sheed and Ward; Washington DC: Georgetown University Press, 1990), p. 211. This extremely useful edition of conciliar decrees has the Latin text on one leaf and, facing it, the English transla-

cardinal electors must decide with a majority of two-thirds, a provision which has remained in force down to the present day, apart from a short hiatus under Pius XII (1939–58).[29] *Licet de evitanda* forced the cardinals to act together to reach a compromise. (It also made for some very long conclaves, but that is another story.)[30] The corporate nature of the body of cardinals was emphasized by Pope Innocent III in a letter of August 1198. It is not just that they form one body in relationship to each other, they even form one body with the pope himself. An attack on a cardinal, declared Innocent III's successor, Honorius III (1216–27), was the equivalent of an attack on the pope himself.[31] So intimate was this relationship, argued the thirteenth-century canon lawyer Cardinal Henry of Susa (Hostiensis, so called because he was Bishop of Ostia), that a sick cardinal cannot have a blood-letting without the approval of the pope of the day.[32] Huguccio (Henry of Pisa, d. 1210), who had been mentor to Innocent III, had, however, earlier put a limit to cardinatial pretensions. Between the death of one pope and the election of the next,[33] he argued, the cardinals cannot be the *caput*, head, of the Church, because the head is one and the cardinals are many. They can only be *vice caput*, in place of the head.

Huguccio's observation was to prove important. Though Peter Damian (cf. below, p. 25) had suggested, or so some people thought, that the rank of cardinal was of divine origin, and that they were hierarchic descendants of the apostles, they suffered from the fact that, unlike bishops, priests and deacons, theirs was not a sacramental order. They wanted to present themselves as the papal senate, to be consulted about major decisions (which they were) and to be able to impose their will on the popes. To this end, after the death in 1352 of Clement VI, the cardinals in conclave drew up a list of what came to be called 'capitulations' to which all electors committed themselves when one of them was to be elected pope. They agreed that the newly elected pope would not create any more cardinals until the number fell below sixteen, that

---

tion. Both pages have the same number, so that p. 211 is page reference for the Latin *and* the English versions of the decree.

29 Pius XII insisted that the majority be two-thirds plus one, apparently so that a cardinal could not be elected with a two-thirds majority achieved only by his own vote for himself. John Paul II, in *Universi Dominici Gregis*, also changed the rule, so that if a two-thirds majority was not obtained after a large number of ballots, the cardinals could decide to have a simple majority. This provision was sensibly reversed by his successor. On *Universi Dominici Gregis*, see Walsh, *Conclave*, pp. 160–4.

30 For the invention of the conclave as such, see *ibid.*, pp. 73–93.

31 Richardson, *Reclaiming*, p. 7.

32 A. Paravicino-Bagliani, *The Pope's Body* (Chicago: University of Chicago Press, 2000), pp. 63–5.

33 The phrase used for the period between the death of a pope and the election of his successor is *sede vacante*, literally, 'the see (or seat) being empty'.

the total number should never exceed twenty, that two-thirds of the cardinals should agree as to the nominees before anyone was raised to the rank, and a similar consent was to be required before a pope could alienate any of the papacy's property. In all there were twelve such conditions,[34] which Innocent VI, though he had sworn to them, promptly repudiated on the grounds that they were contrary to the *plenitudo potestatis*, the 'plenitude of power', which popes enjoyed, and in any case both Gregory X and Clement V had forbidden the cardinals to do anything during a *sede vacante* apart from deciding whom the next pope should be.[35] Capitulations proved an ineffective means of controlling the actions of the pope, but they remained a common practice, and were not ruled as inadmissible until 1696.[36]

The corollary of this very close link between the pope and his cardinals was that the cardinals shared in the revenues that accrued to the papacy from its various sources. Their right to half the revenues of the papacy was granted by Pope Nicholas IV in 1289,[37] though this income was available only to those who were resident at the papal curia. It made them immensely wealthy, because the income of the cardinals was drawn not just from this papal revenue but also from the many benefices which they accumulated over time. These benefices were located all over Europe, as will be seen in the lives which follow: only England made it difficult for Roman clerics to occupy by proxy benefices within the kingdom, in the fourteenth century passing four 'Statutes of Provisors' to limit the procedure. They did not prove wholly effective.

Identification of pope and cardinals was further enhanced by costume. Popes had traditionally worn white, but with a red cloak. During the Council of Lyons in 1245, Innocent IV granted them the right to wear red in the form of a hat (it was first worn by the cardinals during a visit to the monastery of Cluny that November). The red hat became a symbol of their status, and remains so. It was worn for a century or so, but eventually became merely a symbol, carried in a cardinal's train as a sign of their office, and hung over their tomb after death. In 1464 Pope Paul II added a red biretta, a square headdress with three or four peaks, to the cardinal's formal attire. The biretta is sent to the residence of a newly appointed cardinal, or may be in certain circumstances presented to him by the head of state. Although red was the colour associated with the cardinal's formal dress, there were many shades of it, depending on the form of dye which was used. Pope Paul II tried to reserve the most expensive form for the exclusive use of cardinals. This produced purple

---

34 Diana Wood, *Clement VI* (Cambridge: Cambridge University Press, 1989), pp. 103–8.
35 Bernard Guillemin in Mayeur *et al.* (eds), *Histoire* 6, p. 59.
36 Richardson, *Reclaiming*, p. 57.
37 *Ibid.*, p. 36.

(the Roman imperial colour) rather than red, and so tied is that shade to the rank of cardinal that down to the present day the elevation of someone to the rank is frequently referred to as 'being raised to the purple'.[38]

Though cardinals were in theory the deacons, priests and suburbicarian bishops of the city of Rome, their status was not affected by the prolonged absence of the papacy from Rome during the fourteenth century. Popes had often been absent from Rome: the difference in what came to be known as the 'Babylonian captivity' was that for many years he was resident in one place that was not Rome. 'The real problem for the popes', Diana Wood has remarked, 'was that as bishops of Rome, rather than Avignon, they knew they ought to be there, but the dangers of Old Rome contrasted unfavourably with the attractions of New Rome' – Avignon.[39] The cardinals lived across the river from the papal palace, but it did not materially alter their status except that most, though not all, were now French rather than Italian. They were much more affected by the consequences of the election of Pope Urban VI in 1378. He was elected under unusual circumstances that might have been taken to amounting to duress, and his subsequent behaviour was regarded by some at the time as evidence of mental instability. The cardinals were especially alarmed by his efforts to curb their extravagant life-style.[40] The French cardinals – the three Italian cardinals present abstained from voting – at Fondi in the kingdom of Naples elected a rival pope, Clement VIII, on 20 September 1378, who returned to Avignon. This 'Great Western Schism' lasted until the election of Odo Colonna as Martin V at the Council of Constance in November 1417, and did vast damage to the prestige of the Sacred College because the cardinals were regarded, quite correctly, as having caused the schism. They, on the other hand, naturally preferred to see themselves as making efforts to heal the break between Rome and Avignon: cardinals of both 'obediences' collaborated on a reunion council at Pisa in 1409, though the outcome was only more confusion with the election of third contender to the title of Bishop of Rome. At Constance the cardinals were denied their exclusive right to choose a pope. Although twenty-five of them[41] took part in the election they were outnumbered by thirty representatives of the five 'nations' into which the attendees at the Council had been

---

38 Richardson, *Reclaiming*, pp. 137–8.

39 Wood, *Clement VI*, p. 74. How the popes dealt with the problem of Rome in relation to Avignon is discussed by Wood, pp. 74–95.

40 See Kelly and Walsh, *Oxford Dictionary*, pp. 228–30.

41 According to Broderick, there were thirty-one cardinals in all, five of the Roman obedience, eighteen of the Pisan, cf. Broderick, 'Sacred College', p. 14. Salvador Miranda, however, lists twenty-three voting cardinals, and ten non-voting ones. One of those who did not vote was Baldassare Cossa (cf. p. 42), who was in prison (www.fiu.edu/~mirandas/conclave-xv.htm, accessed 16 January 2010).

divided. Before the election occurred there was laid down a list of 18 reforms to be undertaken by the new pontiff, the first of which was 'The number, quality and nationality of the lord cardinals'.[42] Much had been said in the course of the Council about these topics, influenced especially by Pierre d'Ailly (see p. 68) who wanted to see a wider geographical spread of cardinatial appointments. Nothing, however, was explicitly decided.

It was one of the provisions of Constance that councils of the Church should be summoned at regular intervals. One consequently met at Basel[43] in 1431. In 1436 it passed a decree on how many cardinals there could be and what was expected of them.[44] The number was fixed at twenty-four – though a couple more might be added if they were of outstanding holiness of life – with no more than a third of them from a single nation. They had to be over thirty, of legitimate birth, learned and of good repute – though in those who were relatives of princes the degree of learning might be modest. Relatives of popes or cardinals might not be elevated to their ranks (a provision which was systematically ignored), nor might anyone who was physically handicapped. The council then moved on to warn the cardinals against ostentatious display of wealth. It was a vain wish, as the lives of renaissance cardinals were to demonstrate – though there were always admirable exceptions, as the life of Oliviero Carafa (see below, p. 142) demonstrates. A little of what might be included in the display of wealth can be gathered from the bull, never promulgated, of Pius II (1458–64), *Pastor Aeternus*. It repeated the provisions of 1436, noting that cardinals were to be doctors of theology or canon law, and where possible experienced in business. But the Pope also added restrictions on the cardinals' life-style. Those who are already cardinals, he laid down, were to have no more than sixty servants and forty teams of horses. New cardinals were to be limited to forty servants and only four teams of horses. And, moreover, they were not to hunt. Nowhere was it said that cardinals had to be in sacred orders.

In 1514 the Fifth Council of the Lateran also turned its attention to what was required of cardinals, but as befitted a Council under a Medici Pope, Leo X, the requirements proved to be modest. They were urged to behave well, take care of their servants (who must not be over elaborately dressed), look after their benefices, keep the pope informed of what was going on in the region of the Church from which they came, and live in Rome unless sent abroad on a mission by the pope. It also laid down the obligation of secrecy on matters discussed, and votes taken, in consistories. Failure to observe secrecy, said the

---

42 Tanner, *Decrees*, p. 444.

43 It was to move to Ferrara, then to Florence and finally Rome before it concluded in 1445. There was an intermediate council, that of Pavia-Siena, 1423–24.

44 Tanner, *Decrees*, pp. 501–4.

Council, would incur *ipso facto* excommunication, removable only by the pope himself, unless the cardinal incurring it was in danger of death.[45]

Between the Lateran Council and the opening of the reforming Council of Trent in 1545 (it lasted on and off until 1563) the lives of some at least of the cardinals underwent a major change. From the ostentatious display which Pius II had railed against, a group of them became leaders in the renewal of the Church's spiritual life – Reginald Pole, for example (cf. p. 43). Pole and Pietro Bembo (p. 75) were roughly contemporaries, and they were friends, yet their lives could hardly have been more different, and different again from the learned and poverty-stricken Jacopo Sadoleto (p. 78). The reform movement among the College of Cardinals produced saints – one of them a Pope, the uncomfortable Pius V. Charles Borromeo (p. 112) was another cardinal who earned the title of saint, but that was after the Council of Trent. Trent itself had surprisingly little to say about cardinals beyond insisting on their residence in their dioceses if they were bishops, and recommending that the pope choose from all Christian nations when raising men to the purple. It was after the Council, through the reorganization of the papal curia under Sixtus V (1585–90), that a fundamental change took place.

In his apostolic constitution *Postquam verus* of 1586 he set, with the consent of his cardinals, the maximum size of the college at seventy, three times the number of cardinals favoured in the fifteenth century. He also set up the system of 'Congregations', or committees of cardinals and advisors, which is still in place despite frequent changes of name and tasks. The consequence of this reorganization was that consistories became less and less important, and the opportunities for the cardinals to meet and act as a college were fewer and fewer. As a further limitation of their authority, in 1587 Sixtus made the Roman Inquisition the most important of these new Congregations, effectively removing from the College of Cardinals as such any responsibility for the extirpation of heresy.[46]

It may be that the cardinals did not realize the long-term consequences of Sixtus's restructuring, but it did not pass entirely without protest. The occasion was the attempt by Pope Gregory XIV (1590–91) to invest Alfonso d'Este with the duchy of Ferrara, in return for which he would supply an army to aid the Catholics in France. A bull of Pius V, *Admonet vos*, had declared that no part of papal territory could be alienated from the Papal States even temporarily without the approval in consistory of two-thirds of the cardinals. In the conclave which elected him, Gregory XIV had sworn, as had all other

---

45 *Ibid.*, pp. 617–21.

46 The Holy Roman Inquisition had been set up in 1542 by Pope Paul III. It was renamed the Holy Office by Pope Pius X in 1908 and the Congregation for the Doctrine of the Faith by Pope Paul VI in 1967 – though the name 'Holy Office' is still often used.

cardinals, to observe this requirement. He did indeed put this question to the cardinals in consistory in 1591: Alfonso himself did not want to receive the duchy without the approval of the cardinals lest in the next pontificate – and Gregory was clearly ill – a decision in his favour might be reversed. A committee of cardinals was set up to report on the matter. In a sense the issue itself is not significant. What mattered was the response of fifty-nine-year-old Giulio Antonio Santori, who had been a cardinal since 1570. He submitted a memorandum to Gregory claiming the right to offer advice even though the Pope had not asked for it. His arguments harked back to the middle ages, evidence that the cardinals were well aware of past justifications for their status. Cardinals, Santori argued, were not simply advisors to popes, on a par with counsellors to princes. They had, he said, responsibility as a body for the good of the whole Church, and in particular for the good of the Church of Rome. They stood in relation to the pope as the apostles did to Christ, and their status was of divine right. They formed one body with the pope.[47]

In reality they scarcely formed one body with each other. During the sixteenth century there had been two camps, the French and the imperial, for the Empire for much of the century included Spain as well as the German-speaking lands. As Spain and Austria gradually separated – a rather long-drawn-out process – there came to be three camps, imperial, Spanish and French, whose interests merged for time to time in differing alliances. Indeed, as Philippe Levillain has pointed out,[48] there were more than the three groups of cardinals controlled by the princes. There was a further group 'formed by the partisans of the previous pope' and there was yet another, clustered around the Cardinal Nephew, made up of younger members of the Sacred College. The 'partisans' group is readily understandable. The other two need a little more explanation.

Those who represented nations are usually referred to as 'the crown cardinals'. They were men who were appointed at the direct request of the monarchs of the different nations. They believed it important to have someone within the College to represent their interests at the papal court. They were usually nationals of the several countries, but not necessarily so. They could equally well be Italians who for one reason or another – perhaps because they had served as a popular nuncio in Paris or Madrid, for example – were thought to be particularly favourable. A particular case is that of Giulio Alberoni, an Italian

---

47 For this incident, see M. T. Fattori, 'Appunti sulla crisi del Sacro Collegio', in *Cristianesimo nella Storia* 25 (2004), pp. 103–31. Fattori comments that when Clement VIII, Gregory XIV's successor, faced difficult decisions, rather than put the issues to the cardinals in consistory he consulted them one by one.

48 Levillain (ed.), *Papacy* I, p. 394.

by birth who, by dint of good luck and native cunning found himself prime minister of Spain, and was promoted at the request of the Spanish monarch (cf. p. 167). The crown cardinals were of special significance during a conclave, when the various crowned heads (and the Republic of Venice) attempted to influence the outcome. At the extreme, the crowned heads believed that they had the right to exercise a veto over a candidate who looked likely to be elected to the papacy. The origins of this right of exclusion, as it was called, are obscure, and possibly do not go back much further than the beginning of the seventeenth century, but it was certainly acknowledged by the cardinal electors, and occasionally exercised. It was last used by the Prince Bishop of Kraków, Cardinal Puzyna, against the candidature of Cardinal Rampolla in the 1903. He did so on behalf of the Austrian Emperor, in whose then dominions Kraków was located. It was the last time. Soon after his election in that conclave, Pius X in *Commissum Nobis* of January 1904 forbade the cardinal electors, on pain of excommunication, from attempting ever again to exercise a veto over any candidate on behalf of any government.[49]

Closely related to the notion of crown cardinals was the much older, and formally established, role of 'cardinal protectors'. These were cardinals who undertook to foster in the curia the interests of a particular country or institution, for instance – and commonly – a religious order. Thus at the beginning of the thirteenth century Cardinal Ugolino di Segni looked after the nascent Franciscan Order, though this was not a formal arrangement. The first properly instituted cardinal protector came in 1279 – also for the Franciscans – but it was not until the pontificate of Julius II (1503–13) that the role of cardinals as protectors of states was formally approved.[50] The role of cardinal protectors was historically significant, and though it was abolished as a recognized status in 1964 it may still exist on an informal basis.[51]

Levillain's third group of cardinals was the younger ones who clustered around the Cardinal Nephew. As the cardinal was precisely that, the nephew, real or sometimes adopted (see for instance Innocenzo Ciocchi del Monte, p. 211), he was himself a younger man. He was, moreover, an extremely powerful figure in the papal court – one well worth cultivating for those setting out

---

49 There is a lengthy discussion of this topic, with many examples, in Broderick, 'Sacred College', pp. 48–60. He quotes a remark of Clement XI to the imperial Ambassador in 1717 that choosing cardinals while under pressure from national governments was so stressful he was thinking of resigning (*ibid.*, p. 55).

50 William E. Wilkie, *The Cardinal Protectors of England* (Cambridge: Cambridge University Press, 1974), p. 7.

51 See Claudio de Dominicis in Levillain (ed.), *Papacy*, pp. 246–7. One of the problems highlighted by de Dominicis was the tendency of cardinal protectors of religious orders to interfere with the running of them.

on a cardinatial career. While nepotism – the word was coined for the papal court – has now a very bad reputation, and while there were undoubtedly some distinctly unsatisfactory papal nephews, the office itself ought not to be disparaged. The papal nephew was in effect the pope's prime minister, the equivalent of what is now the Secretary of State. It was an office of considerable responsibility, covering both Church administration and the administration of the extensive Papal States, and the pope needed to be able to trust him completely. From the renaissance to the end of the seventeenth century, when the office disappeared, it seemed sensible to trust above all a member of one's own family.

During this period the majority of the cardinals were Italian, for the most part drawn from the Papal States. They had more often progressed through the government of the States than risen through the ranks as priests, resident bishops and so on. Indeed, for most of the history of the cardinalate the greater number of them were Italian. The various nations were not unhappy about this: at least it meant that the Pope was not under the thumb of any particular prince as had happened during the Avignon papacy when there was an overwhelming preponderance of French cardinals. Otherwise the only period when there had been a substantial group of non-Italians had been during the eleventh-century struggles to reform the papacy. The situation changed only in modern times. In the nineteenth century there was a desire to internationalize the administration of a worldwide Church and, perhaps more importantly, to increase the centralization by bringing to Rome prelates from the various countries. This broadening of the geographical basis for recruitment began under Pio Nono, and gathered pace in the twentieth century. The Code of Canon Law introduced in 1917 repeated the medieval and renaissance provisions about cardinals having to be legitimate, not related to the pope or any member of the Sacred College and so on. The revision published in 1983 made no mention of any of these restrictions. Quite the opposite: it stressed the pope's entire freedom of choice.

> Those to be promoted Cardinals are men freely selected by the Roman Pontiff (lays down canon 351§1), who are at least in the order of priesthood and are truly outstanding in doctrine, virtue, piety and prudence in practical matters; those who are not already bishops must receive episcopal consecration.

This lays down one very important difference from past practice. Even in the 1917 Code, a cardinal might be a deacon and remain so (cf. Giacomo Antonelli, p. 184), but now not only has a cardinal to be a priest, he must receive consecration as a bishop. However, a number of cardinals have sought, and been granted, a dispensation from this requirement – as they have also for the further requirement that, if not a diocesan ordinary, a cardinal must reside in Rome (canon 356). It was Pope John XXIII (1958–63) who instructed that all cardinals should be bishops, and it was also Pope John XXIII who first increased the number of cardinals above the seventy laid down by Pope Sixtus V. His successor Pope Paul VI (1963–78) made two important changes. He introduced, not exactly a retirement age for cardinals, but an age (eighty) beyond which they might not vote in elections for the papacy. He also put a limit to the total number of cardinals. He laid down there was to be a maximum of one hundred and twenty, though he suggested that the figure was not to be regarded as absolutely rigid. Indeed, his successor-but-one, Pope John Paul II (1978–2005), regularly created more cardinals that the one hundred and twenty figure allowed. Some of them were over eighty and therefore, according to Pope Paul's apostolic constitution *Romano pontifici eligendo*, as well as his *motu proprio* of 1970 *Ingravescentem aetatem*, did not have a vote in the conclave. On occasion there were more than one hundred and twenty electors, but at the death of Pope John Paul there were only one hundred and twelve, one of whom died in the course of the *sede vacante*.

This raises a final question: throughout the history of the cardinalate, how many have there been? Clearly this is not going to be an easy question to answer given the paucity of evidence in the first millennium of Christianity. John Broderick gives the total for the period from 1099 to 1986 as roughly two thousand four hundred. This is not far from the more detailed enumeration given by Salvador Miranda of the University of Florida in his splendid online survey of the office, 'Cardinals of the Holy Roman Church'.[52] These figures are indicated below in two tables, the first up to 1099 and the death of Pope Urban II, and the second from 1099 down to the present day – slightly further, though rather a lot of cardinals later given the increase under Pope John Paul II, than Broderick's figures go. For the sources of these names, see Miranda's 'Essay of a General List of Cardinals (112–2007)'.[53] As was indicated earlier, there is no evidence of the term 'cardinal' being used in Rome before the mid eighth century (cf. above, p. 3). The names listed for the early centuries are the (known) bishops of the suburbicarian dioceses and the priests of the titular churches in Rome. Finally it should be noted that Miranda organizes his list of cardinals by pontificates rather than centuries, so the dates listed only roughly coincide with the end of one century and the beginning of the next.

---

52 www.fiu.edu/~mirandas/cardinals.htm.
53 www.fiu.edu/~mirandas/essay.htm, accessed 19 January 2010.

Cardinals of the first millennium

112–498	64
498–614	85
614–701	21
701–95	96
795–900	115
900–98	109
999–1099	294
Total	784

Cardinals of the second millennium

1099–1198	447
1198–1303	154
1303–1404	189
1404–1503	198
1503–1605	407
1605–1700	342
1700–99	342
1800–1903	475
1903–2005	640
2005–07[54]	38
Total	3232

The total for both periods is therefore 4016.

As was remarked at the beginning, cardinals in their distinctive red or purple official dress are very distinctive figures in the Catholic world, and to some extent in the world at large. Indeed, in international protocol they take precedence on formal occasions immediately after princes of royal blood. That harks back to the days of the Papal States, and is something of an anachronism in the modern world. The question then remains, are cardinals themselves an anachronism? Their function of electing a pope apart, do they have any function in today's Catholic Church? As has been seen, in the past they constituted a senate, a body who believed they were responsible, alongside the pope of the day, for the wellbeing of the Church, and particularly of the Roman Church. Since Pope Sixtus V reorganized the Church's central administration at the end of the sixteenth century they have largely ceased to operate as a single college.

---

54 At the time of writing, the last consistory

Although cardinals continue to head dicasteries in Rome, and be members of them if not their prefects, as the head himself is generally known, there is no reason why this function could not be performed by other clerics or, indeed, in many cases by lay people, at least in theory. Although the late John Paul II occasionally called special consistories to discuss particular problems, not least the financial situation of the Vatican, the advisory function of cardinals has largely been taken over the synod of bishops instituted by Pope Paul VI. Cardinals are also commonly perceived as the head (or heads if there is more than one in any given territory) of the Catholic Church in a particular country, but there is no reason why this should be so: archbishops as heads of metropolitan sees could play the role just as well.

A cardinalate is like a peerage in the British honours system, and perhaps, like peerages, its future is uncertain. Even the role of the College of Cardinals in electing the pope has been questioned. As has been seen, at the Council of Constance, although cardinals took part in the election of Odo Colonna as Martin V, they were outnumbered by representatives of the five 'nations' or language groups, French, German, Spanish, Italian and English. It is a good and ancient principle of scholastic philosophy that what has been done once can be done again. There is no inherent reason, then, why the same system could not be used in modern times – without the cardinals.

The question is not, however, purely administrative. As this Introduction has attempted to explain, cardinals are the clergy and suburbicarian bishoprics of Rome. That may now be a pious fiction, but it is what entitles them to elect the Bishop of Rome. The person elected to that office has almost (but not quite) always been drawn from their ranks, from the ranks, that is, of the Roman clergy. It is, to repeat, simply a fiction, but to abandon that fiction and to permit the Bishop of Rome to be elected by some constitutional body drawn from the Church at large would, I suggest, irrevocably alter what is the underlying constitution of the Catholic Church. Rather oddly, so it seems to me, such a change is very much part of the liberal agenda. Yet its consequence would be, it seems to me, a much greater centralization of ecclesiastical authority in the Vatican – which is a consequence quite opposed to what I take to be the liberal agenda.

Cardinals, with their titular churches and purple robes are, I suspect, going to remain part of the Catholic scene for many more years to come. But not necessarily for ever.

The Precursors

The cardinals whose lives are recorded below all lived in the eleventh or twelfth centuries. It is perhaps a little inappropriate to call them precursors. As the introductory chapter should have made clear, there were cardinals in Rome itself and, given that cardinals were bishops, priests or deacons attached to particular 'titles', office holders of those titles can be traced back to the very earliest centuries of Christianity in Rome. But for the vast majority of these 'cardinals' before the eleventh century, and indeed for many of them in that century, little or nothing is known of them apart from their names. The Bishop of Rome was quite punctilious about keeping records, and cardinals' names appear at the foot of surviving papal documents, are included in signatories to the acts of Roman synods, or are mentioned by early chroniclers of the period.

It is true that some few names stand out. These are mainly the cardinals who became popes, in which case the *Liber Pontificalis* records the name of their father, and often their place of origin, or the place of origin of the family. Cardinals who became popes are of course omitted from this book, although I have included a couple of cardinals who became popes, or almost became popes, but then were unseated. One such is the earliest person whose life is recounted in this volume, Anastasius Bibliotecarius, Anastasius the Librarian (see p. 37), who almost became pope in 855 and whose life and family both before and after his 'election' is relatively well known. Another, rather later, example was John Gratian. He was possibly related to the wealthy Roman banking family the Pierleoni and was archpriest of St John at the Latin Gate when in 1045 he succeeded his godson Pope Benedict IX, apparently by paying a large amount of money for the privilege. It was an odd thing for him to have done. He was regarded as being a member of the reform party in Rome, and Peter Damian (see p. 25) wrote him a letter of congratulation. He therefore should in principle have been opposed to the act of simony by which he acquired the papacy. Possibly he made the payment because he was eager, as a reformer, to get rid of Benedict, a man of scandalous life who had three stints at being pope, and three times resigned. Whatever the reason for his action, Gregory VI, as Gratian named himself, did not last long, some eighteen

21

months, and despite his brief period of fame little is known about him, before or after his period as pope. There is even doubt about whether he could properly be called a cardinal.

What is perhaps striking about these early cardinals, or rather, the cardinals of the eleventh and twelfth centuries represented here, is that they constitute a rather international collection. Humbert was from Lorraine in what is now France, Peter Damian hailed, like Bernard of Parma, from northern Italy, while Robert Pullen (and Nicholas Breakspear, but in 1154 he became pope Hadrian, or Adrian, IV) came from England. This was of course a change from the time, still maintained by a fiction, that these were Roman clergy: the College of Cardinals was not again to be drawn so widely until the nineteenth century. Otherwise the college was dominated by Italians except for the period of the exile in Avignon for much of the fourteenth century, when the majority of cardinals were French. But from whatever region of medieval Europe they came, they had an advantage that is not perhaps shared by many of the modern members of the Sacred College. Whatever their native tongues, they shared a common language. They could all converse in Latin.

Humbert of Silva Candida

Humbert was born in Burgundy, presumably not far from the monastery of Moyenmoutier in the Vosges mountains where he became a monk. Whether he was a child oblate, or entered as a young man, is unknown. His year of birth is also unknown, though it is likely it was early in the eleventh century. He rose through the ranks of the monks to become abbot of the monastery, part of the reform of monastic life instigated by John, abbot of Gorze near Metz. Another abbey which was part of the same reform was that at Toul, and it was at Toul that Bruno of Egisheim was educated. Bruno, born in 1002, must have been of a similar age to Humbert, and it may have been at Toul that they met. Certainly they were friends, and of a like mind over the necessary reforms not just in monasteries but in the Church at large. Bruno became bishop of Toul in Lorraine, but on the death of Pope Damasus II in 1048 he was nominated by the Emperor Henry III as Pope. True to the reform agenda, he agreed to accept the office only if the nomination was approved by the clergy and people of Rome. He entered the city dressed as a pilgrim to be greeted with acclaim, and was crowned on 12 February 1049. He took the name Leo IX.

Leo now summoned to Rome his friends whom he knew shared his reforming zeal, among them the two monks Peter Damian (see p. 25) and Humbert, along with others, several of them from Lorraine. He appointed Humbert to be Archbishop of Palermo in Sicily. Sicily itself was about to be conquered by the Normans, but at the time Humbert was made Archbishop the island was still in Muslim hands. Humbert therefore was never able to take up his post, but the appointment was an irritant to the Patriarch of Constantinople, from 1043 the combative Michael Cerularius, because before the Arab conquest a century or so earlier Sicily had been a Byzantine enclave in Western Europe. Though the appointment of any Latin bishop to Palermo was likely to be seen by Constantinople as an example of Roman aggrandisement, the choice of Humbert had at least this to commend it: he was one of the few Western prelates who knew Greek, and was well read in the Greek fathers of the Church.

He put his theological learning to good use at the Lateran synod called by Pope Leo in 1050. The theories of Berengarius of Tours on the presence of Christ in the Eucharist were discussed and condemned as contrary to the faith. At a later synod (1059), Berengarius was required to sign a profession of faith in the presence of Christ in the Eucharist in a formula which, it seems likely, was drawn up by Humbert. This was one of the earliest occasions when Rome acted as a guardian of orthodoxy, condemning someone for heterodox beliefs and requiring a retraction.

In 1051 Humbert was appointed Cardinal Bishop of Silva Candida (= 'White Wood'), the early name for the title of Santa Rufina. The account of his appointment is significant, because it is the first time in the eleventh century that the word 'cardinal' seems to be used as a noun rather than as an adjective, rather implying that cardinals had now become as such an expected part of the structure of the Roman Church. In the capacity of cardinal he was used as an emissary by successive popes, sometimes accompanied by Cardinal Frederic of Lorraine at whose election as abbot of Montecassino he presided in May 1057, and who, in the August of that year, was elected Pope as Stephen IX (X). It was Frederic who accompanied him to Constantinople in the fateful visit of 1054.

It has been noted that the Patriarch of Constantinople was something of a problem – he was a problem not just to the Pope but to the Emperor, not least because he started to wear imperial regalia and to call in his sermons for an uprising against the Emperor. When he suddenly died in 1059 there was a strong suspicion that he had been murdered. One of his acts was to close all the Latin churches in Constantinople. Another was to inspire, or so the Latins believed, a treatise by Archbishop Leo of Ochrid condemning some Latin practices, in particular the use of unleavened bread in the Latin-rite form of the Eucharist: the Byzantines used leavened bread. Pope Leo replied. His riposte, composed by Humbert, was hard-line, asserting the supremacy of the Roman Church over all other Christian bodies. It was not framed so as to placate the Patriarch at the best of times, especially as it was based on what appeared to be a secular authority, the Donation of Constantine. This was a forged document, produced in the mid to late eighth century, but neither Pope nor Patriarch knew this. The problem for the Pope was that the Patriarch did not know of the Donation of Constantine at all, and was not likely to give it any credence. A flurry of letters followed, and then a delegation from Rome of Humbert, Frederic of Lorraine and Archbishop Peter of Amalfi, was despatched to Constantinople by Pope Leo, presumably in an attempt to mend relations.

Given his temper, and his firmly pro-Roman view of Church authority, Humbert was probably not the best person to lead such a delegation though, as has been remarked, he knew Greek, which was an advantage. But the party was put at a serious disadvantage by events in Italy. In May 1053 Pope Leo, against the wishes of his reformer friends, personally led a papal army against the Normans in southern Italy. He had hoped that his small force would be boosted by the army of the Byzantine governor of the region, but the governor had already been defeated in battle. On 18 June the papal army was overwhelmed by that of the Normans and Leo captured. He was treated well enough by his captors, but they kept him in their custody for nine months. In Constantinople the Patriarch was ready to exploit the papacy's obvious weakness.

When Humbert and his fellow delegates arrived in Constantinople they were greeted amicably by the Emperor but entirely ignored by the Patriarch. Tension in the city grew, and Humbert realized that he was going to make no headway against the intransigent Cerularius. On 16 July 1054 Humbert stormed into the great church of Hagia Sophia and laid on the altar an excommunication of Michael Cerularius, Leo of Ochrid and of all their followers – it encompassed, in other words, the whole Church. The excommunication was in the name of Pope Leo, but he had died two months earlier, though it is uncertain whether anyone in Constantinople knew that. Nonetheless, the excommunication was technically invalid. Not that it mattered to Cerularius, who summoned a synod and excommunicated Humbert, Frederic and Peter, and threw in the Byzantine governor of southern Italy for good measure. It should perhaps be said that too much has been made of this mutual excommunication. Although it was not formally lifted until 1965, for the most part Popes continued to deal with Patriarchs as if little or nothing had occurred.

Meanwhile Humbert had returned to Italy and to his peripatetic service of the papacy. But he also wrote. The one treatise that can unquestionably be ascribed to him, though undoubtedly there were others, was his *Adversus simoniacs*, 'Against the simoniacs', simoniacs being those who had purchased ecclesiastical office. As might be expected, Humbert took a strong line against them. He argued that any bishop or other cleric who had acquired his office by paying money for it was a heretic, and therefore any acts he carried out were invalid. This included ordinations. Humbert was opposed by Peter Damian, who proposed that such ordinations were valid even if they were illegal according to law. A priest ordained by a simoniacal bishop, therefore, did not have to be re-ordained but only received back into the fold by the laying on of hands. It was Peter Damian's position which was to become the accepted one, but during Humbert's own lifetime it was his view which prevailed.

One of the consequences of Humbert's reasoning was the election decree of Pope Nicholas II, promulgated in the Lateran synod of 1059. It laid down that, to avoid simony in papal elections, only cardinal bishops (a very small number) could vote for the next Bishop of Rome. This decree, which was very likely to have been the work of Humbert himself, was very soon to be modified, but it had momentous consequences, both for elections to the bishopric of Rome, and for the cardinals themselves (see p. 7). In the election of 1057 Humbert had himself been one of the likely candidates. He had been recommended to the reformers by Cardinal Frederic of Lorraine, at this point abbot of Montecassino. In the end it was Frederic who was chosen, but swiftly he appointed Humbert Chancellor and Librarian of the Roman Church (the two offices were at the time more or less synonymous), with overall charge of papal correspondence. The last documents he signed were dated from the Lateran Palace in April 1061. He is believed to have died on 5 May 1061, and to be buried in the Lateran.

Peter Damian

He was known, and wished to be known, as Peter Damian, but his name was simply Peter: Damian was the name of a brother, a priest in Ravenna, who rescued him from the life of a swineherd and gave him an education. He was born in 1007, the last of a large number of children. His family were noble in origin but poor, and after the death of his parents he was brought up by an elder brother who treated him as little more than a slave. It was from this that his brother Damian saved him, sending him to study, first in Ravenna itself, then at Faenza and finally at Parma. He proved to have a nimble mind, and after completing his law studies – not strictly speaking a 'degree' for universities as such had not yet come into existence – he returned to Ravenna to teach.

He had been devout as a child. He now adopted an austere style of life. He thought about becoming a monk of some kind. Then by chance he encountered two monks from the abbey of Fonte Avellana, located not far from Ravenna. This monastery had been founded not long before by St Romuald to observe strictly the Rule of St Benedict which Romuald interpreted as the monks living the life of hermits, but coming together for meals and for liturgical worship; it was similar to that later adopted by St Bruno for his own foundation, the Carthusians. As well as the house at Fonte Avellana, in about 1023 Romuald went on to establish another at Camaldoli, which gave its name to the Benedictine congregation to which Romuald's foundations belong: the Camaldolese.

Peter joined the abbey of Fonte Avellana in 1035, and by 1043, much against his will, had been appointed prior, the second in command to the abbot – except that he had been appointed to the office by the monks so that he might succeed as head of the monastery when the abbot died. He did indeed take charge of the monastery, but continued to insist that he was still the prior rather than the abbot, and never accepted the latter title. He had meanwhile become learned in theology and particularly in Scripture. And he also wrote the first life of St Romuald – it was his first book – for the instruction of the monks who joined the two monasteries, or the other hermitages which he had founded.

He became known for his reforming zeal, not just for the life of monks but for the Church at large. When in 1045 John Gratian succeeded Benedict IX he wrote to the new Pope, who – by, it is said, popular acclaim – had taken the name Gregory VI, congratulating him on taking office and expressing hope for the reform of the Church. Gratian was widely known as a good and honest man, but it emerged that Benedict had been bribed to abdicate the office of Pope with a very large sum of money. Gratian, in other words, seemed guilty of buying the papacy, an act of simony which the reform movement was determined to stamp out. He was forced out of office by King, later Emperor, Henry III of Germany who replaced him with his own man, Suidger, Bishop of Brabant, who became Clement II, the first of the German popes. He, too, like Gratian, was a member of the reform party, and his choice of name, harking back to the first century of Christianity in Rome, was indicative of that. But Peter Damian was disappointed at the speed of the reform, and wrote to tell him so.

After the death of Clement another German was appointed, who again took a name redolent of the early Christian centuries, Damasus II, but he survived only a few months, dying of malaria – though poisoning was suspected. The third German was Bruno of Egisheim. He too adopted the name of a distinguished early pope, becoming Leo IX. Within a couple of months of his appointment in 1049 he held a major reforming synod at Rome which brought together not only like-minded bishops but monks, among them Peter Damian. One of the reforms was the proposal that the ordinations by bishops who had obtained their benefices through simony should be declared invalid. This would have been against a teaching dating at least from the time of Augustine of Hippo's debate with the Donatists in the early fifth century – and, indeed, from even earlier times over the question of rebaptism. Perhaps more telling was the fact that, if such a ruling were to be made, many priests would be forced to abandon their posts, which in turn would lead to chaos. Peter was an advocate of the moderate position – ban simony, but don't expel those ordained by simoniacs – which he expressed in an influential treatise.

In March 1058 Leo's successor but one, the short-lived Stephen IX (or X, there is a confusion over the numbering of Stephens) managed to persuade Peter Damian, against his better judgement, to become Cardinal Bishop of Ostia. There is no evidence of when he had been ordained priest, but he was consecrated bishop by Pope Stephen, on 22 March. The Pope died before the end of the month. He had asked the cardinals not to choose a successor until Hildebrand, later elected Pope as Gregory VII, should return from Germany, but a clique of nobles went ahead with the election anyway and chose one of their own, though he was a member of the reform party. It was the role of the Bishop of Ostia to install the pope, and this Peter Damian flatly refused to do. The action of the Roman nobles quite possibly sprang from fear of their declining influence over the choice of the bishop of their city, and of the rising power of the cardinals. The power of the cardinals was demonstrated in the synod of 1059 under Pope Nicholas II, which Peter Damian attended, when it was decreed that in future the authority to elect Rome's bishop, the Pope, was to lie with the cardinals and with them alone, though the people of the city would be asked to express their approval.

Peter Damian was eager to be released from his responsibilities as Bishop of Ostia and return to his monastery, but Pope Nicholas had a further task for him. In Milan a group calling themselves the Pataria had embraced the reform movement so enthusiastically that they looked like dividing the Church in that city, perhaps even becoming a separate sect. Peter, accompanied by Anselm of Lucca, was sent to exercise a moderating influence. It proved problematic: the 'Patarenes' were, after all, endorsing the changes which the reformers in Rome were attempting to bring about. The mission was not wholly successful, but at a gathering in the cathedral in Milan Peter lectured the assembled dissident clergy about the primacy of the Bishop of Rome, and at least prevented a schism.

He backed the bishop who had been with him on that mission as the successor to Pope Nicholas: Anselm of Lucca became Pope Alexander II. But the election was disputed, and a man of German origins, Peter Cadalus, Bishop of Parma, was elected Pope – effectively by the German Empress, but with the backing of the now totally disenfranchised Roman nobility. An opponent of reform, he managed to establish himself for a time in Rome by the use of force, and Alexander was forced to retire to Lucca. Peter Damian proved to be Alexander's most powerful advocate, first of all before a synod held in Augsburg in 1062, and then at a synod in Mantua in 1064 persuading Hanno, the Archbishop of Cologne and now regent for King Henry IV, to support

Alexander rather than Honorius II, as Cadalus had styled himself. Alexander also played his part, by swearing an oath before Hanno that he had not been guilty of simony.

Peter Damian had only just returned from France, where he had been sent to settle disputes in the Church there: he presided at a synod held at Châlon-sur-Saône and then returned to his Fonte Avellana. In 1067 he was sent to Florence to settle a dispute between the bishops and the monks of Vallambrosa. In 1069 he was again a papal legate in Germany to convince the King he could not divorce his wife, though it took a synod held at Frankfurt, over which he presided, to persuade him of the fact. In 1072 he was once again uprooted from his monastery to act as a papal legate, this time in Ravenna, where the bishop had been excommunicated, and the town divided, because the bishop continued to support the antipope.

In between all these activities he lived as far as he could a simple life as a monk at Fonte Avellana. He also wrote treatises on the spiritual life, sometimes in the form of letters. He commended prayer and penance, and a form of common life even for the secular clergy. He provided the eremitical movement of the time with a structure and a spirituality. He even wrote hymns.

He died at Faenza, on his way back from Ravenna to Fonte Avellana: his feast is celebrated on 21 February, though he died on 22 February 1072. He was buried first in the abbey where he had spent the night, but his remains were eventually transferred to a specially built chapel in Faenza's cathedral. He has never formally been canonized. It was unnecessary: his sanctity was acknowledged even in his lifetime, and veneration began immediately after his death. In 1828 he was declared a doctor of the Church.

Bernard of Parma

Little or nothing is known of the early life of Bernardo degli Uberti except that he came from a wealthy Florentine family, his father's name was Bruno, and he was probably born around the year 1060. It is not until 1085 that he first comes to notice, when he made a donation to the abbey of St Salvi for the repose of the soul of his father: St Salvi was a foundation from the monastery of Vallombrosa. He entered the monastery of Vallombrosa in Tuscany, a monastery then at the height of its success. It had been founded not many years earlier by St John Gualbert with a rather stricter interpretation of the monastic rule than that commonly in force. The monks were meant to be contemplatives and they were to engage in prayer even when, according to the rule of St Benedict which for the most part they followed, they would normally have been occupied in manual work. Another unusual aspect of their lives, later copied by other Orders, was that they did not leave the monastery on any pretext: any outside contact was to be undertaken by lay brothers. It was not, however, a rule that could be observed too strictly: not only Bernard but a number of other monks played a significant part in the church life of the region.

In 1089 Bernard was elected abbot of St Salvi, and then in 1099 abbot general of the confederation of Vallombrosan houses. It was the height of the investiture contest, a time of great tension between Church and State. It was also a time, it would appear, of tension between the papacy and the Vallombrosans, which the appointment of Bernard helped to heal. Certainly Pope Urban II seemed to think so. In a consistory of 1097 he created him a cardinal, and his successor, Paschal II, appointed him papal legate in northern Italy. This was a problematic appointment. Many of the northern bishops were deeply opposed to the Gregorian reform movement and had been supporters of the antipope Clement III, a man of irreproachable character, who had won over a considerable group of cardinals to his side by dint of giving them a greater say in policy-making. (Pope Urban II then felt obliged to do likewise, which had a lasting impact on the developing role of the College of Cardinals.) Even more problematic, as far as the Pope was concerned, was the fact that he was related to the counts of Canossa, and therefore to the Countess Matilda, the most important lay figure of the day as far as the popes were concerned.

Clement III died in September 1100, just before Bernard was named legate. He was also appointed advisor to the Countess Matilda, and was from then on often in her company. In 1102 she renewed the donation of her lands to the Church, a donation which she had first made under Pope Gregory VII. In August 1104 Bernard went to Parma to attempt to reconcile the city to Paschal II: Clement III came from a Parma family, and the city was firmly opposed to the reform. The city was without a bishop, and Bernard decided to preside at mass in the cathedral on the feast of the Assumption of the Virgin, to which event the cathedral was dedicated. He had embarked upon a homily attacking the Emperor Henry IV, who was at odds with the Pope over investiture – but whom the city of Parma supported – when the congregation rioted. The clergy fled from the altar and the papal legate was locked up in a tower, from which he had to be freed by Matilda's troops. Matilda forced the city to make reparation to the legate.

But there then came a surprising change of heart. Bernard was back in Parma in 1105 trying to raise troops to support the Pope against the Emperor. He was unsuccessful. Yet the following year a delegation went to the Pope, it seems, asking for Bernard to be made bishop of the city. The delegation was composed of the leading lay people: the clergy, still looking to the Emperor for protection, were noticeably absent. In October 1106 Paschal held a synod at Guastalla not far from Parma, which was attended by many bishops, including

Bernard as well as some German prelates sent by the Emperor. The conclusion was still the same: the ban on investiture. After it the Pope made his way to Parma, where Bernard was installed as bishop. The following day (the actual date has not been recorded) the Pope consecrated the cathedral. It may well have been on that occasion that the remains of the antipope Honorius II, who had been Bishop of Parma, were disinterred and thrown out of the cathedral, along with those of other bishops who had espoused the cause of the Emperor and opposed the Gregorian reform.

Bernard did not have a great deal of support from the local clergy. He therefore founded a monastery of his own Vallombrosan Congregation in the city, bringing in monks from the Congregation's houses. To counterbalance it, however, the clergy of Parma also founded a monastery of their own. Bernard now gave up the office of Abbot General of the Vallombrosan Congregation, but he continued in the office of papal legate for Lombardy.

In 1111 the German King Henry V entered Italy with an army, seeking coronation as Emperor at the hands of Pope Paschal. Bernard travelled with the King's entourage and at Sutri on 9 February an agreement was reached by which the King would surrender all claim to invest bishops, but in return they would surrender all income from their benefices, except that which arose directly from ecclesiastical sources. This satisfied both sides – or so it seemed – but when the coronation was about to take place in St Peter's on 12 February and the agreement was read out, there was a riot. The coronation was abandoned and a furious King threw the Pope and several of his cardinals, including Bernard, into prison. Most were released two months later after the Pope had made a humiliating climb down, and Henry was crowned in April. Bernard, however, was released almost immediately, at the insistence of the Countess Matilda.

When Henry V came back to Italy in 1117 Bernard, as Paschal's legate, again joined his entourage, but returned to Parma when relations between the Pope and the Emperor deteriorated. Back in Parma he set about the restoration of the cathedral which had been badly damaged in an earthquake. He remained consistent in his support of the Pope, backing Paschal's legitimate successor, the short-lived Gelasius II, rather than the antipope created by the Emperor. The dispute over investiture was finally resolved in 1122 by the Concordat of Worms, which represented the triumph of moderation on both sides. Whether Bernard, one of the leading moderates, was present is not known, but Henry was grateful to the Bishop of Parma and put the monastery of Vallombrosa under imperial protection.

Henry died in 1125. Pope Honorius II backed Lothair III as his successor – he had been recognized as King by the German chancellor. There was, however, a rival candidate, Conrad of Swabia, who marched into Italy and was crowned in Milan cathedral with the iron crown of Lombardy by Anselm, the Archbishop of Milan. Honorius instructed Bernard as his legate to excommunicate both Conrad and Anselm, which he did. Conrad therefore turned on Parma and Bernard had to flee. When he tried to return he was seized and for a short time imprisoned by supporters of Conrad. He then had to flee again, returning only after Conrad had safely left Italy.

There was again a disputed papal election at the death of Honorius, with Bernard backing Innocent II against the antipope Anacletus II. Innocent's position was unsafe, and he had to leave Italy, meeting Lothair at Liège. The German King promised, in return for coronation as Emperor, to support Innocent, though his demand that the right of investiture be restored was ignored. He marched back into Italy, and King and Pope met again at Piacenza in August 1132. The Pope summoned Bernard to join them there, and a council was held. There, too, the Pope again refused to restore investiture. Lothair and Innocent then travelled to Rome. Lothair had troubles in Germany and his army was not large, certainly not large enough to dislodge Anacletus's supporters from St Peter's basilica, so the coronation took place in the Lateran on 3 June 1133.

Bernard was by this time already infirm. He hurried back to Parma, where he died on 4 December 1133. His support for the papacy against the Emperor, when the two were at odds, had not entirely convinced the people of Parma. They chose to succeed him as bishop a man who favoured the imperial party. He was, however, deposed by Pope Innocent in 1135. His successor, Lanfranc, was much more in Bernard's mould. Recognizing that many people already regarded him as a saint he reinterred his remains in an urn which was placed for all to venerate. Bernard's monument can still be seen in the choir of Parma's cathedral.

Robert Pullen

Possibly the most puzzling thing about Robert Pullen, the first (known) English cardinal, is his name. The clerics who haunted the papal court in the middle ages were often shadowy figures, some certainly more shadowy than Robert, who left behind him a substantial body of theological writing as well as some sermons. But the name 'Pullen' is a problem. A variety of meanings have been proposed, from 'brown' to 'cockerel', but the consensus seems to be that it was a form of diminutive, perhaps meaning 'small animal' or 'dingy'. If this consensus is correct then Robert may have adopted it to suggest a humble status, because it is not obviously an Anglo-Saxon name, though it might be of Norman derivation.

That he had Norman roots is certainly possible. He was born shortly after the Norman Conquest, around the year 1080, and definitely somewhere in England – Sherborne in Dorset has been proposed because he had a number of relatives in the Benedictine house there, including his first cousin, Prior Joseph. One chronicler records that King Henry I (ruled 1100–35) offered him the bishopric of Exeter, which he rejected in favour of a teaching career. He may, however, have begun his teaching at Exeter, after studies at Laon in northern France. For five years from 1137 he moved to Oxford. At Oxford, not yet a university, it seems his lectures were remarkable for the attention he paid to the Scriptures which, again in the words of a chronicler, 'had been neglected in England'.

While at Oxford he acquired the archdeaconry of Rochester, and much to the irritation of Bishop Ascelin of Rochester he retained the revenues when he went off to teach in Paris in 1142. The archdeaconry had been conferred upon him by Ascelin's predecessor who, though only an administrator of the diocese, had liberally handed out other livings in his charge, thus sharply reducing the income of the monks of the cathedral chapter. The monks wanted their money back; Ascelin, on the other hand, seems either to have wanted the money back or his archdeacon, who by 1142 was lecturing in Paris, back in Rochester. Robert refused to leave Paris, and won the support of the great saint, Abbot Bernard of Clairvaux, who wrote to Ascelin to excuse his errant archdeacon. The Bishop of Rochester was not mollified. He eventually appealed to the Pope. It was Innocent II who received the case against Robert, but his successor Celestine II who ruled in Ascelin's favour – while giving Pullen time to appeal.

The appeal had to be made before Pentecost 1144, and it may have been this dispute which brought Pullen to Rome – Ascelin and, seemingly, several monks had been there for the original hearing which had gone against Pullen. But the new Pope, the short-lived Lucius II, not only found in his favour but created him cardinal priest of St Martin and, very shortly afterwards, made him chancellor. To be put in charge of the secretariat of the Roman curia seems an odd appointment for someone who was both relatively new to Rome and, as far as we know, had little experience of administration. His name appears on documents in the role of chancellor from the end of January 1145 to the end of September the following year.

Apart from these signatures very little is known about his time in Rome. Bernard of Clairvaux wrote to him after the election in February 1145 of his protégé, the Cistercian abbot Bernardo Pignatelli, as Pope Eugenius III. Bernard did not think Eugenius a particularly suitable candidate for the papacy, and sent a message to Cardinal Pullen asking him to keep an eye on the new pontiff. Pullen himself, added Bernard in a very affectionate letter, was himself sorely missed on Paris. It seems quite likely that it was through Pullen that another Englishman, Nicholas Breakspear, the future Pope Hadrian IV, became a fixture at the papal court, while John of Salisbury, the future Bishop of Chartres whose writings are one of the most important sources for the history of the mid twelfth century, counted Pullen as a friend. Meanwhile the dispute with the bishop of Rochester was dragging on. As a cardinal, Pullen was in a position to resign the archdeaconry from which he had drawn a living, but Pope Lucius, much to the disgust of Ascelin, had allowed him to nominate his successor. In a well-honoured tradition he chose his nephew, who had the curious name of Paris (Parisius). Paris held the post until 1190.

Pullen's reputation as a theologian was, at least in the twelfth century, greater than his reputation as the first English-born cardinal. A number of his works are no longer extant, but nineteen sermons survive, as does a short treatise on 'The contempt of the world'. Most important, however, is his 'Eight Books of Sentences'. The 'Sentences' are opinions (*sententiae*) which he delivered, probably in lectures, on a range of topics from the existence of God to the significance of the sacraments. He held views that were sometimes at odds with the common opinion of his day. He believed, for instance, that the saved received the beatific vision before the resurrection of the body on the last day. In holding this (which eventually became the common teaching) he was directly at odds with St Bernard – despite this, Bernard called his theology 'sane'. His theology was rarely innovative, but he seems to have been the first theologian to hold the view – again, it became the common teaching – that the priestly act of absolution is the effective sign in the sacrament of penance.

The circumstances of Pullen's death are as obscure as the circumstances of his birth. The day of death is thought to have been 2 September, but the year may have been 1146 or 1147, and the place either Rome or, more likely, Viterbo. He is thought to have been buried in Viterbo.

Boso

There was a time when Boso was hailed as the third English cardinal, after Robert Pullen, who is included in this collection, and Nicholas Breakspear, who is not because he became Pope Hadrian (or Adrian) IV. Boso, it was claimed – and this can still be found in some sources – was a relative of Breakspear, shared the same name and like Breakspear's father, though not the future Pope himself, became a Benedictine monk at St Alban's Abbey. The only reason for thinking of a connection between the two, apart from the fact that Boso might just be an English name, appears to be that he becomes a prominent member of the papal staff just at the time that Nicholas turns up in Rome, and the two seem to have been friends. It is possible that they were friendly enough for Boso to accompany Nicholas when Pope Eugenius III, who had created Nicholas Cardinal Bishop of Albano in 1149, sent him as papal legate to Scandinavia, a mission he undertook so successfully that the other cardinals elected him Pope shortly after his return. He was away from 1152–54, and there is no record of Boso having been in Rome at that point; but nor is there any other evidence that Boso went in Nicholas's entourage.

It is, however, far more likely that Boso was an Italian who seems to have liked Englishmen – he was also friendly with Theobald, Archbishop of Canterbury, and his successor in that see, the martyred Thomas Becket. Such clues as there are to Boso's origins point to a town near Lucca. He may have been a canon regular of Bologna, which could also have been a slight link to Breakspear because Nicholas had also been a canon, though of St Ruf near Avignon. His first contacts with the papal court may have been through Cardinal Guido of Pisa, who appears to have employed him as a secretary. Cardinal Guido was papal chancellor, and soon after his death in 1149 Boso's name appears dating papal documents. Hadrian created him Cardinal Deacon of SS Cosma e Damiano in 1156, and appointed him his chamberlain. This was an extremely influential post, almost that of second-in-command, and he presumably sympathized with Hadrian's pro-Norman, anti-imperial policy. When Hadrian died on 1 September 1159, Boso played an active part in attempting to secure the election of the man who had been Hadrian's chancellor, and who had supported the late Pope's policies, Cardinal Orlandi Bandinelli. Duly elected – although an antipope was also elected who was more favourable to the Emperor Frederick I Barbarossa – Bandinelli took the name Alexander III.

Pope Alexander did not make Boso his chamberlain, but instead created him cardinal priest of Santa Pudenziana at the end of 1165, just after the Pope returned to Rome. Alexander had fled to France which, along with England, had declared for him rather than the antipope Victor IV, taking Boso with him: they came back only after Victor's death. But the city was still largely controlled by the antipope's faction backed by the Emperor Frederick, and the papal court soon had to move to Benevento. Alexander had been steadily building opposition to Frederick, helped by the hostility to the Emperor's harsh policies in northern Italy. Frederick was eventually defeated by the Lombard League, and sued for peace. Alexander went to Venice, again accompanied by Boso, and in July 1177 there struck an agreement with the Emperor that he would withdraw the excommunication he had issued against Frederick provided that Frederick recognized Alexander as the legitimate Pope. Despite this treaty Alexander was not able to settle back in Rome, and was still in exile from the city when he died in August 1181.

It is probable that Boso had died somewhat earlier. He had continued the *Liber Pontificalis*, the book of the lives of the popes, providing entries for

Eugenius, Anastasius, Hadrian and Alexander. His life of Alexander, however, only goes up to the events of Easter 1178, and his signature is not found on documents after July of that year. It seems, therefore, that he died in the second half of 1178, though there is some suggestion that he lived on until 1181.

The Nearly Men

As in any election, in a conclave to elect a new pope there is a winner and a runner-up. The idea behind this chapter is to look at the lives of those cardinals down the ages who very nearly became popes. It was inspired by the story of Cardinal Mariano Tindaro Rampolla (1843–1913), Secretary of State under Pope Leo XIII, who, in the conclave of 1903 following Leo's death, was the front-runner until the Austrian Emperor exercised his veto against him (for the story, see the life of Rafael Merry del Val who was secretary to the conclave, p. 190). In the end he was left out because his biography, fascinating though it might have been for his period of office as Secretary of State, was otherwise not greatly interesting. It is, moreover, generally acknowledged that his chances of election were small, despite his early popularity among the cardinals.

The one who came closest to election, and might indeed have become pope had the conclave not been delayed to give the French cardinals time to turn up, was the Englishman Reginald Pole. He had the majority of votes, and was only one short of the two-thirds needed when the French finally arrived and swung the election against him (see below and p. 162). Two other biographies have been added of those who also almost achieved enough support for election, but then failed to gain the final few.

The first two biographies, however, are rather different. In the early centuries of the Church there were frequently antipopes, men who wanted the papacy and won it, but through an illegitimate process. Unfortunately little is known about most of these. One who does stand out is Anastasius Bibliotecarius, Anastasius the Librarian. He was elected illegally, but never consecrated a bishop, so, according to the rules of the day, was not yet the pope. (Confusion arises because eight hundred or so years later the rule was changed so that a person became pope on election, not on consecration.)

There were of course some who were elected and consecrated, and then deposed. This happened often in the turbulent early middle ages, but the most colourful personality was undoubtedly Baldassare Cossa, who in 1410 became (the antipope) John XXIII, and was deposed at the Council of Constance in 1415. He returned to the rank of cardinal, and so with a little stretching of the term, has been counted in among the 'nearly men'. The fate of Baldassare

Cossa raises the question which is often asked, whether a pope can resign his office and retire. It has happened in the past, so it certainly can happen in the future, making the point that the papacy is an office and not a sacramental order. Unlike the office of bishop which, according to Catholic sacramental theology, has to be handed down from one bishop to the next, papal authority is not handed from one pope to the next – though several have tried, and one or two have succeeded, in nominating their successor. A pope who steps down returns to the sacramental order of bishop. Whether he will, like Cossa, also return to the rank of cardinal depends on the pope of the day.

Cossa, as will be seen, tried to hold on to his office but failed. His contemporary Gregory XII, who was of the Roman 'obedience' and therefore regarded by the Vatican as having been the legitimate pope of the day, went quietly when the Council of Constance proposed to depose him. He, like, Cossa returned to the rank of cardinal and the office of bishop. The third of the popes of the day, Pedro de Luna of the Avignon obedience, who called himself Benedict XIII, sped off to his native Spain and kept his rump of a papal court at Peñiscola, a particularly picturesque promontory on the coast near Valencia.

Like the Speaker of the British House of Commons, candidates for the papacy are expected to show at least a modicum of hesitation before accepting the job. Not all take it on with the alacrity shown by the Medici Pope Leo X (1513–21), who is reported to have said 'God gave us the papacy, let us enjoy it.' When a pope is finally chosen he is led away for a few minutes' reflection before being vested in his robes of office. He is taken to what is called 'the crying room'. The tears may be of grief at the task ahead or, in the case of some, tears of joy at having at last landed the top job in the Church. For the 'nearly men' any tears shed might be those of relief – or just possibly of frustration.

Anastasius the Librarian

The life of Anastasius is difficult to unravel. He must have been born sometime in the second decade of the ninth century, which makes him chronologically the first of the cardinals to be included in this book. He was well related – one of his uncles, Arsenius, became Bishop of Orte and was employed as a papal emissary – but that is about all that is known of his family. His early life is equally unknown. It is, however, a reasonable assumption that he was educated by Greek monks in Rome (there were some nine Greek-speaking monasteries in Rome in the ninth century) because he was himself fluent in Greek, an extremely rare accomplishment in the Rome of his day.

Perhaps it was because of his remarkable learning that Pope Leo IV created him cardinal priest of St Marcellus either in 847 or 848. It can scarcely have been because of great sympathy between the two men. It is evident from what happened afterwards that Anastasius belonged to the pro-imperial party in Rome (the Empire at the time being that of the Franks) because soon after his elevation he had to flee Rome and take refuge in imperial territory in northern Italy. The Emperor Lothair, and his son and successor Louis II, both had strained relations with Pope Leo, not least because he had failed to wait for Lothair's consent when he accepted the papacy. Leo demanded that his errant cardinal return to Rome, but when he refused, the Pope had him excommunicated at a council in Rome on 16 December 850. The excommunication was renewed almost exactly two years later, and on this occasion Leo had erected above the entrance to St Peter's an image of Christ and of Mary anathematizing Anastasius.

Leo IV died on 17 July 855. There was some confusion at the election of a successor because the first choice, Hadrian, refused the office. The people's second choice was Benedict, but he had to await imperial approval. It did not come. The papal messengers were intercepted by Arsenius, and, at Orte, Arsenius's see to the south of Orvieto, Anastasius was elected Pope. He then marched on Rome with imperial backing, seized the Lateran basilica and papal palace, and threw Benedict III into prison. He then had the picture Leo had erected at St Peter's pulled down. But he never had popular support. Neither the people nor the clergy wanted him: he had, after all, been excommunicated. The traditional consecrator of popes, the Bishop of Ostia, refused to take part in any consecration ceremony, and after three days the imperial representatives in Rome, who had hitherto been backing Anastasius, allowed the consecration of Benedict to go ahead.

But then, what to do with Anastasius, the would-be antipope? At this period a person became pope not on his election, but at his consecration, and as Anastasius had not been consecrated, he was simply a claimant to the papal throne rather than an antipope. It appears that he was degraded from his office of priest, and imprisoned in the abbey attached to the church of Santa Maria in Trastevere. He was soon restored to the rank of priest, however, even possibly by Benedict himself, and Pope Nicholas I, who in 858 succeeded Benedict, made him abbot of the monastery. Nicholas fostered his talents, employed him as a papal secretary, and used him for liaison with the Frankish court, to which he had remained close despite his vicissitudes.

Nicholas was succeeded by Hadrian II in December 867, and Anastasius continued in office though he was not wholly confident in Hadrian's firmness of purpose. He was afraid in particular that Hadrian might be browbeaten into annulling Lothair's marriage, which Nicholas had refused to do. Hadrian did not in fact yield, and he rewarded Anastasius with the office of *bibliothecarius sanctae romanae ecclesiae* – Librarian of the Holy Roman Church. This was an exceedingly important position. It had less to do with books than with papal correspondence: he not only signed letters on behalf of the Pope, in many instances he also dictated them. He was, in other words, helping to formulate papal policy. But then, for apparently no fault of his own, his career once again came to a sudden stop.

Before his election to the papacy Hadrian had been married. His wife was named Stephania, and they had a daughter, whose name is unknown. In March 868 a certain Eleutherius seized the daughter, who was already betrothed to someone else, and raped her – then murdered Stephania. Eleutherius was put to death for his actions by the imperial representatives at Rome, but Anastasius was thought to be somehow implicated in this crime. Eleutherius seems to have been the son of Bishop Arsenius, in which case he was Anastasius's cousin, or it is just possible that he was Anastasius's brother. Unless there was some kind of conspiracy it is difficult to know why the Librarian was involved, but he was nonetheless deprived of his office and once again reduced to the status of a layman. He went into exile, possibly at the court of Louis II. When there was a council in Constantinople in 870 he was present, but he was part of the imperial delegation rather than that of the pope: he had been charged with the task of arranging a marriage between the daughter of Frankish Emperor Louis II and the son of the Byzantine Emperor Basil.

Anastasius was degraded in mid October 868, but the crime was committed much earlier in the year. Why the delay? One reason may have been that Pope Hadrian could not do without him in the course of that year. The apostles of the Slavs, Cyril and Methodius, had come to Rome bearing what they claimed were the relics of the first-century Pope Clement, over which there was much rejoicing. During their stay (Cyril died in Rome in 869) they celebrated the liturgy in the Slavonic rite which they had been instrumental in creating, and Anastasius was heavily involved in organizing it.

Although at Constantinople in 870 he was not a member of the papal delegation, as has been remarked, he seems to have kept a watching brief on the various issues which divided Rome from Byzantium. There was the question of papal authority over the Patriarch in Constantinople and the affairs of the Eastern Church, but there was also the question of territory – specifically, in this instance, responsibility for Bulgaria, where both Rome and Constantinople had been vying for jurisdiction. Shortly after the council proper the representatives of the Eastern Churches met behind closed doors and decided this issue in favour of Constantinople. Naturally the Roman delegates were furious, and none more so than Anastasius. When he was back in Rome (and restored to papal favour) he spent much of the remainder of his life translating lives of saints and other documents from Greek which upheld the authority of Rome over Byzantium – and, for that matter, the authority of the pope over the Frankish Empire.

The date of Anastasius's death is not recorded. The last dated mention of him is on 29 May 877, but there is no mention of another *bibliotecarius* for almost another two years. After a remarkably tumultuous career he seems to have died either late 877 or sometime in the course of the following year.

Baldassare Cossa (Pope John XXIII)

When in 1958 Giuseppe Roncalli was elected pope and chose to be known as Pope John XXIII, from the historians among the cardinals there was a sharp intake of breath. There has already been a Pope John XXIII. The Vatican's year-book, the *Annuario Pontificio*, in its chronology of all the popes lists him as an antipope. Whether he was this or a legitimate pontiff depends very much on the interpretation of events over almost half a century from 1378. During this period, the time of the Great Western Schism, there were always two contenders for the title of pope, and sometimes three. The earlier John XXIII belongs to the period from 1409 (he himself was elected in 1410) when there were three competing pontiffs. He was deposed in 1415 and, given the events of his extraordinary earlier life, returned to the rank of cardinal with surprising dignity.

Baldassare Cossa was born on the island of Procida, or possibly Ischia, near Naples, about the year 1360: his father was lord of Procida and moved among the nobility of the region. His mother was distantly related to Pope Boniface IX of the Roman 'obedience', who died in 1404. He had three brothers. Living as they did on an island, their trade was the sea, hence he gained a reputation for piracy which was possibly undeserved. On the other hand, his reputation as a womanizer was well earned. He had a liaison with his sister-in-law and with many others besides. He was wholly unsuited to the office of cleric, but with a relative as pope it was inevitable that one of the Cossa sons would pursue a clerical career. Baldassare was the chosen one, and armed with the indispensable doctorate in canon and civil law from the University of Bologna, bought for him, it is thought, by his father, he was on his way. The doctorate came in 1389, by which time he was already a canon of Bologna cathedral. He was given a minor position in the service of Boniface IX, and by 1392 he was a papal chamberlain. Four years later he was made archdeacon of Bologna, an office which included oversight of the University.

In 1402 Cossa borrowed 10,000 ducats from the Florentine banker Giovanni di Bicci, a member of the Medici family. He had decided it was time to acquire a cardinal's hat. This was duly bestowed by Pope Boniface, with the title of S. Eustachio, on 27 February of that year. He was then sent as legate to Bologna. This was not an easy task: first of all the city had to be wrested from the control of the Visconti. Cossa set out with an army, and returned it to the control of the papacy by September 1403. He stayed on as legate to govern the city. It is of this period that some of the more lurid aspects of Cossa's career are recounted. He ruled with great severity, he paid back the Medicis, added substantially to his own bank account (though the papal one was run down), and is said to have seduced at least two hundred women.

Cossa's legation, bestowed by Boniface, had been confirmed by successive popes of the Roman obedience, Innocent VII and Gregory XII. There was increasing pressure on each side to come to some agreement. The Roman Pope Gregory and the Avignon Pope Benedict XIII negotiated a reunion of the two obediences, but neither was prepared to give way. In frustration a group of cardinals decided to call a council of their own to settle the matter. Cossa perhaps saw an opening. Certainly he hurried to associate himself with the 'unionist' bloc, and joined the gathering held at Pisa from March to August 1409, first withdrawing all his funds from the Medici bank. It was not Cossa who was elected Pope (or antipope) at Pisa but Pietro Philarghi, who took the title of Alexander V. Cossa's skills were needed elsewhere. Gregory XII was backed by Ladislas Durazzo, King of Naples, who was occupying Rome. The Pisan group decided to back a rival claimant for the Neapolitan throne, Louis of Anjou, and Cossa marched to Rome at the head of an army. He captured it after a siege, but did not stay. Instead, accompanied by Pope Alexander, he returned to Bologna, where a deputation of Romans arrived begging the Pisan Pope to return to the city. On 3 May 1410, while still in Bologna, Alexander died. Some suspected Cossa had arranged an assassination, but it is more likely that the Pope died of natural causes.

The cardinals now met at Bologna, and chose Cossa as pope on 17 May: he was ordained priest a week later and consecrated a bishop the following day, immediately before his coronation in Bologna's cathedral on 25 May. He took the title John XXIII. He owed his election to his prominence in the unionist group of cardinals, but also to the need to have a skilled military commander in charge if Rome was going to be retaken from Ladislas, who had re-established himself there. Backed by Medici money once more, the troops of Louis of Anjou, accompanied by John, again marched on Rome and captured it, but Louis's hold on the city was precarious. John XXIII had to make peace with Ladislas. To do so he was obliged to pay him a large sum of money, which he again borrowed from the Medici bank, this time pledging as security a jewel-encrusted gold mitre and other papal accoutrements.

The peace did not last. Ladislas marched back to Rome and John had to flee to Florence. He turned for help to the newly elected King of the Romans, and candidate for the imperial title, Sigismund. John had enjoyed fairly wide-spread support among the European powers, but only because they wanted a united Church, which the Pisan effort at reunion had seemed to promise. As it seemed increasingly unlikely that John could deliver unity, support melted away. As a condition of his own support, Sigismund demanded a general Council. Reluctantly John was obliged to give in, though it was Sigismund who formally summoned the Council to meet in Constance. John began to have second thoughts when Ladislas suddenly died and he was no longer under pressure, but it was too late to prevent the Council from happening. Again he borrowed money, and to ensure that nothing went wrong, Giovanni de Bicci sent his son Cosimo de'Medici to accompany to Constance the Pope in whom he had invested so much of the Medici wealth.

Pope John XXIII opened the Council on 5 November 1414. It soon became clear that, although he was the 'unionist' Pope, he was highly unlikely to survive in office. Disguised as a groom he fled the city on the night of 20/21 March 1415: councils, he reasoned, could not proceed without the Pope. He was proved wrong. Sigismund kept it going, and it solemnly proclaimed the superiority of a Council over a Pope. John did not get far. He was captured and brought back and put on trial: he was charged with poisoning Pope Alexander, of simony, of acting tyrannically and of generally living a dissolute life. All fight had been knocked out of him. He was deposed and for a while imprisoned: he was released after three years only when the Medici bank once again produced the money Sigismund demanded as ransom.

Giovanni de Bicci found the money for Baldassare Cossa's ransom on one condition: that he come to Florence and be reconciled with the new Pope, Martin V, who was living there. The reconciliation duly took place, and Martin created Cossa Cardinal Bishop of Tusculum (the modern Frascati). The Medici hoped Martin would be grateful, and be impressed by their loyalty to Cossa, an extremely problematic client. But the new Pope was not impressed – there was the matter of the jewelled mitre of which, it seems, the Medici kept possession.

The elevation of Cossa from Cardinal Deacon to Cardinal Bishop took place on 23 June 1419. Six months later, on 22 December, he died. As a condition of one of his loans he had agreed to make the Medici not only executors of his will, but also its beneficiaries, and despite Cossa's vicissitudes it seems he still had a fair amount of money left to repay his creditors. He also had a finger of St John the Baptist, which Giovanni di Bicci kept with him for good luck for the rest of his life. Giovanni di Bicci continued to demonstrate his loyalty to his former client: he hired Donatello and Michelozzo to construct a magnificent tomb in the baptistery at Florence. It bears the inscription *Ioannes Quondam Papa XXIII*, 'John XXIII, once the Pope'. Pope Martin V was not amused.

Reginald Pole

While there has so far been only one English-born pope, Reginald Pole came very close to being the second. He was born at Stourton Castle in Staffordshire, possibly on 3 March (the exact date in uncertain) 1500. His father was chamberlain to Prince Arthur, the eldest son of Henry VII and heir to the throne. His mother was Margaret Plantagenet, Countess of Salisbury, who was daughter of the Duke of Clarence, the somewhat less than wholly loyal brother of King Edward IV. The Countess was later to be appointed governess to the Princess (later Queen) Mary. Pole was the third son, and as such had a rather distant claim on the English crown. Not that this claim particularly troubled Henry VIII, to whom Pole was therefore related. Henry appears to have paid for his education. His early schooling was either at Christchurch, Canterbury, or at the Charterhouse at Sheen. He then went to Magdalen College, Oxford, with the King's support, and Henry also provided him with a couple of benefices. After graduating from Oxford he went on to Padua, again with a pension provided by the Crown.

In Padua, where he was treated as an important visitor, he met Pietro Bembo (see p. 75), through whom he came to know a large group of humanists and scholars of whom some, such as the Church reformer Gianpietro Carafa (later Pope Paul IV), were to play a significant role in his life. He also met others who were to espouse the Protestant reform. He was in Padua, apart from visits to Rome and elsewhere, until July 1526. He had become a fellow of Corpus Christi College, Oxford in 1523, a position which helped to pay for his upkeep while in Italy. After his return home he was provided with further benefices, including the deanery of Exeter.

The major topic of the time was the divorce of Henry VIII from Catherine of Aragón. It was inevitable that he be drawn into the controversy, and while pursuing further studies in Paris in 1529–30 he was asked to enquire as to the opinion of the teachers of the University of Paris about the legitimacy of Henry's case. It seems he received a favourable response to Henry's query, though his own opinion at this time is more difficult to determine. He certainly outlined to the King some of the problems involved, but without apparently incurring the King's anger was able to leave England again early in 1532. But neither had he received any ecclesiastical preferment, even though at one time it had seemed likely he would be offered the archdiocese of Canterbury, vacant since the death of Cardinal Wolsey.

Pole again made his way to Padua, but only after six months living in and around Avignon where he encountered Jacopo Sadoleto (see p. 78). Again he moved in humanist circles, but he also dedicated a great deal of time to the study of Scripture: he had earlier learned Greek and while in England had set about acquiring a knowledge of Hebrew. Henry VIII wanted to know what Pole thought about the divorce proceedings, and about the King's supremacy over the Church in England. While in Padua he produced a response, *A Defence of the Unity of the Church*, which he sent to Henry, suggesting that a committee be set up to study it. But Pole was treading dangerous political ground. The imperial ambassador proposed that Pole, still technically a layman, should marry the Princess Mary. Such a union would give Pole a double claim to the English throne and therefore, in a politically unstable England, he might form a rallying point for dissidents. Henry was right to be concerned, Pole right to be alarmed.

Shortly after sending his book off to England, Pole was summoned to Rome, ordained deacon, and created cardinal deacon with the title of SS Nereo ed Achilleo. He was then put by Pope Paul III on the commission tasked with proposing, as they did in 1538, a plan for the reform of the Church. But he was also given a political agenda. It was in theory a wide one, encompassing the forthcoming Council (of Trent) and the Turks, but his real task was to support the rising in England against Henry's policies known as the Pilgrimage of Grace. He had money for the rebels, and the Pope backed him with a bull promising a crusading indulgence to anyone who overthrew the English King.

His journey to the Channel coast was slow and difficult – neither the King of France, who had treaty obligations to Henry, nor the Emperor was happy with the thought of Pole being present in their territory. And in addition there were several attempts on his life by English agents. Pole eventually gave up his efforts to reach England and returned to Rome, where he was appointed to the commission of cardinals preparing for the Council. He also travelled with the Pope and on his own on diplomatic missions to persuade the Emperor to form an alliance with the Pope against Henry. But Charles V was opposed unless the French joined in, and he was unhappy with Pole's call to the English nobility, of which his family was of course part, to rise up against the King: such an act of *lèse majesté* was not going to be popular with any sixteenth-century monarch. The danger to his own family was evident: his mother was executed on 27 May 1541.

Back in Rome, while political matters still occupied him somewhat, he became deeply involved in a circle of men and women who were spending time reflecting on their spiritual life. There were those who were convinced that the views of members of the circle verged on the heretical, and Peter Vermigli going over to the Reform did not help. But Pole's friendship with Pope Paul III protected him. The Pope demonstrated his confidence in Pole by charging him with preparing the Council of Trent and naming him as one of the three papal legates. It was Pole who gave the opening address, although he did not play a substantive part in the proceedings.

It was in the conclave of March 1555, which resulted in the election of Julius III, that Pole was almost elected Pope: indeed, he would have been chosen had he not rejected the proposal to dispense with a final formal vote. But the French were against him, and the required two-thirds majority could not be found: Pole spent the conclave writing a short treatise on the pastoral office of the pope. After Julius's election the new Pope appointed Pole to the Inquisition, despite the fact that he seems to have objected to its methods; he did not attend its meetings with much regularity. At the head of the Inquisition, however, was Pole's old acquaintance from his first years in Italy, Gianpietro Carafa, an austere zealot who was distinctly suspicious of Pole's involvement with Rome's humanist and spiritual circles. Julius forced Carafa to be reconciled with Pole, but immediately afterwards Pole left Rome to spend time in prayer at a Benedictine monastery on Lake Garda.

He never returned to Rome because in July 1553 the Catholic Mary Tudor became Queen of England, and Pole was appointed papal legate to her court. Charles V opposed the appointment of Pole as legate, almost certainly because Pole had opposed his plan, eventually realized, to marry his son Philip of Spain to Mary. Why Pole was against this Catholic marriage was never clear. If he feared Spanish intervention in English affairs, it was a fear which many of his countrymen shared. Because of imperial opposition – and to some extent France's opposition likewise – it took Pole until 20 November 1554 to reach England. He said he would not set foot in the country until the crown had agreed to restore Church property, which Mary was prepared to do, though Philip was less enthusiastic. Protestant England was reconciled with Rome ten days later, on 30th November.

In December 1556 Pole summoned a synod to meet in London. It lasted well into the following January and proved to be in some respects, especially in the emphasis it placed upon a better-educated clergy and the establishment of what would come to be called seminaries, a forerunner of the reforming sessions of Trent. He also commissioned a catechism, but it was prepared late, and only in Latin. Immediately after the synod a visitation was launched into the English Church, and into the two universities. In the course of the synod, on 11 December 1555, Pole was named administrator of Canterbury, Archbishop Thomas Cranmer being still at that time alive. Pole was not yet a priest, let alone a bishop. He was ordained on 20 March 1556, and consecrated two days later in Greenwich, but came into full possession of the see only after Cranmer's death, burned at the stake in Oxford on 21 March. Queen Mary also proposed making him Chancellor of England, but he objected and so, in Rome, did Pope Paul IV.

Paul IV, elected on 23 May 1555, was Gianpietro Carafa. Despite their earlier enmities, Pope Paul had been very complimentary towards Pole when promoting him Archbishop of Canterbury. But suspicion rankled. And then there was the problem of Spain. Pope Paul, a Neapolitan by birth, had an almost irrational hatred of Spain's domination of southern Italy, and launched a war against Spain in the course of which the papal armies were decisively defeated. It did not help matters that Philip of Spain arrived in England in March 1557 while the war was going on. Pole, as a papal legate, refused to meet him publicly, but that was not enough for Pope Paul who withdrew Pole's Legatine authority the following month. Mary and Philip, and the English parliament, all backed Pole, but Paul had now announced in a consistory that he was suspect of heresy. Pole wrote a long defence of his position and said he would come back to Rome to face imprisonment (one of his friends was already a prisoner in Castel Sant'Angelo).

It was never to happen. According to the Treaty of the Cave after the defeat of the papal forces by Spain, Pole was supposed to be reinstated as legate, but Paul's antipathy to him only increased and he was summoned to Rome. He did not go. He died at the Archbishop of Canterbury's London residence, Lambeth Palace, in the early evening of 17 November 1558, and on 15 December was buried in Canterbury Cathedral. Mary Tudor had died twelve hours earlier.

Giuseppe Renato Imperiali

Imperiali came from a powerful and ancient noble family originally of Genoa, though he was born on 29 April 1651 at Oria, near the family stronghold of Francavilla in the diocese of Brindisi. The Castello Imperiali still dominates the town, though the family acquired it only towards the end of the sixteenth century, by purchase from Charles Borromeo (see p. 112). Several of the family became cardinals – Giuseppe was the nephew of one, and the uncle of two. Surprisingly little seems to be known about him. Nothing is known of his education, though he held the customary (for the time) doctorate in civil and ecclesiastical law. Nothing is known either about his rise through the ranks of the clerical state. When he became a cardinal deacon in February 1690, with the title of S. Giorgio in Velabro, he had to be granted a dispensation because he had not up to that time received even minor orders. He acquired orders immediately, however, and in double-quick time: he had to get another dispensation to be ordained out of season, and without pausing between the reception of one order and the next.

He entered the papal service about 1670 and served in a number of posts – including that of commissary general for the armed forces of the Papal States. After his elevation to the purple he was used in a number of diplomatic posts as well as serving for a time as legate (i.e. papal governor) in Ferrara. He was apparently a skilled administrator, for he was a member of the Congregation of Good Government charged with overseeing reforms in the papal territories. Crucially, however, he appears to have been one of the *zelanti*, the group among the cardinals which favoured freeing the papacy from political involvements, and concentrating much more on its spiritual function (*zelanti*, as the word suggests, derives from 'zeal'). Among other things this meant that they supported the Society of Jesus against the efforts by the Bourbon courts of France and Spain to pressure the papacy to take action against the order.

The conclave of 1730 lasted from 5 March to 12 July (two cardinals died in the course of it, though only one in the conclave itself). Imperiali was within one vote of being elected when Cardinal Bentivoglio vetoed him, acting in the name of the King of Spain. He died on 15 January 1737, but he seems to have played no major role in the workings of the Holy See after the conclave, instead devoting himself to the care of his large and extremely valuable library.

Hyacinth Sigismund Gerdil

Gerdil was a member of the Clerks Regular of St Paul, a religious order commonly known as the Barnabites because when it began it was closely associated with the church of St Barnabas in Milan. (The Barnabites, though relatively unknown in Britain and Ireland, flourish in Italy and the United States and elsewhere – they even have a house in Kabul, Afghanistan.) He was born at Samoëns in the diocese of Geneva on 23 June 1718 to Pierre, a notary, and Françoise Perrier. Though this region is now part of France, until shortly before Gerdil's birth it had been the independent duchy of Savoy, by the time he was born it had become part of the Kingdom of Sicily, and shortly afterwards it became part of the Kingdom of Sardinia.

He received his early education in what had been Savoy, at Thonon and at Bonneville, where his father's brother, himself a Barnabite, was teaching. It was there that he entered the order, taking his vows in September 1733. He had been baptized Jean François: he now adopted as his name in religion Giacinto (Hyacinth) Sigismondo. His intellectual abilities had already been remarked, and he was sent for theological studies to Bologna, where he excelled. So much so that he came to the notice of the Archbishop of Bologna, Prospero Lambertini, the future Pope Benedict XIV. After his studies he was sent to teach philosophy at various Barnabite houses in Italy, being ordained priest at Casale in June 1741. Soon afterwards he published a critical study of the English philosopher John Locke and a year later a defence of the Oratorian priest and philosopher Nicolas Malebranche. The following year, in September 1749, he was made professor of philosophy at the University of Turin.

Many other works followed. Gerdil's interests ranged well beyond what was then contemporary philosophy to political theory, moral theology (he was given the chair of moral theology at Turin in 1754), even science. For his scientific work he was made a member of London's Royal Society as well as of other learned societies in Bologna and Rome. Admired by the King of Sardinia, Victor Amadeus III, he was appointed tutor to his two sons, the future King Charles Emmanuel V and Victor Emmanuel I, who succeeded his brother on Charles's abdication. In 1759 he resigned his teaching post and in 1764 became provincial superior of the Barnabites in Savoy and Piedmont. He maintained his interest in philosophy, however, and continued to publish even after leaving the university, including an attack on the educational ideals of Jean-Jacques Rousseau, and on Rousseau's *Contrat Social*, describing his theories as the complete reversal of a proper social order – which in his eyes was definitely not democratic.

There is some doubt about the date on which he was created cardinal because whenever it was, it was *in pectore*, that is to say, kept to himself, by the Pope. It may have been in the last consistory of Clement XIV, held on 26 April 1773, or it may have been in Pius VI's consistory of 23 June 1777 – it was in any case published in the December of that year and in March 1778 he received the title of cardinal priest of St John at the Latin Gate (he shortly afterwards exchanged it for that of St Cecilia). Whenever the elevation happened, he had been called to Rome – where he lived in the headquarters of the Barnabites – by Pope Pius in March 1776 to advise him as to what he should do about Victor Amadeus III, who was now pursuing a policy of suppressing religious houses and confiscating their wealth. The King, however, bestowed on him a couple of abbeys which had not been suppressed, and he directed their progress through a series of pastoral letters despatched from Rome.

Once in Rome he was immediately involved in the doings of the papal curia, becoming a consultor of the Holy Roman and Universal Inquisition. He became titular Bishop of Dihona in February 1777, not long before it was made known that he had been created a cardinal. As cardinal he became Prefect of the Congregation of the Index, a role which he took very seriously. At the time there were threats to the unity of the Church in Germany, Austria and northern Italy. The Bishop of Pistoia, Scipione de'Ricci, held a synod in his diocese in 1786 which proposed a series of reforms to the Church, some of them not unlike those introduced by the Protestant reformers of the sixteenth century. The bishop described Gerdil as the only moderate voice among the Roman cardinals. He was, however, one of the committee of cardinals who helped prepare Pius VI's bull condemning the Synod of Pistoia. During the last quarter of the eighteenth century Gerdil's many writings were frequently concerned with this kind of threat to traditional Catholic doctrine and practice.

But there were even greater challenges ahead. He advised the Pope in his condemnation of the Civil Constitution of the Clergy, produced in the wake of the French Revolution, though he was prepared to see, as the King of France had requested, dioceses divided even against the wishes of the French bishops. To divide dioceses in this way was, he believed, within the prerogative of popes. More offices in the Roman Curia were given to him, but the one to which he was most attached was the appointment, in February 1795, as Prefect of the Congregation for the Propagation of the Faith (Congregatio de Propaganda Fide) which was, and is, responsible for the Church's missions. It was a very difficult time. The French wars made communication with missionaries extremely difficult. Even more problematic was raising money to support them: Gerdil sold some of his own possessions for the purpose, including books.

After the occupation of Rome by the French in February 1798 he was obliged to leave the city and made his way – eventually – back to Turin, where he was given refuge by the King and, after the King's death, by his former student Charles Emmanuel. When the latter abdicated, however, he went to live at the abbey of St Michael at Chiusa that Victor Amadeus had bestowed on him. He continued to write, producing in 1799 a treatise on political sovereignty.

After the death of Pope Pius VI in French custody, the cardinals made their way to Venice, as they had agreed, for the conclave: thirty-four of the forty-five members of the college managed to make it to the city. They were dominated by the fear of France, on the one hand, and the fear of the Emperor in Vienna, upon whom they had to rely for their security. The conclave was a long-drawn-out affair, from the beginning of December 1799 to mid March of 1800. It took time because it was deadlocked, but also because the Emperor of Austria vetoed two likely candidates, one of them Cardinal Hyacinth Sigismund Gerdil. It was probably not that the Emperor had anything particularly against Gerdil, more that he wanted a particular candidate, Cardinal Mattei, who had proved weak in opposing French annexation of the Avignon, and the confiscation of sundry art treasures. What Mattei had done once in favour of the French, reasoned the Emperor, he might do again in favour of Austria. Gerdil was not elected, but nor was Mattei. The choice fell upon Barnabà Chiaramonti, who took the name Pius VII.

Gerdil accompanied the new Pope back to Rome, where he took up his old offices and continued to write in defence of Catholic doctrine: three more volumes appeared after his return to Rome. One of them, however, was posthumous. After a short illness he died in Rome on 12 August 1802. At his own wish he was buried in the church of S. Carlo ai Catinari where, in 1777, he had been consecrated bishop.

Pietro La Fontaine

Cardinal La Fontaine was for twenty years Patriarch of Venice, an office in the Church from which a good many popes have been chosen. He was a cardinal only for one conclave, that which elected Pope Pius XI, but in it he played a significant, if entirely passive, role. He came close to becoming the successor to Pope Benedict XV.

He was born in Viterbo on 29 November 1860. His father Francesco was by origin from Geneva, but had served in the army of the papal states, married Maria, the daughter of the manager of the estates of Prince Doria Pamphili, and had settled down to the gentle trade of a clockmaker. Pietro showed early signs of a vocation to the priesthood, and entered the local seminary. He was ordained priest in Viterbo in December 1883. He did pastoral work in the diocese – he was a skilled preacher – but most of his work lay in the seminary itself, as a teacher then as spiritual director and eventually, though fairly briefly, as rector. His service to the diocese had impressed the powers that be. In December 1906 he was chosen by Pope Pius X as Bishop of Cassano all'Ionio in Calabria.

These were difficult years in the Church, the height of the struggle against Modernism. Modernism is not easy to define. It took different forms in different places, but in essence it was an attempt to reconcile Catholic teaching with contemporary scholarship. Perhaps the most striking aspect of Modernism was the attempt to interpret the Bible employing the same tools that historians had begun using to study ancient texts. Many of the findings of the new Biblical criticism were condemned by Rome (needless to say they are now commonly accepted), and those who held them were reported on and removed from their teaching positions. Bishop La Fontaine's own personal theological stance was severely traditional, and well in tune with that of the Vatican. He was appointed the Vatican's emissary, traversing Italy and visiting seminaries to report on the teaching and the teachers, seeking out any deviation from the acceptable Roman norm. The records of his investigations, however, reveal him to be a prudent and moderate inquisitor.

He was rewarded for his efforts by promotion. He was nominated successively to be vicar to the archpriest of the Lateran basilica (1908) and of St Peter's itself (1910). He was appointed a consultor to the committee which was drawing up the Church's code of law, and in 1910 he became secretary to the Congregation of Rites, the Vatican body overseeing the Church's liturgy. All of these Roman offices meant that he could no longer exercise the duties of a resident bishop, so he was in 1910 made the titular (honorary) Bishop of Caristo. In March 1915 Benedict XVI made this loyal servant of the Church Patriarch of Venice, an office which traditionally is held by a cardinal: he was created cardinal priest of Ss Nero ed Achilleo (a title which he later changed to that of the XII Apostoli) in December 1916.

Pietro became Patriarch of Venice just months before the Italians, who had remained neutral at the outbreak of the First World War, entered the battle on the side of France and Britain in the hope of regaining territories which had been ceded to Austria a century earlier, at the close of the Napoleonic wars. In November 1917 the Italians were heavily defeated at the battle of Caporetto, and fell back to the Piave River. The war was now being fought on territory that fell within the diocese of Venice. The cardinal was heavily involved in the relief of the consequent sufferings of the people of the Veneto, getting government help, urging the fixing of prices of foodstuffs, encouraging the wealthy Venetians to support the poor, and giving liberally to the poor from his own funds. His charitable activities won him the affection and respect of the people of his diocese.

The conclave which followed the death of Benedict XV opened in Rome on 14 February 1922. It took fourteen ballots to elect Achille Ratti as Pius XI, but almost until the last La Fontaine was a likely choice. There was a body of electors who wanted a sternly conservative candidate, but it soon became clear that such a person was not going to be chosen. La Fontaine's reputation for orthodoxy could not be questioned: he had been an inquisitor during the Modernist controversy. But he had also gained a reputation for his humanity, both as an inquisitor and during the war. He was therefore proposed by the intransigents among the Sacred College as the one of their number who might possibly win over some of the less conservative cardinals. There were sixty cardinals in all at Benedict's death (one, the Cardinal of Toledo, died the same day as the Pope), but the Cardinal of Quebec did not arrive in time, and others excused themselves on health grounds. There were in the end fifty-three electors. La Fontaine received votes on the first ballot, but some dropped away before the conservatives lighted on him as a possible compromise candidate. The number of his votes peaked at twenty-two when the number required for election was only thirty-six. Even at the end he was running second to Ratti. (For more on this controversial election, see the biography of Pietro Gasparri, p. 194)

It was not easy for a churchman to live an uneventful life in the Italy of the 1920s and early 1930s, but La Fontaine did his best. He served as papal legate, or representative, at several Eucharistic Congresses, once travelling as far as Vienna. He was an early sympathizer with Benito Mussolini, and welcomed the rise of fascism on the grounds that it was good for the Church. But as time went on he was increasingly confused by Mussolini's stance, and complained of fascist attacks on Catholic organizations.

This gentle man who had, as a pastime, written poems and even plays which friends put to music, died at the Villa Fietta, the minor seminary of the diocese of Venice at Paderno del Grappa, on 9 July 1935. He was buried on the Venice Lido, in a chapel dedicated to the Immaculate Conception of the Virgin. He himself had built the chapel, amid the tombs of the Italian soldiers who had been killed at the battle of the River Piave. In February 1960 the then Patriarch of Venice, Cardinal Urbani, began the process leading to his eventual canonization. It has not progressed very far.

The Dynasts

No one who has studied the lives of cardinals, or even the lives of the popes, can fail to have noticed that some names appear time and again. It is almost as if there were certain families who had a special claim to high rank in the Church. The most notable among these families was – and indeed is, because it still survives though it no longer provides cardinals, the Colonna family. In all there were eighteen cardinals who bore the name Colonna, from Giovanni, born c. 1185, who became a cardinal in 1206 or possibly half a dozen years later, to the last, Pietro Colonna Pamphili, born in 1725 and who became a cardinal in 1766. The lives of eight of them are recounted here, including both Giovanni and, briefly, Pietro. Strangely, perhaps, only one of them was elected to the papacy: Odo Colonna became Pope Martin V in 1417.

In attempting to give some impression of the dynastic aspect of the cardinalatial office, it is really only possible to provide an outline of one of the families who exercised a claim to the purple. But there were many more. The Orsinis, for example, although they were perhaps less colourful than the Colonnas, produced well over a score of cardinals and two popes. The first of these popes was Celestine III (1191–98), whose name was not Orsini but Boboni; it was, however, the same family. One of Celestine's first acts was to create his nephew Niccolò a cardinal, and in the consistory of 1193 he made a cardinal of a canon of the Vatican basilica named Bobone. The family was extremely powerful in Rome, and it was the senator Matteo Rosso Orsini who, in the papal election in the summer of 1241, locked the cardinals (there were only twelve of them involved) in a falling-down palace and kept them there for two months in increasingly squalid conditions until they agreed on a candidate. It was an Orsini, therefore, who inadvertently invented the idea of the conclave.

There were intermarriages between the two families, but for much of the middle ages they were enemies, or at least in an uneasy truce. The Orsinis were the stronger clan within the city, and dominated the commune. In the long-drawn-out quarrel between Pope and Emperor, the Colonnas tended to side with the latter (they were therefore leaders of the Ghibelline party), and the Orsinis with the papacy (the Guelphs).

Like the Colonnas, the Orsinis provided cardinals down almost to modern times. The last was Domenico Orsini d'Aragona, who was created a cardinal deacon in September 1743, just a year after his wife had died. He had to be granted a dispensation to raised to the purple without having received even minor orders, but he did receive them, and went on to ordination to the priesthood. He died in 1789. He was a nephew of Pope Benedict XIII (1724–30), who had renounced his dukedom to become a Dominican. The cause for Benedict's canonization was opened shortly after his death, but stalled because of the Pope's association with Niccolò Coscia (see p. 217). It has been recently reopened. None of the Colonna cardinals were members of religious orders, but several of the Orsinis were, two of them apart from Pope Benedict becoming Dominicans, and one of them a Benedictine.

Although the lineage was not as long-lasting as that of the Orsinis or Colonnas, perhaps no cardinatial family was more dynastic than that of Farnese. Alessandro Farnese was made a cardinal in 1493 because his sister Giulia was the mistress of Pope Alexander VI, Rodrigo Borgia: he was derisively known as 'cardinal petticoat'. Though he later completely changed his life and became an upstanding member of the reform movement, Alessandro in turn kept a mistress who bore him three sons and a daughter. His eldest son, Pier Luigi, who married an Orsini, unfortunately imitated his father's worst excesses. When Alessandro became Pope in 1534 he made Pier Luigi's son, also called Alessandro, a cardinal, and later created Pier Luigi the first Duke of Parma. Pope Paul also made Alessandro's younger brother a cardinal.

There were several other families with a handful – or more – of cardinals in their ranks, the della Rovere family, for example, the Aldobrandini, the Fieschi, the Gonzaga and others. So prevalent was family relationship in the Sacred College that a rule was introduced forbidding close relatives being members of the College at the same time. It was frequently dispensed with.

Giovanni Colonna

Of the great Roman families who struggled among themselves for control of the city none was more powerful, or more enduring than the Colonnas. They are said to take their name, and their heraldic symbol, from Trajan's Column, located not far from their Roman property next to what is now the Jesuit Gregorian University. The reality is a mite more prosaic. The family appears to have come from the town of Colonna in the Alban Hills, and to have spread from there to be overlords of several neighbouring towns, not least the town of Palestrina, which was to figure large in the history of the family. They produced a good many cardinals and one pope, Martin V (1417–31), elected in the unusual circumstances of the Council of Constance. The first of these dynastic cardinals seems to have been Giovanni Colonna.

His date of birth is unknown, though it was probably in the last couple of decades of the twelfth century. He is first mentioned as a member of the papal chapel in the early years of the thirteenth century and may have been created Cardinal Deacon of SS Cosma e Damiano in 1206, though according to other sources he became cardinal priest of S. Prassede in 1212, and to yet others in 1217. In that year he was given the task of accompanying the new Latin Emperor of the East, Peter de Courtenay, to Constantinople, setting sail from Brindisi. But he and the Emperor were captured by the Despot of Epirus, and while the cardinal was released at the Pope's request and continued his journey, the Emperor died still a prisoner.

When he reached Constantinople Giovanni gave his support to the Empress Yolande, Peter's widow, but after her death in September 1219 he was, as papal legate, effective ruler of Constantinople and of what remained of the Eastern Empire of Byzantium. He proved to be remarkably efficient in this role, smoothing out problems between Rome and the local barons. He took particular care to undermine the influence of Venice, which had been pursuing its own policies in the East. He ensured that all the major churches in Constantinople would have a vote in the election of a new Patriarch, and not just the clergy of Hagia Sophia, who were judged to be too sympathetic to the Venetians. He returned to Rome in 1222, bearing with him for his titular church of S. Prassede, the appropriate gift of a column – the column, it was claimed, to which Christ had been bound during the flagellation. It is still venerated there.

For the next few years he held a variety of posts under the Pope, and when Rainaldo of Spoleto attacked the Papal States, Giovanni was put in charge of part of the papal army. He showed himself remarkably competent as a general, and equally remarkably loyal to the Pope, apparently paying some of his troops' expenses out of his own pocket. But by that time he had become the wealthiest of all the cardinals. When the populace of Rome fell out with the Pope, he was one of the cardinals who helped to negotiate a peace deal.

Matters were more complicated when the Emperor Frederick II wanted the Pope, Gregory IX, to excommunicate the Lombards who had risen against him. Gregory refused. Frederick then defeated the Lombards in battle, setting out, it seemed to Gregory, to take over the whole of Italy. A truce was negotiated, but collapsed when Gregory refused to exclude the Lombards from it. At this point Giovanni changed sides: his family had, in any case, always rather favoured the imperial cause. Frederick asked the cardinal to take part in the attack on Rome from his family territory of Palestrina. The inveterate enemies of the Colonnas, the Orsinis, now rose to power in Rome, and besieged the

Colonna stronghold in the city. But at this point, August 1241, the Pope died.

This presented Giovanni with a problem. As a cardinal he had the right to participate in the election of a new pontiff, but in Rome he was at risk. Matteo Orsini guaranteed his safety, and he took part in the conclave which chose Celestine IV, but Celestine died after little more than a fortnight in office. Most of the other cardinals took this opportunity to flee the city, but Giovanni did not and was imprisoned by Orsini. He then refused to take part in the new conclave on the grounds that it would not be a free election. With all the problems in Rome there was an eighteen-month gap between the death of Celestine and the election of Innocent IV – an election which took place not in Rome but at Anagni – but by that time, at the Emperor's insistence, Giovanni had been released. He participated in the conclave, but from then on largely disappears from history. He died on 12 January 1245, but where he died, and where he is buried, remains a mystery.

Giacomo and Pietro Colonna

Giacomo, born around the middle of the thirteenth century, belonged to the Palestrina branch of the sprawling family. He pursued a typical ecclesiastical career, studying law at Bologna, and early on acquiring the archdeaconry of Pisa. He was promoted by Pope Nicholas III to the title of cardinal deacon of Santa Maria in Via Lata on 12 March 1278, and archpriest of Santa Maria Maggiore. Pope Nicholas was a relative, an Orsini, and was quite possibly counting on the Colonna family's pro-imperial, anti-Angevin stance to support him as he tried to curb the ambitions of Charles of Sicily, and broker an alliance between the Angevin Charles and the Habsburg Rudolph, who was Emperor-elect. He hoped thereby to ensure stability in the Papal States. This policy was reversed by Pope Martin IV who, being French, was understandably pro-Angevin. Under Martin's successor Honorius IV it was reversed again.

Then came the Franciscan Pope Nicholas IV. He decided early on in his pontificate that he was going to turn to the powerful Colonna family, who in any case had already strong links to the Franciscans (Giacomo's sister Margherita was for a time a member of St Clare's convent in Assisi before founding her own community) to safeguard papal interests. He promoted another Colonna to the rank of cardinal, Pietro, the son of Giacomo's brother Giovanni, and made Giovanni himself the sole senator for Rome itself. It seems quite likely that Pietro had been married before being raised to be Cardinal Deacon of S. Eustachio in May 1288, but whether his wife was persuaded to enter a convent, leaving him free to take orders, or whether the marriage was simply dissolved by the Pope is not recorded. Like Giacomo, Pietro's life before entering the papal curia is little known. It is thought likely, however, that he studied law at Padua, and held canonries at both Padua and Verona.

From the time of Pietro's promotion the lives of the two Colonnas, uncle and nephew, were intertwined. They were given various important posts in the administration of the Papal States, and in diplomatic missions. So much did the Pope depend upon them that a cartoon was circulated which showed the Pope imprisoned within a column, the Colonna heraldic device, with only his head sticking out. It was during this period (1288–92) that Giacomo, in his capacity of archpriest of Santa Maria Maggiore, had the apse of the basilica decorated with mosaics.

The two Colonnas both took part in the long election – it lasted well over two years – which culminated in the choice of the holy but wholly incompetent Pope Celestine V, who, rooted out from his hermitage was effectively wished upon the cardinals by Charles, the Angevin ruler of Sicily. Holiness apart, Celestine's only redeeming feature was that he recognized his own incapacity, and after six months resigned the office of Pope. Pietro and Giacomo participated in the election of Benedetto Caetani as Pope Boniface VIII.

If the reign of Nicholas IV had marked the apogee of Colonna influence on papal affairs, that of Boniface VIII marked its nadir. Boniface's reign had started well enough for them, but they had exploited the interregnum to consolidate and extend Colonna-held territory in central Italy. In doing so they were obliged to rethink their relations with Charles of Sicily. They were, therefore, ill at ease with Boniface's hostility towards the Angevin ruler, and although Giacomo had approved the resignation of Celestine, and supported the election of Boniface, the two cardinals now began to raise questions about the validity of the resignation, and to spread a rumour that Celestine – who by this time had died – had been murdered on the orders of his successor, which is just about possible, but highly unlikely.

Matters came to a head when on 3 May 1297 a nephew of Giacomo's seized a papal convoy carrying treasure. Boniface summoned the two cardinals to meet him, but the encounter resolved nothing and they fled to a Colonna stronghold. They now made a public declaration that Boniface's election had been invalid, and called for a general council of the Church to unseat the Pope. Boniface promptly stripped both Giacomo and Pietro of their cardinatial rank, declared them to be schismatics, and on 14 December 1297 announced a crusade, a holy war, against the two and all the Colonna supporters. The following October the Colonnas were forced to submit, the cardinals among them, but they did not feel secure, and Giacomo seems to have fled to the countryside. But Boniface had made an enemy even more potent than the Colonnas: he had angered King Philip the Fair of France. One of the French King's ministers, backed by the Colonnas, led an armed attack on the Pope and his entourage while they were at Anagni, and although the people of the town came to the Pope's aid and freed him, he was a broken man. He returned to Rome under the protection of the Orsinis, but shortly afterwards died there, on 12 October 1303.

The two Colonnas were no longer ranked as cardinals, and the other members of the Sacred College were in no mood to reinstate them, so they had no part in the election of the saintly Benedict XI. He removed from them all the ecclesiastical sanctions which had been imposed, but did not restore to them their rights and privileges, nor their many benefices. Under Nicholas IV, Pietro had been papal legate (ambassador) to the court of the King of France. He now appealed for support to the French King, but Philip was so preoccupied with exacting posthumous revenge on Boniface with the aid of Boniface's successor that he was no help.

Still not being of cardinatial rank, the two Colonnas were barred from the election of the short-lived Benedict's successor, Clement V. Clement was more forgiving. He restored them to the status of cardinal, and gradually lifted the other disabilities with which they were burdened. They received further benefices, but Giacomo seems not to have been restored to the papal court, by this time at Avignon, until 1310. Two years later he was once again made archpriest of the Liberian basilica (Santa Maria Maggiore), and resumed his task of artistic renovation. Once again fully cardinals, Pietro and Giacomo took part in the subsequent election of Pope John XXII. They were rewarded with further benefices, but seem to have played little further part in papal policymaking. After their bruising encounter with Boniface they had effectively been sidelined.

Giacomo died at Avignon on 14 August 1318: it was reported to have been an edifying demise. His corpse was taken to Rome and interred in the Liberian basilica on which he had lavished so much time and money. He had included himself, Pietro, and Pope Nicholas IV among the figures represented in the mosaics he had installed, together with the saints he believed he had seen in a vision after the death of his devout but peripatetic sister Margherita. Pietro took over his role as archpriest of the basilica; he was already, from 1306, archpriest of the Lateran basilica, which he also undertook to restore. Pietro died in Avignon on 7 January 1326, and like his uncle was buried in the Liberian basilica. He chose to be interred next to the tomb of Nicholas IV. In his will he left money for a hospital for incurables in Rome. The hospital was dedicated to San Giacomo.

Margherita had died at the very end of 1280. She was declared to be a 'blessed' by Pope Pius IX in 1847, though veneration of her was restricted to the Franciscans. That was extended to the diocese of Palestrina by Pius's successor, Leo XIII, in 1883.

Giovanni II Colonna

Very little is known about the early life of this great nephew of Giacomo. Along with his father he was taken prisoner at Ravenna in November 1290 when he must have been quite a young man, possibly little more than an infant. Then he only turns up again in 1327, being named as a papal notary. As a notary it must be presumed that he had studied law somewhere, presumably at Bologna, but there is no record of this. Later that same year, however, he was promoted to the rank of Cardinal Deacon of S. Angelo in Pescheria in the consistory of 18 December. Since the death of Pietro nearly two years before there had been no Colonna cardinal, which was problematic if the Pope, John XXII, wanted to maintain good relations with this most powerful of Roman families. In the same consistory he also promoted a distant relative of Giovanni's – but just to keep the balance he also made a cardinal of Matteo Orsini, a member of a rival family to the Colonnas. Indeed, the Orsinis had seized Giovanni's titular church, reduced it to ruins, and had to be expelled by force.

The rank of cardinal was generally seen as a means of enrichment, for the cardinal himself and for his family. Giovanni was no exception. He received a string of benefices bestowed on him by the Pope, archdeaconries, canonries and so on. He also became, like his uncle and great uncle before him, archpriest of the Liberian basilica, Santa Maria Maggiore. Again like Pietro he left money for the hospital for incurables. He was also associated with the basilica of St John Lateran.

The power of the Colonnas in Rome was demonstrated in the strange career of Cola (short for Nicola) di Rienzo. He claimed descent from the Emperor Henry VII, but his mother was a washerwoman and his father a tavern keeper. A cultured man, at least in the history of ancient Rome, he wanted to restore the city to its former glories. In 1343 he visited the papal court at Avignon, and won papal favour. When he returned home he fomented a revolt against the powerful families, above all the Colonnas, and picked out Giovanni in particular. On 20 November 1347 there was a clash between Cola's supporters and the Colonnas which led to the deaths of several of the family – a fact which Cola put down to divine retribution. But his own fall was not far off: after being denounced by the Pope he fled the city and the country. He was imprisoned in Prague and eventually handed over to the Pope, but by that time Cardinal Giovanni, who seems to have orchestrated his downfall, was dead. He died in Avignon of the Black Death on 3 July 1348, one of six cardinals to die of that plague over the Avignon Summer. Perhaps as a consequence of the manner of his death, his burial place is unknown.

A good deal of what is known about Giovanni and Cola di Rienzo comes from the letters and poetry of Francesco Petrarch. The poet had got to know

Giovanni's brother while at university, and they had become friends. He was introduced to Giovanni by his brother in 1330, and became a member of the cardinal's household until, in 1347, inspired by Cola's claim to be restoring the ancient liberties of Rome, he returned to Italy. Despite the Colonna opposition to Cola, Petrarch always spoke, almost with affection, of the cardinal he had served for seventeen years.

Agapito Colonna

There were, as has been already remarked, several branches of the Colonna family, one of the most powerful of them hailing from the city of Palestrina. It is the modern name for the ancient city of Praeneste, located some twenty miles east of Rome, and its patron saint, the saint to whom the cathedral is dedicated, is St Agapitus – hence the popularity of the name in the Colonna family. This Agapito, whose date of birth is unknown but was possibly c. 1330, was the son of the Colonna who took part in the attack on Boniface VIII at Anagni which shortly afterwards occasioned Boniface's death. After his father's death he travelled to Avignon, where he joined the household of Cardinal Giovanni Colonna (see above), there to be taught for some years by Petrarch, who regarded him as an intelligent and diligent scholar.

He studied law at Bologna, where he stayed until 1363. There he became vice-chancellor for the faculty of Canon Law, as well as Archdeacon of the city itself. He had already gathered sundry benefices, and was to gather more until, in July 1363, he was named Bishop of Ascoli Piceno. He was still only in deacon's orders, but was consecrated a bishop at the beginning of 1364. He did not, however, spend much time in his episcopal see. He was sent by Pope Urban V on a number of diplomatic missions, in which efforts he was not notably successful. Nonetheless he was in the entourage of the Pope when Urban returned to Rome from the papacy's long exile in Avignon towards the end of 1367.

For a year or so he remained at the papal court before being sent back to Germany to negotiate peace between Otto of Brandenburg and the Duke of Austria, the Pope's aim being to facilitate the entry of the Emperor Charles IV into Italy. Agapito was then to be found for a time in the imperial court at Lucca, which was a relatively safe place. Rome was not. The Romans had revolted against papal rule, and Urban thought it best to return to Avignon. Before setting out from Montefiascone, where he had taken refuge, the Pope appointed Agapito his legate in the Iberian Peninsula, with the task of bringing peace to the warring Spanish kingdoms and Portugal, and to preach a crusade. He also appointed him to the diocese of Brescia, a much more lucrative post than that of Ascoli. St Bridget of Sweden, who had prophesied Urban's early death should he return to Avignon, was proved right. The Pope died in that city little more than two months after his return. His successor, Gregory XI, made Agapito Bishop of Lisbon. His peace-making in Spain had been an undoubted success, and Gregory sent him off on a similar mission to Hungary. The objective was always the same: a crusade against the forces of Islam, which was impossible unless there were peace among the Christian princes.

When Gregory decided to return the papacy to Rome, arriving there in January 1377, Agapito followed him. He came to play an important role in the conclave which followed Gregory's death on 27 March 1378. He was one of the few Roman prelates to have returned to the city from Avignon, and he was the natural channel for the anxieties of the citizens of Rome who feared that the election of a non-Roman, or at least a non-Italian, would result in the papacy once again leaving their city. The election of Urban VI took place on 8 April, but the mob invaded the Vatican before the outcome could be made known. The cardinal electors fled for their lives, one of them, Robert of Geneva, who was a close friend of Agapito, taking refuge in one of the Colonna family's Roman palaces. Agapito himself, however, remained at the new Pope's side, and in the manoeuvrings which followed the election was used by Urban to help gather together such of the cardinals as had not fled the city.

The election was controversial. Urban's apparently bullying tactics alienated especially the French members of the Sacred College, and they slipped off to Anagni, claiming that the choice of Urban had been made under duress from the Roman mob, and was therefore invalid. Agapito now served as an intermediary between Urban and the dissidents, though without success. On 20 September, Robert of Geneva was elected as Pope Clement VII by the dissident cardinals gathered in the cathedral of Fondi. Agapito, who had at last been created cardinal priest of S. Prisca two days earlier after trying to fight off the promotion – he said he wanted a quiet life – was completely taken aback.

He remained loyal to Urban for the few years that were left to him. He served the Pope in particular by attempting to broker a peace between Venice and Genoa, in which enterprise he was unsuccessful. While in northern Italy he attended the King of Hungary at Verona and, after returning to Rome, was again sent off by the Pope on a mission to Aragón. When he came back he was invested by a grateful Urban with yet another benefice, the archdeaconry of Durham. He died in Rome either on the 11th or the 18th of October 1380. He was buried, as was his brother Stefano, created a cardinal on the same day as Agapito and who had died two years earlier, in the basilica of Santa Maria Maggiore: Stefano in the chapel of the Nativity, Agapito under the pavement before the high altar.

Ascanio Colonna

A list of Colonna cardinals would include several between Agapito and Ascanio – one of them, Odo, became Pope Martin V in 1417. Ascanio stands out, however, not least because his father, Marcantonio, Prince of Paliano, was the admiral of the fleet which in 1571 defeated the Turks at the battle of Lepanto, a rare victory in the struggle to defend Christian Europe. Paliano is a small town, south-east of Rome, which then lay within the Spanish-ruled Kingdom of Sicily. It was, and is, dominated by the fortress of the Colonnas. It was, however, not in Paliano itself but at the nearby village of Marino that Ascanio was born, on 27 April 1560.

At the age of just over sixteen Ascanio went with his father to Spain, and it was in Spain, at the universities of Alcalá and then of Salamanca, that he studied, graduating with a doctorate *in utroque iure*, i.e. 'in both laws', civil and ecclesiastical. At the death of his father in 1584 he inherited a palace and other territories: destined for a clerical career, the abbacy of the monastery of Santa Sofia in Benevento had already been obtained for him. His family background may have been in Italy, but Ascanio was very much an Hispanophile, an admirer of the Spanish monarch Philip II, who returned the compliment. Philip petitioned Pope Sixtus V to create him a cardinal, on the grounds of his religious devotion, and his learning. This Sixtus was disposed to do, raising him to the rank of cardinal deacon in the consistory of 16 November 1586. But the news of the intended promotion was slow reaching Philip, and the King sent another letter to the Pope, making the same request, which he gave to Ascanio to carry to Rome: Ascanio only learned of the Pope's decision while on his journey, receiving the traditional red biretta when he disembarked at Genoa. He was invested with the deaconry of SS Vito e Modesto in Rome on 17 February 1587. He now, in the accustomed manner, began to acquire further benefices, the most important being that of Archpriest of the basilica of St John Lateran. To that he added the abbacy of the monastery of Subiaco and, already a Knight of Malta before he left Spain, he became Prior of the Order for Venice in 1594, and finally Grand Prior.

But there were also other, rather more durable, acquisitions. Cardinal Guglielmo Sirleto was regarded by his contemporaries as one of the most learned men of his time; he became Librarian of the Vatican Library, which he greatly enriched. He also collected books for himself. At his death he is thought to have had some 7,000 manuscripts or printed books in his library. These were acquired by Ascanio, who then added to them books and manuscripts from the monastery of Santa Sofia, where he was titular abbot. His books, which were, much used by scholars of his day, including by Cardinal Cesare Baronio (see p. 83), were housed in specially prepared rooms in his Roman palace.

He himself was no mean scholar of Greek. The Council of Trent had ordered a new edition of the Vulgate, the official Latin translation of the Bible, to be prepared. This had been undertaken, by a commission set up by Pope Sixtus, but it was going, in the Pope's view, painfully slowly. He took it over himself, and rushed it into print in May 1590. There was an immediate outcry. It was full of errors, some typographical, others more serious. Sixtus died in the August of the same year, and there were in quick succession two conclaves, in both of which Ascanio took part. The cardinals' first choice, Urban VII, lasted less than a fortnight, his successor Gregory XIV less than a year, while Gregory's successor lasted under two months. That brought Clement VIII to the papal throne. Clement listened to the criticisms of the text of Sistine Vulgate voiced by Ascanio (among others), and had a new version produced, which lasted down to the mid twentieth century.

Ascanio's relative, Cardinal Marcantonio Colonna, who had served on the revision committee for the Vulgate, had in 1591 risen to be Vatican Librarian, and Ascanio played some part in the management of the collection, possibly relying on the skills of his own library staff. But as time went on he felt he was not getting in Rome the recognition he deserved. He therefore determined to return to Spain – which he called his second homeland – and with the reluctant permission of the pope took himself off to the court of Philip III, his former patron, Philip II having died in September 1598. He set off two years after Philip II's death, travelling in some style and sharing part of the journey with Marie de' Medici as she made her way to France to marry King Henry IV.

When Ascanio met the Spanish King at the court in Valladolid he lost no time in asking some significant mark of regal favour: he was granted the title of Viceroy of Aragón. This was a somewhat problematic posting because it required him to dispense criminal justice, which was forbidden to clerics. He had to ask the pope for permission. But it had other problems. It was, he came to the conclusion, more expensive than it was profitable, and in mid 1605 he returned to Rome.

He had no sooner arrived back in Rome than he became embroiled in controversy. As has been remarked, Cardinal Baronio, who was by this time the Vatican Librarian, had used Ascanio's library while he was engaged upon his multi-volume history of the Church, the *Annales Ecclesiastici*, composed as a response to the version of Church history produced by the Lutheran 'Centuriators of Magdeburg' – so-called because they divided the history up century by century. Baronio sent one of his volumes to Ascanio for comment. His account of the conflict between the papacy and the Spanish monarchy over the Kingdom of Sicily infuriated the avowedly pro-Spanish Cardinal Colonna. He produced a riposte, which appeared in print only after his death, accompanied by Baronio's own refutation of Ascanio's interpretation of events. He again intervened, only this time taking the Pope's part, in the clash between the papacy and the Venetian Republic: Paul V had excommunicated the Venetian senate for having usurped, he believed, clerical authority. The whole of the Republic was put under an interdict which most of the clergy (the Jesuits excepted, and they were exiled) openly flouted. Baronio also supported the papacy, so in this at least he and Ascanio Colonna were on the same side.

He died on 17 May 1608, and was buried, alongside the only Colonna Pope, Martin V, in the family chapel in St John Lateran. His library was sold, but it eventually became part of the Vatican's collection. As well as books, however, he also left a son.

Prospero Colonna di Sciarra

Much of papal politics in the eighteenth century was dominated by the fate of the Jesuits. In the Far East their adaptation of the Roman liturgy to the customs of the local population had resulted in the 'Chinese Rites' controversy, during which their efforts at enculturation were condemned by successive popes – though they managed for a time to find a way round the papal ukases. In Europe, and especially in France, they were under attack from the Jansenists, a powerful rigorist movement within the Church. It was inevitable that the cardinals surrounding the Pope would be drawn into these disputes.

Prospero Colonna rose quickly through the ranks of papal functionaries. He had been born in Rome on 7 January 1707, the son of the Prince of Carbognano, of the Palestrina branch of the Colonnas who also had the name di Sciarra. He studied in Rome, but also in Parma and Padua, gaining the usual doctorate in laws civil and ecclesiastical. He was made a Protonotary Apostolic when only twenty-three and a consultor for the Congregation of Rites two years later. He was given various offices in the administration of the Papal States, in particular being put in charge of the food supply, where he collaborated with the aged Pope Clement XII, and especially Pope Benedict XIV, in freeing up trade within the Papal States by the removal of local tariffs and other barriers to the movement of goods. He was particularly close to Benedict who, on his election, named him as Prefect of the Papal Household. In his first consistory Benedict created both Prospero and his younger brother Girolamo cardinal deacons, first granting a dispensation from the rule against having two brothers in the Sacred College at the same time.

The Pope then made him Prefect of the Congregatio de Propaganda Fide, the part of the Vatican administration concerned with the missions. It was at the Congregation of Propaganda that he had his first major brush with the Society of Jesus. Clement XII had issued a new condemnation of the Chinese

Rites, but he had also banned Spanish discalced Franciscans from working on the southern part of what is now Vietnam, thus leaving the field open to the Jesuits: this expulsion order was now revoked by Prospero. His apparent hostility to the Society marked him out, in the eyes of the French ambassador, as someone favourable to France, and he was hoping that, after the death of Benedict XIV, Prospero might be made Secretary of State. France instructed Prospero, who was cardinal protector of France, how to vote in the conclave – namely against any candidate who might be thought favourable to the Jesuits. The tactic did not work. Not only was the next Pope, Clement XIII, sympathetic to the Society (he had been taught in Jesuits schools) but he chose as his Secretary of State Cardinal Torrigiano, who was also distinctly pro-Jesuit.

Both the Portuguese government and the Parlement of Paris now took action against the Society without waiting for the Pope, the Parlement demanding that the French Jesuits be separated off from the rest of the Society. *Sint ut sunt, aut non sint* ('Let they stay as they are, or not exist at all'), Clement is reported to have said, and he condemned the Parlement in a specially convoked consistory, where he also complained that the French were usurping the rights of the Church. Prospero thought it politic to stay away from that particular consistory, and although he could not prevent the Pope criticizing France, he managed to prevent Clement's address being published, on the grounds that the only result would be that the Parlement condemned it. In any case, nothing would stop the Parlement. In December 1764 it obtained from the King an edict suppressing the Society throughout the whole of France. Should he officially inform the Secretary of State and the Pope of the edict, the French ambassador enquired of Prospero Colonna? Better not to do so, answered the cardinal.

He died soon after this, on 20 April 1765. His funeral took place in the church of San Marcello, and he was buried in the family chapel at Santa Maria Maggiore.

Pietro Colonna Pamphili

There were sixteen children in the family of Prince Fabrizio Colonna of Paliano. Pietro was the third, the second being Marcantonio, both of them destined for an ecclesiastical career. Pietro was born at Rome on 7 December 1725, and in 1747 became the first holder of the benefice handsomely endowed by Prince Pamphili Aldobrandini, who made it a condition that the holder of the benefice should add 'Pamphili' to his name. By the time he was ordained priest in January 1760 he had held a number of significant posts in the administration of the Papal States. He had also graduated, in 1750, from the University of

Rome, La Sapienza, with a doctorate in civil and ecclesiastical law.

The day after his ordination to the priesthood he was named titular Bishop of Colosso, and consecrated a fortnight later, in preparation for his appointment as papal nuncio to Paris. It was a difficult time for the Church in France, and Pope Clement had chosen carefully. There was a whole series of major issues with which he had to contend. First there was the suppression of the Jesuits in France in May 1761, then the conflict between the Pope and the Jansenists, who continued to refuse to accept the papal bull *Unigenitus* which condemned one hundred and one Jansenist theological positions, and there was the removal of the prohibition against Catholics marrying Protestants in Alsace, which Pietro feared was a harbinger of tolerance for Protestants in the whole of the kingdom. Typically, however, he advised caution. The people, he warned Rome, wanted toleration.

His advice was much appreciated. He was asked to draw up a memorandum on the conduct of the nunciature in Paris, and he was created cardinal priest of Santa Maria in Trastevere in September 1766 – his brother Marcantonio was already a member of the Sacred College, so a dispensation had to be granted for two close relatives being in the Sacred College together. His red biretta was sent to Paris, but he himself returned to Rome soon afterwards where, in the manner of cardinals, he fulfilled several functions in various Congregations and collected further benefices. In 1769 he took part in the conclave which elected Clement XIV, and in the conclave of 1774 he backed the man who became Pius VI, though in the first ballots both Pietro and his brother received a number of votes.

He died unexpectedly on 4 December 1780. He was in Verona, attending the wedding of one of his relatives, and was interred in the cathedral.

The Scholar Cardinals

It is particularly difficult to write about the scholar cardinals. Or rather, it is particularly difficult to choose about whom to write. There were, and are, a great many of them. It was always part of the job description. As was remarked in the Introduction, Pope Alexander III (1159–81) instructed his legate in France to seek out learned men who might be appropriate candidates for the Sacred College. In 1436 the Council of Basel insisted that room in the College had to be found for learned men, though it added that, for the scions of princely families, the level of learning might be set quite low.

Those whose lives are recounted below, however, were all men of considerable scholarship. Pierre d'Ailly was a theologian, and chancellor of the University of Paris. One might indeed have expected cardinals to specialize in the study of theology, but that was often not the case. As will be seen in a good number of the biographies, the main study was frequently legal, a requirement if someone was to choose a career in the administration of the Papal States, or indeed in the administration of any of the governments of Europe (see the chapter on the Politicos, p. 153). Some of the more interesting characters among the cardinals were humanists by training, their specialized knowledge being that of the Latin and Greek classics. Pietro Bembo was such a one, and so was Jacopo Sadoleto, though Sadoleto, as will be seen, also tried his hand at theology, and not wholly successfully. He even ran into trouble with Rome as he attempted to grapple with some of the theological issues that were raised by the reformers.

It was of course Sadoleto's desire to defend his Church. Two other scholars mentioned in this chapter were in their own ways more successful. Cesare Baronio might well have preferred to be a theologian, but circumstances forced him into the guise of an historian, at which he acquitted himself extremely well. Roberto Bellarmino was indeed a theologian, but he became better known in his own day as a controversialist, and in modern times for his involvement in the case brought against Galileo.

Few, if any, of the cardinals were greatly skilled in the natural sciences, and given their necessary training in the humanities this is scarcely surprising. Giuseppe Garampi was initially very interested in science, but then he was interested in everything, archaeology, numismatics, bibliography. As will be seen, the massive Vatican Archives would be much less accessible had it not been for his labours in cataloguing them. As a bibliographer he collected a vast library. This was typical of many a cardinal, even those whose learning was not of the best. And often enough they bequeathed them to seminaries. Possibly the best known of these collections was that put together by Cardinal Aeneas Sylvius Piccolomini, who is not included in this volume because he became in 1485 Pope Pius II. It is not so much the collection of (very) early printed books and manuscripts that is so remarkable, as the setting in which it was housed, in the extraordinary setting of a room off the cathedral (duomo) in Siena, painted by Pinturicchio to designs very likely made by Raphael. It was created by Aeneas's nephew, Cardinal Francesco Piccolomini Todeschini, who at the time was Archbishop of Siena, and who also is not included because he became Pope Pius III.

They were men of the renaissance, but there had been scholar cardinals from the earliest times, not least the earliest cardinal mentioned in this book, Anastasius Bibliotecarius (p. 37), or the other 'precursors', Humbert of Silva Candida (p. 22), Peter Damian (p. 25) – who is a doctor of the Church – the Englishman Robert Pullen (p. 31), and saints such as Bonaventure, who was one of the greatest theologians of the middle ages, or Gregorio Barbarigo (p. 101) who bought a Hebrew typeface for the printing press he established in his seminary. Whether the same degree of humane learning has invariably been present in even some members of the College of Cardinals down to the present day is, perhaps, a moot point.

Pierre d'Ailly

Pierre d'Ailly was born at Compiègne not far to the north-east of Paris, some-time around the year 1350. He died in Avignon, seventy years later, on either the eighth, or more probably the ninth, of August 1420. He was buried some days later at Cambrai where he was bishop. He lived through possibly the most troubled period of the papacy. When he was born the Pope had lived for over four decades in Avignon rather than in Rome. In 1367, however, Pope Gregory XI had returned to a somewhat inhospitable Rome. At his death in 1378 there was a disputed election. Urban VI was elected, but the French cardinals some-what belatedly came to the conclusion that they had voted under duress and that consequently the election was invalid. So they elected their own Pope, who took the title Clement VII and returned to Avignon. This state of affairs, one Pope in Rome, another in Avignon, lasted for most of d'Ailly's life. The situation was further complicated when, in an attempt to end what became known as the Great Western Schism, cardinals of both the popes, those of Rome and those of Avignon, held a council at Pisa and elected a third Pope. From June 1409, therefore, there were three 'obediences' as they were called: those of Rome, Avignon and Pisa. The monarchs of Europe took their pick. The King of France naturally opted for Avignon, the English, as opponents of the French, for Rome. The Schism was finally resolved in 1417 at the Council of Constance when all three popes were declared deposed (one did not go quietly) and a new one elected. In sorting out all this confusion Pierre d'Ailly played an important part.

He came from a fairly middle-class family and went – on a scholarship – to the University of Paris, joining the College of Navarre in 1363. He followed the traditional medieval curriculum, graduating as Master of Arts five years later. The course of theology which he now embarked upon was much longer-drawn-out: he was finally awarded the title of doctor of theology on 11 April 1381. By this time he was teaching in Paris, and four years after his doctorate he became the rector of the College of Navarre. He was a prolific writer, not just on philosophy and theology but on geography, even astrology. There were sermons published, and also of course the lectures he delivered at his college.

As rector he became heavily involved in the politics of the university, but he was also deeply committed to the pursuit of benefices. He was quick to seize the opportunity offered by the arrival of Clement VII in Avignon. He went off to see him in 1379, even before the University of Paris had decided which of the rivals to the papal throne deserved its support. His sycophancy paid dividends. He became a very rich man through his collection of livings, culminating in October 1389 with his appointment to the post of chancellor of the cathedral of Notre Dame. The following year he added to his lustrous list of titles that of chaplain and confessor to King Charles VI, Charles the Mad as he came to be known.

Mad or not, Pierre's relations with the King were problematic. Although he – and the University – had given their support to the Avignonese papacy, there was an understandable belief that the schism was disastrous for the Church, and should quickly be resolved. The way forward, d'Ailly believed, was to hold a general council of the Church. In May 1381 he told the King so. This proved to be an unwise move. Not only was it contrary to the King's policy of support for Clement VII, it would also have undermined the Italian ambitions of the King's great uncle, Louis of Anjou. Pierre thought it wise to retire for a while from Paris and take up residence in Noyon, where in September 1381 he became a canon.

He had clearly worked-out ideas about ending the schism. Either both popes should resign, allowing the election of a third, unifying candidate, which was the route tried at Pisa, or – his favoured option – there should be a council of the Church to settle the matter. Popes, he pronounced, had always erred. The Church could not be built upon them but only upon Christ and the Scriptures. Christ gave his authority to priests and bishops, and only they, meeting in a universal council, could be regarded as infallible. Once the council was established it should, he argued, set about a radical reform of the Church. This was the theory which came to be known as conciliarism, and which attracted a great deal of support, though obviously not from the popes themselves. Not that Pierre was particularly voluble about these radical notions. After all, the Pope was the source of benefices. After Clement's death in 1394 and the election of Benedict XIII he was once again in Avignon, presenting the French King's greetings, and collecting a whole new array of benefices, both for himself, his family and his friends. In April 1395 he was made Bishop of Le Puy. Though he drew its revenues, d'Ailly never resided in the see, and eighteen months later exchanged it for the bishopric of Noyon. Unfortunately for him, there was already a Bishop of Noyon who refused to move, so Benedict appointed him to the bishopric of Cambrai. This was a far better prospect because it made him a prince bishop of the Holy Roman Empire. It had, however, the disadvantage of bringing him into conflict with another of the King's great uncles, Philip the Bold, Duke of Burgundy. Philip was conspiring against Charles while Pierre, though no longer the King's confessor, was now a member of his council of state.

The King, and the University, used Pierre as an emissary to Pope Benedict. They wanted a resolution to the Church's internal conflict, but the Pope was adamant. Pierre's loyalty was tried, but he remained for now on the Pope's side: he had preached a sermon on the Trinity before Benedict, and the Pope had as a consequence extended the celebration of the feast of the Trinity to the whole Church. When in November 1406 there was a meeting of the clergy in Paris, he spoke in favour of the Avignon Pope and carried the day, despite an attack on d'Ailly personally by a particularly eloquent member of the opposition. In 1406 a new Roman Pope was elected, Gregory XII, and it seemed an opportune moment to reopen negotiations. D'Ailly was sent to Rome. He got on well with the pontiff, but was unable to persuade him to resign.

The way of the council had long been d'Ailly's preferred way to end the schism. He therefore approved of, and attended, the gathering at Pisa which elected the short-lived Alexander V. True to his convictions he now espoused the cause of Alexander and then of his successor, one of the more unlikely pontiffs in the history of the Church, the former pirate Baldassare Cossa (see p. 40), who became Pope John XXIII. It was this Pope John who, in June 1411, elevated him to the rank of cardinal priest of S. Crisogono. John blessed him further: he became administrator of the diocese of Limoges, which he swapped for the bishopric of Orange: he was still, of course, receiving the income from the see of Cambrai. He served as John's legate to Venice and, more significantly, to the Emperor Sigismund. Sigismund was unhappy with the situation within the Church, where there were now three popes vying for the support of the various European monarchies. He determined to call a council of his own, to meet in the imperial city of Constance in December 1413.

Pierre d'Ailly was himself unconvinced of the value of the papacy of Pope John, even though he had taken part in electing him. But he was still a subject of the King of France, and Charles did not want another council. So it was not until almost a year after the meeting had begun at Constance that d'Ailly finally arrived there. He made it clear from the outset that he was abandoning John XXIII, but rather oddly took little part in the discussions which effectively implemented the conciliar theory which he had formulated, asserting the supremacy of council over pope. Instead, smarting under the recent defeat at Agincourt and the alliance between England and the Empire, he launched an ultimately unsuccessful attack on the right of the English to a separate vote in the council. He also busied himself with another conciliar issue, the condemnation of Jan Hus as a heretic. And above all he, with two other cardinals, were appointed to head a commission on the reform of the Church, a subject dear to the heart of this many-beneficed prelate.

After the council he was appointed by the new Pope to be his legate at Avignon, where he had a palace, given to him by the deposed John XXIII. He died there on 9 August 1420. Two years later he was buried in his cathedral at Cambrai where he had, as far as time allowed, been a zealous, if for the most part absentee, bishop.

Juan de Torquemada

Juan de Torquemada has a famous, or better an infamous, name, but it was not he who was Spain's Grand Inquisitor. That was his nephew Tomas, and Tomas was never made a cardinal. Theirs was a distinguished Castilian family: Juan's father Alvaro was governor of Valladolid, then one of the most important cities in the kingdom. He was born in 1388 and in 1403 entered the Dominican Order at Valladolid as, later, did Tomas. He studied at Valladolid, and was later sent to the University of Salamanca. But his life changed dramatically when in October 1416 the regent of Castile, Catharine of Lancaster, sent Fray Luis de Valladolid to the closing stages of the Council of Constance. Juan was sent as Fray Luis's travelling companion. It was a critical moment in the young friar's life. The Council had been summoned by the Emperor to settle the Great Western Schism, when there were two, and then three, contenders claiming to be the rightful Pope. The Council resolved the issue by deposing all three (one refused to go quietly) and electing Odo Colonna as Martin V, but in the process it also asserted the superiority of the Council over the Pope, a theory of Church governance which came to be known as conciliarism. Juan was to battle conciliarism for the remainder of his life.

First, however, he had to complete his studies. His superiors sent him to Paris to study theology. He became a Master in 1425, and returned home to Valladolid, where he was elected prior. He then went to Toledo, also as prior, the senior post in a Dominican house. In 1431 he was chosen to be the representative of the Dominicans of Castile at the Order's general chapter in Lyons, and at Lyons he and the Master General of the Order were chosen to be the Dominican representatives at the Council which Martin V had announced would meet at Basel in 1431: the King of Castile, Juan II, also appointed Juan as his observer at the gathering. He was personally in favour of reform of the Church along the lines that the bishops gathered at Basel were proposing, except for their central demand, the superiority of council over pope. He opposed, for instance, the Council's proposal to limit the right of popes to appoint bishops and abbots. He was a moderate, where the Council was radical, with the result that he became an apologist for the papacy. In March 1434 the Pope, now Eugenius IV, rewarded him for his support by making him Master of the Sacred Palace, a title originally bestowed on St Dominic and held by a Dominican ever since. In effect, Juan became the Pope's personal theologian.

As the Pope's theologian he opposed the Council's efforts to cut the papal curia down in size and to abolish the fees and taxes which contributed to its expenses. When the Council fathers demanded that popes swear an oath to follow conciliar dictates, he again objected, but it was the decision to move the meeting to Ferrara in 1437 that finally split the Council. The issue was the opening of reunion negotiations with the Greeks, which the hard-pressed Emperor in Constantinople, John VIII Palaelologus, hoped would win him Western backing against the Turks. The Pope and the Greeks wanted the meeting to be in Italy, the majority of the Council fathers wanted it to be held in Avignon or in Savoy. Juan naturally sided with the Pope, and went off to win over King Juan II of Castile to the papal cause. The Council reopened in Ferrara while Juan was still in Spain, but he made his way back there for a short time before he was sent off again, this time to Germany, in the company of Cardinal Albergati (see p. 94) to persuade German prelates to back the Pope rather than support the rump of the Council of Basel, which was now proposing to depose Eugenius and elect an antipope (which indeed it did: Felix V, in November 1439). The Germans were to meet in Frankfurt in November 1438, but because of plague the Diet was transferred to Mainz the following March. While in Germany Juan wrote a pamphlet attacking the conciliarists, and at Mainz made a speech in which he defended, unsuccessfully as far as the Germans were concerned, the infallibility of the Pope.

After Mainz Juan returned to Florence, where Eugenius's Council was now meeting. He debated with the Greeks on two major issues between Catholics and Orthodox, and the Greeks – with one important exception – declared themselves satisfied. On 5 July 1439 the decree of reunion, *Laetantur Coeli* (= 'let the heavens rejoice'), was issued. Juan was also the Pope's spokesman when Eugenius organized a debate on the relationship between Pope and Council, while Cardinal Cesarini, who had presided at Basel, spoke for the Council: Cesarini confessed himself convinced by Torquemada's arguments. On 18 December 1439 Torquemada (or, in Latin form, Turrecremata) was created cardinal priest of San Sisto and though, in 1460, he became cardinal Bishop of Palestrina, on 5 May 1463 Cardinal Bishop of Santa Sabina and in 1446 opted for the title of Santa Maria in Trastevere, he remained known as the Cardinal of San Sisto.

He was once again sent away on a diplomatic mission, this time to the court of the French King, Charles VII, at Bourges. The ostensible reason was to mediate in the war between England and France, but his main purpose was to win Charles over to the Pope's side against the on-going Council of Basel. When he arrived at Bourges Charles was absent, away putting down a revolt against him, and while awaiting his return Torquemada produced a pamphlet on the usurpation of lawful authority, guaranteed to appeal to any King, and especially to one against whom there had just been an uprising. Charles was won over: only the Germans and the Council fathers remaining at Basel backed Felix V.

It was Juan de Torquemada who, in March 1447, cast the deciding vote in the deeply divided conclave that finally elected Pope Nicholas V. Despite this support, he played only a small part in the pontificate of the new pope. His time was taken up by other concerns. He was deeply involved in the reform of his own religious order, the Dominicans, and also of the Camaldolese monks of whom he was cardinal protector. He was made administrator of the diocese of Palestrina in 1455, and also abbot of the Benedictine monastery of Subiaco, which he busily reformed. He campaigned in 1449 against the attempt of King Juan II to deprive *conversos* – Catholics in Spain who had converted from Judaism – of their rights. So vigorous was he in defence of the *conversos* that the unfounded rumour sprang up that his own family had originally been Jews. But his chief activity at this time was to produce a commentary on the *Decretum*, a compendium of canon law by the twelfth-century jurist Gratian. Torquemada was no canonist, and found it hard going, and, on and off, it occupied him for much of the remainder of his life. In 1453 he took time off from the commentary to write a treatise on the Church. It was not the first such, but it was one of the most thoroughgoing and, like the commentary, was intended to demolish the arguments of the conciliarists.

He took part in the conclave of 1455 which elected Callistus III, and again the following year in the conclave which elected Aeneas Piccolomini as Pope Pius II. He had opposed the election of Piccolomini, but apparently he bore him no ill-will. Certainly he was more involved in papal affairs during the pontificate of Pius than he had been in the two previous papacies. Pius and he both nurtured the vain hope that the Catholic powers might yet again unite in a crusade against the Turks. It was he who helped the Pope compose the letter to the Sultan Mehmet II which contained a detailed refutation of the doctrine of Islam. In it the Pope promised to make Mehmet an emperor should he convert to Christianity. Happily the letter was never sent: its text displayed a woeful and naïve ignorance of Muslim beliefs. That was in 1461. A couple of years earlier Juan had produced his own attack on Islam, which gave a similarly distorted account. He also worked for the release of Christians taken captive by the Turks.

He held a number of benefices in Spain, including administrator of the see of Orense, though the King of Castile, now Enrique IV, would not at first let him occupy it. He rebuilt the Dominican house of San Pablo in Valladolid which he himself had first entered, and donated to it part of his library – the major part went to the main Dominican church in Rome, Santa Maria sopra Minerva. He founded in Rome, with an offshoot in Florence, the Brotherhood of the Annunciation, which undertook to find dowries for poor young women. He also wrote a book of devotions based upon the psalms. His most significant devotional work, however, was a series of meditations based on the paintings he commissioned for the cloister he had built at Santa Maria sopra Minerva, to which he moved from Trastevere. He had the book printed in Germany although the earliest printers in Italy, refugees from the wars in Germany, had first settled in his monastery at Subiaco. In 1466, after the success of this venture into the new technology, he decided to issue an illustrated edition based on the paintings. This volume was printed in Rome, the first illustrated book produced in Italy.

He was by now plagued with gout, the pain of which reduced him to great rages. He was extremely ill at the time of the conclave of 1464, but still insisted on being carried into it. He survived for another four years, dying at Santa Maria sopra Minerva on 24 September 1468. He was buried in the church, in the chapel of the Annunciation which he had commissioned, and where his memorial may still be seen.

Pietro Bembo

For reasons that will soon become clear, it is highly improbably that Pietro Bembo will ever be declared a saint. Were it to happen, however, he would make an outstanding patron for printers. As some will have already recognized, he has given his name to a type font, but italic type was also first used in a book which he had helped to produce.

The publisher of both works was Aldus Manutius of Venice, and it was in Venice that Bembo was born on 20 May 1470, the son of a senator, Bernardo Bembo, and of Elena Morosini, also from an old noble family of the city. Bernardo served as Venice's ambassador to Florence and to Rome, and in many other political and diplomatic roles on behalf of the Republic, on some of which missions his family – certainly Pietro from time to time – accompanied him. Much as he was attracted to the society in which his father mixed, Pietro had no wish to enter into the political life of the Republic. Instead, when still quite young, he went off to Messina to learn Greek, in true humanist fashion, from the famous Constantine Lascaris, a refugee from Greece since the fall of Constantinople to the Turks in 1453. Other than that, his early education is difficult to assess, though later he was to attend the University of Padua, and later still become closely involved in the University's academic life. The visit to Messina was the occasion for his first book, or at least the book's inspiration: *De Aetna*, a description of the volcano, was the work printed in 1496 by Manutius in the special typeface he had invented which thereafter has been known as 'Bembo'. He continued to work with Manutius on books by other authors, as an editor and corrector of manuscripts: it was an edition of Petrarch on which he had worked that appeared in the new 'italic' script.

He was working with Manutius during the two-year period 1497–98 when his father was Venetian ambassador at the d'Este court at Ferrara, and Pietro was with him. Though from time to time in his life he expressed a desire for a solitary life, even at one time taking up residence in a hermitage, he much enjoyed the ambience of Italy's ducal courts, especially those of Ferrara and Urbino. While he was at Urbino he was working on his second book, written, as was his first, in the form of a dialogue, but this time a dialogue on love. It was entitled *Gli Asolani* after the town where it was supposed to be set, and it proved highly popular. It was dedicated to Lucrezia Borgia. In 1502 Lucrezia, the much-loved daughter of Pope Alexander VI, was married, a dynastic arrangement rather than a love-match, to Alfonso d'Este, heir to the dukedom of Ferrara. She arrived there with a retinue of 180 and a guard of 200 soldiers supplied by her brother Cesare (see p. 150). For some years Bembo carried on a clandestine love affair with Lucrezia from his nearby villa, though this relationship was, it seems, never a sexual one. Alfonso was suspicious – though he ought to have been more concerned about Lucrezia's next dalliance with her brother-in-law Francesco Gonzaga, to whom she turned after Bembo.

Francesco's sister Elisabetta was married to Guidobalda de Montefeltro, Duke of Urbino. Their court, the most splendid in Italy, was as has been mentioned, also attended by Bembo. It was the setting for Baldassare Castiglione's *Il Cortigiano*, 'The Courtier', which, after the manner of the time, was also set in the form of a dialogue: Bembo is one of the characters in the dialogue. Urbino played an important part in Bembo's life. When he settled for a time in Rome in 1511 (he had visited before with his father) in the hope of making his fortune, he lived there with a friend from the Montefeltro court, Federico Fregoso, Archbishop of Salerno. He was relatively impecunious, and needed preferment. He (and Sadoleto, see p. 78) found it as a secretary to Leo X, the Medici pope elected in 1513. Leo used him as an ambassador to Venice in December 1514 in an unsuccessful attempt to prevent the Republic entering an alliance with France. This embassy did not enhance the standing of his father in the Republic, who was forced to retire from public life. Perhaps not a great hardship: he was already 82 years old, and was to die soon afterwards. While Bembo was in Rome he entered a relationship with Ambrogina Faustina Morosina della Torre, a Vatican courtesan, which was to last until her death on 6 August 1535 at the age of 38. They had three children, two boys and a girl, of whom the elder boy died at the age of 8, to the great distress of his parents.

But by that time Bembo was no longer living in Rome. In 1521 he retired from papal service on the grounds of ill health to settle in a villa on the outskirts of Padua. He was chronically short of money despite the numerous benefices he had accumulated in papal service. Some were small; in other instances he found it difficult to lay hands on the income. Potentially the most lucrative was a benefice on the main square in Bologna belonging to the Knights of St John of Jerusalem (now known as the Knights of Malta). The only problem with it was the requirement that he should, in order to profit from it, himself become one of the Knights, a military religious order. He kept promising to take vows as a Knight, but failing to do so. The accession of Leo X's successor, the austere and reform-minded Dutchman, Hadrian VI, in 1522, forced his hand. His first son was born not quite a year after he had taken his vows.

It was during this period that he produced his most successful and indeed important book, *Le prose della vulgar lingua*, which had taken him in all twenty-five years to write. There was then hardly such a thing as Italian, simply a collection of dialects. Bembo chose to promote the Tuscan dialect as the most suited to literary purposes, and this book, as well as discussing grammatical and other issues, is in praise of it. He took it to Rome as a gift to the new Pope Clement VII, elected in 1523. It made him the most famous literary figure in the whole of Italy, and brought him a greater income, with which he was able to buy a house within the city of Padua itself, where he became involved in the University and where he was also able to run an informal school for boys. Several humanists frequented his Padua residence, not least Reginald Pole (see p. 43).

Though never himself one of the *spirituali* as Pole was, he was close to many of them, not least to the poet Vittoria Colonna who had been one of Bembo's earliest admirers but had rather transferred her attentions to the English prelate: when Pole settled at Viterbo for a time, she moved there to be close to him. There were many who were ready and able to commend Bembo to Clement VII as a candidate for a cardinal's hat, especially after the death of his mistress. His Venetian background was important: there were always one or two Venetians in the Sacred College. In the past Bembo had, with his father's backing, looked for positions in the service of the Republic to remedy his frequently chronic lack of funds. The posts had never been offered. But now he was offered the office of librarian of the Republic's Nicean Library. It was the collection of Cardinal Bessarion, another refugee from Constantinople, who had been Bishop of Nicaea – hence the name of the library. He was a relatively successful librarian, managing to have the library building extended. He was also asked to write the history of the Republic. It covered the period from 1486 to 1513. He wrote in Latin, but later translated the book into Italian.

So he had become a famous man, and on 20 December 1538 he was created a cardinal *in petto*, literally, in the breast, in other words it was not made public for almost a year, not until 10 November 1539 when he was announced as Cardinal Deacon of S. Ciriaco alla Terme. (He later became cardinal priest, first of S. Crisogono and later of San Clemente.) Some accounts of his life suggest that with the cardinalate he became a reformed man. He did nothing of the sort. Back in Rome he fell in love with another married woman (Morosina had also been married, though nothing is known of her husband, who may have died before she began her relationship with Bembo). He had, to please his colleagues among the cardinals, begun to write penitential sonnets as a kind of balance to his love poetry of earlier years, but he now started to write poetry for his new love. It was a problematic relationship, not least because her son had murdered his bride on their wedding night, and then fled to a monastery. Bembo found himself pleading for his safety with the abbot.

The rank of cardinal did not bring him any great wealth; on the contrary, cardinals were expected to live in a certain state of grandeur as befitted their rank and Bembo, as ever short of money, especially as his father's death had left him with considerable family debts, found it difficult to finance himself. In Rome he had to live in borrowed accommodation, and to reduce his staff. In 1541 he was appointed to the see of Gubbio (though he was never consecrated a bishop and possibly was not even a priest), and he found himself having to live there because it was a cheaper option than living in Rome. Two years later he was transferred to the diocese of Bergamo where, as he pointed out to the canons of Bergamo cathedral, his father had once been governor and he had lived for two years. In the manner of the day he appointed someone to run the diocese for him, and never visited his new see.

He died on 18 January 1547 after an accident. He was riding through an arch into his Roman lodgings when his horse lurched and he banged heavily against the wall. It did not seem a serious incident, but he was already frail and did not recover. On the instructions of Pope Paul III he was buried the following day in the Roman church of Santa Maria Sopra Minerva, near the tomb of Pope Leo X. His epitaph was composed by his son Torquato who had, like his wayward sister Elena, caused their father considerable anxiety during his life.

Jacopo Sadoleto

It is difficult to categorize Sadoleto. In his day he was rightly regarded as one of the most learned members of the College of Cardinals. Though they may no longer be read by anyone other than historians of the period, his collected writings were published several times in the course of the seventeenth and eighteenth centuries. He even wrote a treatise on the Church, despite having come late to theology. He was a would-be ecumenist and a reconciler of warring factions in Europe. Unlike many of his clerical contemporaries he appears to have lived an admirably chaste life apart from a youthful and fairly brief flirtation with Lucrezia Cugnatis, better known as Imperia, the most sought-after courtesan of early sixteenth-century Rome. Yet his devotional life remains something of a mystery, and though he wanted to spend his years in his diocese rather than in Rome, it was not because he wished to commit himself to the pastoral care of his flock at Carpentras. Rather it was because that city provided him with an oasis of tranquillity in which he might pursue his scholarly interests.

He was born on 12 July 1477, the second (just possibly the first) of the five sons and one daughter of Giovanni Sadoleto and his wife, Francesca Machiavelli. His birthplace was Modena, where Giovanni was a lawyer, but in 1488 the family moved to Ferrara, where Giovanni became Professor of Law at the University, and later Ferrara's ambassador to Naples and to France. Jacopo attended the University in Ferrara, and there came to know Pietro Bembo (cf. p. 75). The Sadoleto family was prosperous rather than rich, bourgeois rather than noble. If Jacopo was to make his way in the world as a cleric, then he had to journey to Rome and find a patron who would help him complete his education. The patron he found, though it is not clear how, was Cardinal

Oliviero Carafa (cf. p. 142). At the University his favourite discipline had been the Latin classics. In the household of Carafa on the Piazza Navona he came to study the Latin and Greek fathers of the Church. He also wrote poetry at this period, though he ordered all his verses to be destroyed except one, a poem marking the discovery on the Esquiline Hill of the statue, now in the Vatican, of the Laocoön: clearly he shared Carafa's passion for archaeology. In 1511 he wrote home that he was shortly to become a priest (he already enjoyed a modest revenue as a canonry of San Lorenzo in Damaso), but the date of his ordination is unknown.

The death of Carafa left him bereft of a patron, but only a month later both he and Bembo were offered posts as secretaries of briefs (letters) by the newly elected Leo X, the first of the two Medici popes he was to serve in that office. It was not a job which greatly attracted him, but as an expert Latinist it was one to which he was well suited. He became rather more than a secretary, dealing with correspondence from around Europe: his signature is to be found, for instance, on several papal letters dealing with that traffic in indulgences which so aroused the ire of Martin Luther and precipitated the Reformation. He displayed no personal antipathy to the practice. In this curial position he was able to collect yet more benefices, and with the proceeds to purchase a vineyard on the Quirinal Hill, where he found relief from the chores of office by entertaining other humanists gathered in Rome. Roman life, then, had its compensations, and when in April 1517 the diocese of Carpentras was conferred upon him he made some effort to refuse the benefice. This may have been a convention: he did not protest too much, and came to enjoy the greater wealth which the diocese produced. He was dispensed from residing in his see, but nonetheless showed a more than usual – for a non-residential bishop – interest in the diocese which was run for him by vicars, and promoted at the Rome the interests both of the diocese and of the town.

In years to come he was severely to criticize Pope Leo for his failure to deal with Luther, wholly forgetful that, as secretary of briefs, he had a part in framing the papal response. But none of that was heard while Leo was alive. He was close to the Pope, and when Leo walked barefoot from St Peter's to Santa Maria sopra Minerva as a penitential act to launch a crusade, it was Bishop Sadoleto who was chosen to preach the sermon in Santa Maria. It was a theme which was close to his heart and one on which he did not waver: Europe was in danger of being enslaved to the Turks. A Holy War was needed to save Christendom.

He left Rome on the death of Pope Leo, and did not immediately return on news of the election of the Dutch Pope Hadrian VI, who was himself absent in Spain at the time of the conclave. He returned to the city after Hadrian had belatedly arrived, having heard rumours, which proved false, that the new

Pope wanted him to return to his old office. Rather than stay jobless in Rome he requested permission to go to his diocese: he arrived back in Carpentras in May 1523. Hadrian's pontificate proved short: it was followed by the election in November 1523 of another Medici Pope, ruling as Clement VII. Almost immediately Clement sent for Sadoleto, who returned to his former post, but now with the added responsibility for papal nuncios in Germany and Eastern Europe: Italian policy the Medici Pope disastrously kept to himself. Sadoleto's approach was one of careful neutrality between Francis I of France and the Emperor Charles V, but Clement preferred an anti-imperial policy. The sack of Rome on 5 May 1527 by Charles's forces was preceded by a more modest, but still terrifying, sack by soldiers of the imperialist Colonna faction the year before, during which the papal apartments, and Sadoleto's in Trastevere, were ransacked and the Pope together with Sadoleto had to take refuge in Castel Sant'Angelo. Clement's decision to join the League of Cognac (an alliance of France, Milan, Venice, Florence and the Papacy) against Charles was the last straw for Sadoleto. He left Rome in mid April 1527 and travelled to Carpentras by sea via Civitavecchia and Nice. En route plague developed on his ship, and it was forbidden to disembark cargo in Nice. Such books as Sadoleto had salvaged from the Colonna attack had to be left on board, and were never seen again. He arrived at Carpentras on 3 May, to remain there until September 1536.

He was much criticized for leaving Rome, and spent some time defending himself, but in Carpentras he gave himself over to scholarship. During his earlier sojourn in his cathedral city he had written a commentary on Psalm 50 which had won plaudits from, among others, no less a humanist luminary than Erasmus. Now he wrote a commentary on the 93rd Psalm in which he reflected upon the nature of the priesthood, something of a departure for someone who had an excellent education in the classics and philosophy, but little or no structured knowledge of theology. He wrote a dialogue on education and a defence of philosophy – which last irritated his friend Reginald Pole (see p. 43), who thought he ought to give more time to theology. But when he did so in a commentary on St Paul's Letter to the Romans he ran into trouble both with the Sorbonne and with the Vatican censors because of his treatment of the doctrine of justification, where he tried to answer Martin Luther. He sent his second cousin and close companion Paolo Sadoleto to Rome to defend him, and the Vatican withdrew its ban.

The disastrous pontificate of Clement VII ended in 1534 and was followed by the election in October of Alessandro Farnese as Pope Paul III. Sadoleto was favourably disposed to Paul, but had no desire to return to the papal curia, which he had come to dislike if not actively to despise. Nor was he at first wholly in favour of Paul's wish to call a Council at Mantua to address Church reform, though once it became clear the Pope would not be moved from the idea he announced that he would go. But preparations had to be made. A commission was set up to prepare for it, and Sadoleto and Pole were named as members. In September 1536, therefore, he left Carpentras and arrived in Rome, after a stay at Modena, at the end of October.

Sadoleto was chosen to preach at the opening of the commission's proceedings. He took the opportunity to launch a scathing attack on Pope Paul's predecessors, especially on the two Medici popes, and on the unreformed clergy. Despite this, or perhaps because of it, he was named a cardinal priest in the consistory of 22 December 1536, later receiving the title of San Callisto, which he exchanged twice, first for that of Santa Balbina and then for that of San Pietro in Vincoli. His promotion did not particularly please him because of his dislike of the Vatican curia, to which he was now irrevocably tied – or so it seemed. The commission's report, *Consilium de emendanda ecclesia* ('Advice on what is to be reformed in the Church') was presented to the Pope and cardinals in March 1537. It is known that Sadoleto produced a dissenting opinion, though this has not survived, and its contents were not reported.

A couple of months later he took matters into his own hands by writing to the Protestant reformer Philip Melanchthon. It was an irenic letter, addressing Melanchthon not so much as a theological adversary as a fellow scholar and member of the circle of humanists. Melanchthon was impressed by the letter, especially by the quality of its Latin, and distributed copies among his friends. He considered replying, but in the end failed to do so. Sadoleto also gave his support to the proposals for Church reform put forward by the dean of Passau, Rupert Mossheim. The German bishops were not impressed. Sadoleto, they thought, simply did not understand the situation, and his approaches, though well meant, were naïve.

In January the following year Sadoleto was made a member of the committee discussing the structure of the future council, still scheduled for Mantua, but was too ill to attend. One prerequisite for such a gathering, Pope Paul believed, was peace among the European princes, and he organized a meeting of the King of France, the Emperor and himself at Nice. Sadoleto was too ill – it was possibly malaria – to set off in the Pope's entourage, but caught up with it before it left Italy. The Nice meeting was not wholly satisfactory (Francis and Charles refused to meet each other), but on 18 June 1538 a treaty was signed guaranteeing a ten-year truce.

Pope Paul went back to Rome, but Cardinal Sadoleto once more made his way to Carpentras and for four years refused to be moved though urged to return to the Vatican curia. He pleaded poverty. He had collected a number of benefices, and the diocese of Carpentras produced reasonable revenue, but with his advancement came increasing calls upon his income from his numerous relatives. It was easier to bear the financial burden in Carpentras, but as he pointed out several time to the Pope, he found it much more difficult to do so in Rome where he had to live in the expensive cardinatial style. If the Pope wanted him back in Rome, he said more than once, he would have to subsidize him. Meanwhile he turned his attention once again to reconciliation with the Protestants, writing a letter similar to that to Melanchthon to the rector of a Protestant college in Strasbourg, Johannes Sturm, and a rather less irenic, if not positively polemical, letter to the Council and people of Geneva. To this last John Calvin was eventually persuaded to reply, which he did with vigour, exposing Sadoleto's somewhat unsure theology. The cardinal also composed a treatise on the Christian Church in which he blamed the upheavals of the recent past on the corruption of the clergy. Pole, who had spent some considerable time in Carpentras at the beginning of 1538, wrote from Rome to say that his treatise had not been well received.

Very early in 1542 a letter was sent to all cardinals not resident at Rome instructing them to make their way there as soon as possible because of the forthcoming Council. Sadoleto arrived in Rome, by way of Modena, at the end of April and soon found himself drafting the document which was to summon the Council to meet, no longer in Mantua but at Trento, on 1 November. There were other problems requiring his attention. There was a growing threat of heresy in Italy, and Modena had been particularly affected. Pope Paul wanted to take drastic action, but Sadoleto asked that he be allowed to handle it his own way and, on his way to the court of Francis I, he again visited his home city. He called a meeting of the town council and succeeded in reconciling dissidents to Catholic orthodoxy. He then continued his way to Francis's court as papal legate to negotiate peace. Francis had unilaterally broken the truce agreed at Nice and had declared war on Charles V. Sadoleto's mission was a failure. Charles was incensed that the Pope was treating both Francis and himself equally, though it was not he who had broken the truce. The Pope therefore instructed Sadoleto to withdraw from Francis's court. He did so willingly, and once again made his way to Carpentras. Because of the plague he had to stay outside the city, from where he wrote to the Pope saying that if Paul wanted him in his curia, he must give him more money. Paul simply ordered him back to his side.

Once in Rome he argued that the Pope had to meet the Emperor, something many of his fellow cardinals opposed, because otherwise the Council would never take place. Pope Paul agreed, but the Council was nevertheless postponed and Sadoleto once again made his way back to Carpentras. But this time his peaceful, scholarly leisure was not to be. He found himself in conflict with the papal legate in Avignon, who was claiming jurisdiction over Carpentras. He was also beset by the incursion of heretics, both Protestants and members of the much older Waldensian sect, some of whom had adopted the doctrines of Calvin. His attitude to the latter was for the most part tolerant, in which he differed from his cousin Paolo, but though he had argued against the use of force, he did not complain when they were forcefully suppressed. He was also concerned about the fate of the peasants in his diocese, whose lands had been marched over by armies, and who were obliged to supply the troops with food. Sadoleto had once before complained to Rome about the privileges granted to Jewish moneylenders who, he believed, were exacting undue charges from the peasants, and now he complained again that nothing had been done to relieve the poverty in the countryside. But despite these pressing issues, he still found time to write a treatise on original sin, and another on purgatory. He also asked that he be allowed to retire and that the diocese be handed over to Paolo, who ten years before had been named his coadjutor bishop with right of succession. The request was ignored.

In the meantime, the opening of the Council had been set for Trento on 25 March 1545. Again Sadoleto was ordered to Rome and again he pleaded poverty, but to no avail. In March 1545 he set off for Rome, arriving there in May. As a concession to his poverty he was given an apartment in the Vatican Palace, though he later moved to Santa Maria sopra Minerva and finally to Santa Maria in Trastevere. He was already ill, but took considerable interest in the doings of the Council fathers, which were often not to his liking. He objected, for instance, to their readiness to accept as it stood St Jerome's Latin version of the bible, the Vulgate, despite what he believed as a good classicist to be the inadequacy of its Latin. And he was incensed when they voted, and the Pope approved, to move to Bologna. He did not object to the move in principle, but thought that in the interests of concord the Emperor ought to have been consulted.

He was of course right, and the Council continued to meet in Trent, but Cardinal Sadoleto played no part in it. He died in his apartment at Santa Maria in Trastevere on 18 October 1547. There was a funeral service in San Lorenzo in Damaso, and he was buried in his titular church of San Pietro in Vincoli. But no sign of his tomb is extant, for just a century later, in 1646, his remains were transferred to the cathedral at Carpentras.

Cesare Baronio

In 1559 the Centuriators of Magdeburg published the first three of their twelve volumes on the history of the Church. It was written, as the full title indicates, by a group of 'learned and pious men' in the city of Magdeburg in Germany. The group was composed of Lutherans; they came by their name 'Centuriators' because they wrote the history devoting each volume to a single century, a convenient arrangement if not exactly one which corresponded readily to the exigencies of historical periods. They were, given the polemical atmosphere in which they composed their account, distinctly anti-Catholic. They began from the premise that the pope was Antichrist, and their purpose was to demonstrate that the purified Church of the Reform was a true descendant of the Church of the first centuries. A Catholic response was needed. The man who supplied it was Cesare Baronio, or Baronius as he is commonly known.

He was born on 30 October 1538 in Sora, a small town in the Lazio region of Italy which, at the time of his birth, was in the Kingdom of Naples and still boasted a cathedral which had been consecrated by the English Pope Hadrian IV (it was destroyed by an earthquake some years after Baronius's death). His family was of Neapolitan origin, and was fairly wealthy. After a time studying in nearby Veroli, he went in 1556 on to Naples to study law, but left there because of an outbreak of hostilities between France and Spain. He moved to Rome, where he continued his studies at the university, La Sapienza, obtaining a doctorate in canon and civil law.

He took up residence in a house on the Piazza Duca, now the Piazza Farnese, not far from the church of S. Girolamo di Carità, where Philip Neri lived. He was a priest who had just begun what became the Congregation of the Oratory, an organization of clergy living in common and dedicated to preaching and hearing confessions in the churches of Rome. The Congregation was still in its very early stages in 1557, hardly more than an elaborate prayer group. In 1557 Baronius met Neri, and was attracted, as many were, to the gentle character of the future saint, and committed himself to the nascent organization. In December 1560 he wrote to his parents saying that he had decided to become a priest: he was ordained on 27 May 1564.

Rejecting the canonry he had been offered in his home town, he instead went to live at the church of San Giovanni dei Fiorentini, the church in Rome for those from Florence – as was Philip Neri himself, who had by now also taken up residence there. He stayed there for a decade, doing pastoral work. When the Congregation of the Oratory was given formal approval by the Pope in 1575 it was also entrusted with the church of Santa Maria in Vallicella, to which, in April 1577, this group of Oratorians now moved. It was there that Baronius spent most of the rest of his life, and it is where he died.

The Council of Trent had ordered a reform of the liturgy. One of the liturgical books which was in desperate need of revision was the *Martyrologium Romanum*, the Roman Martyrology. This is a volume containing very brief lives of the saints, organized according to their feast days. Pope Gregory XIII commissioned Baronius to undertake this revision, and his new edition was published in 1586 – he himself revised it for another edition in 1589. It was a work of considerable historical scholarship, and bore his name on the title page. This is no longer there, but the latest version of 2001 still starts from Baronius's text.

Many of the saints mentioned in the Roman Martyrology are from the early centuries of Christianity. Work on the Martyrology, therefore, neatly fitted with the response to the Centuriators of Magdeburg. The first volume of this massive, twelve-volume *Annales Ecclesiastici* appeared in 1588, the final one in 1607, not long after Baronius's death. A work of massive erudition, its approach was somewhat more irenic than the one to which it was a response. It was in the *Annales* that the expression 'the dark ages' was first used for the early Middle Ages – Petrarch had used it earlier to describe a much broader period of time, from the classical era down to the renaissance.

In 1593 Philip Neri chose him to be his successor as head of the Congregation of the Oratory. Baronius was unwilling to take on this role, and insisted that there be an election: he was elected. It was at this point that Pope Clement VIII first attempted to make him a cardinal. Baronius managed on this occasion to avoid the dignity, but he became instead the Pope's confessor, in practice a rather more influential figure. It is said that it was Baronius who persuaded the Pope to be reconciled with the once Protestant Henry of Navarre who had become the Catholic King of France. He was once again pressed to become a cardinal, and this time he accepted: he was created a cardinal priest in the consistory of 5 June 1596, and was given the title of SS Nereo ed Achilleo, which basilica on the Coelian Hill he set about restoring – as he did the nearby church of St Gregory.

He had to move his quarters into the Vatican – Clement had also made him Librarian of the Roman Church – but he lived there as simply as he could and, during the Holy Year of 1600, he opened his rooms to accommodate pilgrims. In the conclave of the last fortnight of March 1605 he was very close to being elected. He was opposed by the Spanish contingent, however, because they judged that he had been unfair over their country's claims to the Kingdom of Naples: himself from Naples, Baronius was not sympathetic to the Spanish monarchy. His sympathies lay more with the French, and he persuaded his supporters in the conclave to switch their votes to the Florentine Alessandro de' Medici who also favoured France but, perhaps more importantly for Baronius, was also a disciple of Philip Neri. The new Pope did not live to see the end of the month, so there was a second conclave. But this time he was not a contender: it had been recognized that Baronius was not a viable candidate.

Had he been elected, however, he too would have been a short-lived pontiff. In 1606 he returned to live at Vallicella. It was there that he died on 30 June 1607. He was declared 'venerable' on January 1745, the first step on the way to a beatification which never happened. The process for his eventual canonization, however, has recently been reopened to mark the 400th anniversary of his death. Galileo recorded with approval a remark he made, presumably in conversation with the astronomer: 'The bible tells us how to go to heaven, not how the heavens go.'

Roberto Bellarmino

There are to be found 'Bellarmine jugs', flagons with pot bellies and a bearded face depicted on the front. They are sometimes said to represent the large and stout figure of this saint, but Bellarmino was a small man, and the jugs reflect not so much his physical size as the role in played in the polemics of Catholics against Protestants at the end of the sixteenth and the beginning of the seventeenth centuries.

He was born in the town of Montepulciano in Tuscany on 4 October 1542. His father Vincenzo was of a noble family, but without much money. His mother Cinzia Cervini was the sister of Marvello Cervini who was already, at the time of Roberto's birth, a cardinal and was to become on 9 April 1555 Pope Marcello II, the last Pope to retain his own name, and the one commemorated in Palestrina's famous *Missa Papae Marcelli*. Roberto Francesco Romolo was educated by the Jesuits in their recently opened college in Montepulciano, and at the end of his school days, already skilled in debating (as well as in playing the violin), he decided to please his devout mother, but annoy his father, who had hoped he would restore the family fortunes, by himself entering the Society of Jesus. This he did in September 1560, and then was sent to the Roman College of the Society to study philosophy.

On October 1563 he was sent to Florence, and later to Mondovi in Piedmont. There used to be a Jesuit saying, 'I don't know Greek. I have never even taught it': in Mondovi Bellarmino taught Greek and learned it at the same time. After his experience of teaching classics, in 1567 he was sent to the University of Padua to study theology. So far his career had been typical of a Jesuit student, but after only two years at Padua he was sent to the University of Louvain. His scholastic ability had much impressed his superiors, and rather than Bellarmino spend his time in Catholic Italy they wanted him to attend a university where he might gain greater experience of the religious disputes of the day.

He was ordained, not in Louvain but at Ghent, but then returned to Louvain where, at the age of twenty-eight, he became a professor of theology. He was an enormous success as a teacher, and his lectures drew Protestants as well as Catholics. So skilled did he become in the disputed questions of the day that, in 1576, he was recalled to the Roman College to take the newly created chair of 'controversy': he was appointed at the direct request of Pope Gregory XIII. His lectures over the next few years became the vast volumes entitled *Disputationes de Controversiis Christianae Fidei adversus hujus temporis hereticos* ('Disputations on the controversies concerning the Christian faith against the modern heretics'), but known, not surprisingly, simply as *De Controversiis.* Sold widely across Europe, they were a polemical defence of Catholic doctrine against the criticisms of the Protestant reformers, but conducted for the most part with courtesy, intellectual rigour, and based where appropriate upon a thorough knowledge of history. Their success can be judged by the very many editions in which the volumes were published.

One person who was not wholly approving was the Pope, by this time Sixtus V. Specifically he did not approve of Bellarmino's treatment of the authority of the papacy in politics, which in the Jesuit's view was only indirect. Sixtus had been happy to accept the dedication of *De Controversiis*, but now he was threatening to put the first volume on the Index of Forbidden Books. Not that there was a personal animus: Pope Sixtus had already chosen Bellarmino to accompany an emissary into France to advise on theological matters during the religious wars. In any case, the Pope died before anything could be done about putting *De Controversiis* on the Index, and his successor, Gregory XIV, thought otherwise, giving the book a special approbation.

Gregory died after less than a year, and his successor survived only a few months. Clement VIII, who was elected in January 1592, made Bellarmino his personal theologian, as well as a consultor to the Inquisition and a member of the body which approved the appointment of bishops. Being the Pope's theologian was not without its problems. The Council of Trent had called for a revision of the Vulgate, the Latin text of the Bible produced some twelve hundred years earlier by St Jerome, which was regarded as the standard, authorized version of the Bible by Catholics. Frustrated by the time it was taking, Pope Sixtus had launched upon the task himself and published an edition which proved to be full of errors. Bellarmino was made a member of the commission to oversee a revision of Pope Sixtus's work. This was tricky, because Sixtus had announced that his version was definitive. In the preface which he wrote for the new version, Bellarmino suggested, perhaps somewhat disingenuously, that the new edition was needed, not because of papal errors but because of printers' mistakes.

In addition to these tasks, Bellarmino had played a number of roles internal to the Jesuits. From 1592 to 1594 he was rector of the Roman College, and was then sent to be provincial superior of the Naples province. More importantly, from 1588 he had become spiritual director to the young Jesuits in training (including to a future saint, Aloysius Gonzaga). This experience led him to produce two catechisms in Italian, a short one aimed at children, and a longer one for adults, both of which remained in use in Italy for nearly three hundred years.

In Pope Clement's consistory of 3 March 1599 he was made a cardinal priest, with the title conferred later of Santa Maria in Via Lata. As a cardinal he became embroiled in the controversy between Jesuit theologians and Dominican ones about grace (known as the controversy *de auxiliis*, grace being an essential help or aid – *auxilium*) and its relationship to free will. Not unnaturally he sided with the Jesuits: one of the chief of those involved had been his student at the Roman College. His preliminary advice to the Pope was not to become involved. The matter, he believed, could not be decided for certain, at least not at that time, and more space had to be given for theologians to debate the matter. In the meantime, however, the protagonists on both sides should be forbidden from calling each other heretics. This was the conclusion finally arrived at, but Clement's first response was that it ought to be decided by disputes in his presence. They failed to resolve the matter before Clement died, but Bellarmino, having given contrary advice to what was happening, was something of an embarrassment in the papal curia. He was therefore consecrated bishop on 21 April 1602 in the Sistine Chapel by Pope Clement himself, and dispatched from Rome as Archbishop of Capua. He went immediately, and conscientiously fulfilled the duties of the office for the next three years.

Clement VIII died on 5 March 1605 and his successor was elected on the first day of the next month. He did not survive the whole of April, and was in turn succeeded by Pope Paul V, who was elected on 16 May. Bellarmino took part in both of the conclaves, and was a much-canvassed candidate. But the austere life he led was something of a challenge even to the reformed cardinals of the early seventeenth century, as was also the fact that he was a Jesuit: no Jesuit had up to that time, nor has yet, been elected to the papacy. The new Pope, Paul V, wanted to keep Bellarmino in Rome, so he resigned his diocese and undertook a whole new set of duties in the papal curia, particularly in the office of the Inquisition. It was in that capacity that he became involved in one of the Vatican's best-known *causes célèbres*, the case of Galileo.

Galileo had enthusiastically embraced the theory advanced by Canon Nicholas Copernicus, in a book dedicated to Pope Paul III, that the world went round the sun, not vice versa. The problem with the heliocentric system, however, was that it appeared to contradict Scripture. Bellarmino, who was a friend of the astronomer, told him that he would be much better presenting this theory as a hypothesis – which, given the state of knowledge and of research at the time, is what it was. Galileo nonetheless insisted, and a panel was set up by the Inquisition. The panel ruled that the heliocentric view was formally heretical, and it fell to Bellarmino to inform Galileo of this decision, in which he himself had played no part. This all took place in the early months of 1616, and Copernicus's book was effectively put on the Index on 5 March.

Galileo himself, on the other hand, at this point went uncensored. Rumours to the contrary went flying round Rome, so before he left Rome to return to Florence, Galileo appealed to Cardinal Bellarmino to clear his name. The cardinal wrote him a formal letter in which he said that the astronomer had neither been condemned, nor asked to abjure his views – nor, indeed, had he abjured them 'as far as we know', wrote Bellarmino. And that was the extent of his role. Under Bellarmino Galileo was not condemned, or required to abjure his views. All that happened long after the cardinal's death and Galileo, who had kept Bellarmino's letter, cited him in his defence.

His chair at the Roman College had been in controversy, and controversies of one kind and another continued to engage him. When Venice arrested a number of clerics in contravention of the law of the Church which required those in holy orders to be tried by the Church, he took on those in the Republic who defended its actions. When an oath was imposed upon the English as a test of their loyalty to King James I, Bellarmino took on James himself – no mean controversialist in his own right – as well as others who came to the King's defence.

Jesuits are required to make an annual retreat. In the closing years of his life the cardinal used those retreats to write five short spiritual works, the last of which became the best known, *De arte bene moriendi*, 'On the Art of Dying Well'. It was published in 1620, and Roberto Bellarmino himself died a year later, on the early morning of 17 December 1621. He was buried in the church of the Gesù, the headquarters of the Society of Jesus. In 1923, however, his remains were moved a few hundred yards to the church of San Ignazio, to be close to the burial place of his one-time pupil St Aloysius Gonzaga, whose cause for canonization he had been instrumental in starting.

His own canonization was much longer in coming. His cause was introduced in 1627, but he was not beatified until 1923, and only canonized in 1929. Two years later he was declared a doctor of the Church. His feast day is celebrated, as is normally the custom, on the anniversary day of his death.

Giuseppe Garampi

Like Sadoleto (see p. 78), Cardinal Garampi is not easy to categorize. He might perfectly reasonably to be added to the list of cardinatial diplomats, but he could equally well, and one suspects it might have been his preference, be remembered as a scholar.

He was born in Rimini on 29 October 1725, the second son of Count Lorenzo Garampi – the title had been acquired by purchase by Lorenzo's father. Lorenzo himself had been a student at Bologna, where he had become friendly with Prospero Lambertini, the future Pope Benedict XIV. As a young man Giuseppe became a member of the Academia dei Lincei – the Academy of Lynxes, Lynxes being reputed to have particularly sharp sight. It had originally been founded in Rome in 1603, the world's first scientific society, with Galileo as an early member. But in its first incarnation it scarcely survived its founder, and was started again in Rimini in 1745. Giuseppe had an interest in science, but a greater interest in history.

The year after he joined the Academia he received minor orders, making him technically a cleric, and left for Rome, where he was ordained priest in March 1749. He studied ecclesiastical history in Rome, and the year before he became a priest he joined the Academy of Ecclesiastical History, which Benedict XIV had founded. He dedicated his first book to Benedict, a critical study of the legends of Pope Joan. Benedict now made him the assistant, with the right of succession, to the prefect of the Vatican Archives. The prefect died in July 1751, and Giuseppe Garampi succeeded to the office, to be followed shortly after by the office of prefect of the Archives of St Peter's (1752), and by the office of prefect of the Archives of Castel Sant'Angelo (1759). Thus he united in himself the duty of care of the greater part of the archival collections of the Holy See, and can be regarded as one of the main creators of the modern Vatican Archives.

To use the Archives, catalogues are needed. One of Garampi's projects was a survey of all the dioceses in the world, of the churches of Rome, of the papacy and of the cardinals. He never completed the work – nor did his successor – but the index which he produced to help researchers on this undertaking still exists and is still in use. When the Archives were opened to scholars in the late nineteenth century the then Archivist decided to reorganize the index. The cards were sorted and glued to sheets of paper which were, in turn, bound into large volumes – 125 of them, the 'Schedario Garampi', which consist of more than 800,000 cards.

This index was itself a massive undertaking, but Garampi had a number of other projects on the go while he served as archivist. He wrote on Clare of Rimini, carefully distinguishing fact from fiction; he embarked on a massive study of papal coinage; he demonstrated, from a study of seals, that a particular region had long been the property of the papacy. He also travelled round Europe making contact with other collections of documents, and with those who cared for them.

On the first of these journeys he was absent from Rome for nearly two years. His purpose, however, was not simply to visit libraries. He was also on a diplomatic mission for the Holy See, meeting important European figures, including the Empress Maria Theresa at Vienna. One of his tasks was to look after the Vatican's interests at the Augsburg conference of 1761 which, had it been successful, would have meant that the Seven Years War would have lasted only five. Six months after his return he was sent to Frankfurt for the coronation as Emperor of Maria Theresa's son, Joseph II. He became an expert on the politics of German-speaking territories. Above all he had to advise on the growing hostility of the German princes towards the rights of the papacy in their territory. He wrote a pessimistic report on the decline of religion in Germany under the increasing influence of the Enlightenment. In particular he read *On the status of the Church and the legitimate power of the Roman Pontiff* by Justinus Febronius, published in Frankfurt in 1763. Febronius was the pen-name of Johann Nikolaus von Hontheim, an assistant bishop of Trier. Hontheim had been approached by three German prince-bishops to investigate their grievances against Rome. Hontheim's conclusions were that papal power as currently exercised was a medieval accretion, and the affairs of a church in a particular principality should largely be the responsibility of the local bishops and the civil authority: the doctrine became known as Febronianism, though in Emperor Joseph's Austria, where a version of it was also embraced, it became known as Josephism.

Hontheim's book was promptly put on the Index, but the doctrine it contained survived until the French Revolution gave both the Church and the sovereigns of Europe something more pressing to think about. For his activities on behalf of the Holy See Garampi was granted a doctorate in laws by Pope Clement XIV, and then sent off to Poland, which had just been very largely divided up among its neighbours Prussia, Austria and Russia. He arrived a year before the Society of Jesus was suppressed by Pope Clement, a special problem in Poland because Catherine the Great of Russia insisted on the Jesuits continuing to exist and run their schools in the part of Poland which she had just acquired.

A new Pope, Pius VI, sent Garampi from Poland as his representative to Vienna, making him at more or less the same time Bishop of Montefiascone and Corneto; just before setting off for Poland he had been appointed to the honorary (titular) archiepiscopal see of Beirut. In Vienna the Archbishop had some modest success in stemming the tide of Josephism, financing the publication of books defending papal rights, but his relationship with the government was increasingly frosty. Were the Emperor to continue his programme of religious reform, he told Rome, the Church would suffer a crisis similar to that it had undergone in the sixteenth century. His concern at the ferocity of the attack on the papacy pushed him increasingly into the party of the 'zelanti' or the 'intransigents', among the Roman curia, though they were not his natural allies. He, too, as a scholar, had been influenced by the Enlightenment.

His constant travels had allowed him to collect books from all over Europe, and many of them were by authors who were hostile to the Catholicism he embraced. His library was immense, containing manuscripts and incunabula as well as contemporary writings. He gave some 30,000 volumes to the seminary of his diocese of Montefiascone, and left a great number more to the Gambalunga library in his home town of Rimini. Another collection of between thirty and forty thousand was sold after his death.

In February 1785 he was created cardinal priest of SS John and Paul, and shortly afterwards returned from Vienna to his diocese. He proved to be an admirably pastoral bishop, with a particular concern both for the education of the clergy of the diocese, and for the welfare of the poor. But he continued also with his scholarship. An Etruscan tomb, decorated with frescoes, was discovered at Corneto (today Tarquinia), and was called 'the cardinal's tomb' because of his interest. He also kept up his extensive correspondence with people he had come to know as he journeyed around Europe. He was particularly well informed about the situation in France after the Revolution, and about the impact of the Revolution on the Church.

He was frequently at the Vatican, discussing the rapidly deteriorating situation of Catholicism. It was in Rome that he died, in the German-Hungarian College of which he was protector, on 4 May 1792. His funeral took place in the church of S. Apollinare and he was buried there, though in November the same year his body was moved to the basilica of SS John and Paul, of which he had been the titular cardinal priest.

The Saints

In the second half of the eleventh century, in a rather mysterious document known as *Dictatus Papae*, which could perhaps be translated as 'What the pope has laid down', someone, possibly Pope Gregory VII, declared that all popes were saints: as far as the Catholic Church is concerned, Gregory VII is certainly among that select number. But no one ever said anything about the holiness of saints. The Council of Basel (see p. 12) tried to fix the number of cardinals, but added that more might be added if justified by their holiness of life.

As this volume bears witness, many of those who were raised to the purple lived anything but holy lives, at least in the rather prissy fashion in which holiness is judged in modern times. Quite a number whose lives would be judged by current standards as verging on the scandalous, to say the least, were quite devout. The most obvious example of this being Cardinal Rodrigo Borgia, who is not included here because he became Pope Alexander VI – though his son Cesare is included elsewhere (see p. 206), whom no one would judge to have been holy, and who resigned from the cardinalate.

The first cardinal whose life is recounted below is unusual because he, alone of the cardinal saints, was a martyr. He has become a publicly proclaimed saint because he died for his beliefs, whereas the others in this chapter were judged to have lived lives of heroic virtue. What that may mean varies from period to period. It is interesting that the two most recent cardinals to have been declared holy and beatified – a halfway step to eventual full canonization – not only dedicated themselves to the service of the poor, but put into practice the Church's social teaching, which had been given a new impetus by Pope Leo XIII.

John Fisher was, of course, a sixteenth-century saint. But there were a number of cardinals ranked among the officially holy who date from much earlier times. Peter Damian (see p. 25) has been included under another category. More saints are also to be found elsewhere, Cesare Baronio (see pp. 83) or Robert Bellarmino (see p. 86) for example. Baronio has not been formally canonized: he has only be named as 'venerable', which means that the cause for his canonization has been accepted by Rome. In Baronio's case, that happened a long time ago, but it has recently been revisited. Another cardinal for whom there is an on-going process for canonization is Rafael Merry del Val (see p. 190), and though it might seem to be going nowhere, the process could be reopened by those in the Vatican who want to reassert the values of conservatism. Merry del Val would make a very odd saint, for though there is no question about the exemplariness of his private life, it could be suggested that aspects of his public life showed signs of a very unsaintly vindictiveness.

All those whose lives are told below were saintly men. Only two of them, however, have been officially canonized, John Fisher as a martyr and Gregorio Barbarigo. For whatever reason, the causes of Pierre de Berulle and the admirable Jean Louis Lefebvre de Cheverus have not been introduced. The first cardinal below, Niccolò Albergati, and the final two in this section, Ciriaco María Sancha y Hervás and Andreas Carlo Ferrari, have been declared 'blessed'.

Niccolò Albergati

Niccolò's life as bishop and cardinal began in the late middle ages and ended in the renaissance, but anyone more different from the traditional picture of a worldly cardinal prince of the period would be difficult to imagine.

He was born in Bologna in or about the year 1375. His family was quite wealthy, and in 1386 he became a student of the University of Bologna. Bologna was renowned in the middle ages for its school of law, and it was law that he began to study. In 1395, however, he opted for the life of a quasi hermit, becoming a monk of the Carthusian order at the monastery of S. Girolamo of Casara, near Florence. He was professed – took his solemn vows as a monk – the following year and was ordained priest in June 1404. In 1407 he became prior, or second in command, of his monastery. His virtues must have been widely known because at a General Chapter of the order in 1412 he was elected visitor of all the Carthusian monasteries in Italy, and subsequently became prior at several of them. In the process he was able to reunite the order which, in the course of the Great Western Schism, had been divided among the 'obediences'. That he achieved in 1417 when with the election at the Council of Constance of Odo Colonna as Pope Martin V, the Schism was over.

He became a well-known figure in the Church in Italy and in 1417 the people of Bologna together with their clergy elected him their bishop. This election proved to be a long-drawn-out process. Niccolò Albergati did not want the office and had to be instructed by his superiors in the Carthusians to accept it. But then the election had to be ratified not only by the cathedral chapter, but also by the metropolitan Archbishop of Ravenna. The election was made at the beginning of January; he was not consecrated until early July, in the

Carthusian church in Bologna, and then it was almost another year before the Pope confirmed his appointment. He was very much a reforming bishop, and promptly held a diocesan synod. He was one of a handful of such prelates in Italy at the time, and a number of clerics were attracted to his service, including two future popes who had both served him as secretaries (the Popes-to-be Nicholas V and Pius II).

Bologna was a problematic city of which to be bishop. Technically part of the Papal States, it operated when it could as an independent city-state. Albergati was loyal to the papacy, but he found himself having to negotiate a concordat between the city and the Pope. But the agreement fell apart when the commune, led by one of the Bentivoglios, rebelled against the papacy and Albergati had to flee disguised as a monk – which of course he was. On this occasion he was absent a relatively short time, between 26 March and 24 July 1420. While in Bologna he continued to live as much of the monastic life as he could achieve, residing not in the episcopal palace but in a small house he acquired and which he ran like a monastery.

Two year later he was appointed a papal legate to attempt to bring about peace between the Kings of England and France, travelling to France for that purpose. In recognition of his services, on 24 May 1426 Pope Martin V named him cardinal priest of Santa Croce in Gerusalemme. At this point he resigned the office of Bishop of Bologna, and instead became administrator of the see: he took up the office of bishop again in July 1440. After making him a cardinal, the Pope used him frequently as a negotiator in an attempt to broker peace among the warring Italian states. As often as he was successful, and a peace formula agreed, just as often one or other of the states broke the agreement. Bologna itself was still troublesome, and in August 1428 Albergati once again had to flee the city after a renewed effort by the Bentivoglios to recover control. He was away absent only a few days on this occasion, but the disturbances did not cease with his return. The Pope placed Bologna under an interdict, which meant there could be no religious services held there: Albergati decided he had again to leave. The commune was incensed by what it saw as desertion and elected another monk to replace him – the replacement bishop later resigned.

At the death of Martin V he took part in the conclave which elected, on 3 March 1431, Pope Eugenius IV. Eugenius had a high regard for Albergati, making him legate to Florence, Venice and Milan, and in 1435 sent him as his legate to the Congress of Arras held to make peace between the French and the English. It did not achieve that end, but to the delight of the French succeeded in separating Burgundy from England, the Duke of Burgundy acknowledging the King of France, to whose crown England had laid claim. He was then sent to the Council of Constance, the rump of which was still sitting in effective defiance of the papacy. As a representative of Eugenius he was not accepted as one of the presidents, but then Eugenius named him as a president of the Council, which moved to Ferrara (January 1438) but which continued in Florence (February 1439), and which brought about a temporary reconciliation of the Eastern and the Western Churches. As a sign of his esteem, the Pope also named him Grand Penitentiary in 1438. He then sent him in 1438 as his representative to the Diet of Nuremberg. After Nuremberg Albergati returned to Florence, where the Pope still resided. In the end Eugenius remained in Florence until 1443, largely because of the unrest in Rome fomented by the Colonnas, against whom the Pope was waging war in an effort to regain the territory Martin V had so generously bestowed on his Colonna relatives.

When Eugenius and the cardinals finally left Florence for Rome, Niccolò Albergati followed behind. He was by now a sick man, suffering it seems from kidney stones. He died in the Augustinian house in Siena on 9 May 1443, in the presence of Pope Eugenius, who took part in the funeral mass. He was buried in the Carthusian monastery in Florence, and the Carthusians promptly came to regard him as a saint. In 1744 Pope Benedict XIV decreed that he should be venerated as a blessed. His feast is now celebrated on 10 May.

John Fisher

In many ways John Fisher has been overshadowed by his fellow English martyr Thomas More. More, a family man and a man of affairs, is a far easier subject for biography, but in some respects Fisher was the more significant figure in the controversy over Henry VIII's divorce. It was he who took perhaps the more principled stand, and one based on a thorough knowledge of Scripture.

He was born possibly in 1469 in Beverley in Yorkshire, where his father Robert was a prosperous merchant. His earliest schooling would presumably have been in Beverley, but at the age of fourteen he went to Cambridge University, graduating as a bachelor of arts in 1488 and as a master of arts in 1491. In the same year he became a Fellow of Michaelhouse, a college which was later incorporated into Trinity College, and in December was ordained priest by the Archbishop of York. He was still under age for the priesthood, and needed a dispensation. He was presented with a living as vicar of Northallerton. In 1494, however, he resigned the benefice because he had been made senior university proctor. On university business he visited the court of King Henry VII at Greenwich, where he met the King's mother, Lady Margaret Beaufort. It was an encounter which was to change his life. He became her spiritual director, and through her he was presented with the living of Lith.

But he did not become a parish priest. He stayed on at Cambridge, proceeding to a doctorate of divinity in 1501 and being promoted to the post of university vice-chancellor. It was remarkable progress for one who was probably not yet thirty-five years of age, but it is very likely that he owed it to his close ties to the Lady Margaret, a generous benefactor to Oxford as well as Cambridge, but because of Fisher's friendship, particularly to the latter. She created a professorship in divinity and, in 1502, he became the first to hold the post. In 1504 he was made Bishop of Rochester, being consecrated in November in the chapel at Lambeth Palace by the Archbishop of Canterbury. In acknowledgment of his new dignity the university made him chancellor, electing him every year until 1514 – when he offered to stand down to make way for Thomas Wolsey – and then for life.

His impact on the university was immeasurable – quite literally so, because it is impossible to know how much it was Fisher's influence that led the Lady Margaret to found two colleges, Christ's and St John's, or that led King Henry VII to bequeath money to complete the outstandingly beautiful Gothic chapel at King's College. But it was in the foundation of St John's, which opened its doors in 1516, that Fisher played his major role. It was a struggle to get it started, because everyone, from the Lady Margaret's staff to the King himself, now Henry VIII, was trying to get their hands on some of the bequest meant to endow it. Fisher drew up its regulations, laying down that its students were only to speak Latin, Greek or Hebrew within its walls. He also made provision for these languages to be taught. He persuaded Erasmus to teach Greek and theology in Cambridge from 1511 to 1514; he himself founded a chantry at St John's to support scholars; he prevailed upon the King to provide money for lectureships in Greek and Hebrew, as he himself did not know these languages, and made an effort to learn them.

Meanwhile Fisher got on with running his diocese. He was an exemplary bishop, personally carrying out regular visitations of the parishes, conducting ordinations, confirmations and the other responsibilities of an Ordinary: despite his role at Cambridge he was no absentee bishop. He was to have been one of the English representatives at the Council of the Lateran in 1512, but the political situation on the continent made it impossible for him to leave the country. The only time he did so was in 1520 to attend the Field of the Cloth of Gold, the meeting between the Kings of England and France. He disapproved of the extravagant display.

He also disapproved of the teachings of Martin Luther and the other German and Swiss reformers, doctrines which would come to be termed 'Protestant'. When the papal bull condemning Luther was proclaimed in England he preached at the ceremony of publication. In 1523 he published a refutation of the reformer's basic doctrines: his *Confutatio* was widely available throughout Europe, and it helped to frame the Catholic response. The King himself had produced an attack on Luther, and when others wrote against his defence of the seven sacraments, Fisher responded with a defence of the King's book. He also wrote on the presence of Christ in the Eucharist, one of the most hotly debated topics of the time. His writings, however, were not all polemical attacks on the reformers' theology. He also wrote a controversial work on the Scriptures.

But from the late 1520s he became increasingly embroiled in the King's wish to divorce Catherine of Aragón to marry Anne Boleyn. When first approached on this 'Great Matter' by Henry he gave a theologian's response. The King told him he was troubled by the fact that he had married his deceased brother's widow, and that he did not believe a Pope could – as he had done – grant him a dispensation from this act, which was forbidden by Scripture. At first Fisher seems to have believed that the King's scruples were real, and hastened to reassure him that, although the Scriptural evidence was confused, he had no doubt that the Pope possessed the authority to issue the dispensation Henry had sought. Which, of course, was not the response Henry wanted to hear.

A tribunal was set up at Blackfriars to hear the King's case. Cardinals Campeggi from Rome, and Wolsey were to preside. It got nowhere because the Queen refused to appear before it and appealed directly to Rome. But written arguments had been submitted, including an outspoken defence of the marriage from Fisher. The King was furious. When in 1529 Henry introduced bills to force the clergy into line, Fisher spoke out against them, implicitly accusing the Commons of falling into heresy. He and two other bishops were briefly put in prison.

In 1531, when the King proposed to declare himself supreme governor of the Church, Fisher led the opposition, and it is thought that it was he who added to the bill before the convocation of clergy the words 'as far as the law of God allows'. After the passing of the bill he continued to oppose Henry, as did those who were close to him in London and Cambridge. An attempt was made to assassinate Fisher by poisoning his soup, but he was an austere man who ate little. The soup was given to the poor: two people died, others were taken ill. Then someone tried to shoot him, but missed.

On April 1534, after the Pope had rejected the divorce petition, Fisher was required to take the oath attached to the Act of Succession which recognized Henry's offspring by Anne Boleyn as heirs to the throne. But attached to the oath was a repudiation of the authority of the Pope. Fisher refused to take the oath, and was imprisoned in the Tower. In May 1535 the Pope created him cardinal priest of San Vitale. Whether this was an act of defiance, recognition of his constancy or simply an attempt so to raise his profile in Europe that the King would not have him executed is not known. But if the last, it did not work. Rather the contrary, because the King was enraged. On 17 June Fisher was tried and condemned to death. His health had long been failing, and on

22 June he had to be carried in a chair to the place of execution. Nevertheless the climbed the scaffold unaided, and addressed the crowd saying that he died for the Catholic faith.

He died only a few days before Thomas More. He was beatified in 1886 along with over fifty other English martyrs, and was canonized in 1935 alongside Thomas More. Their feasts are celebrated together on 22 June.

Pierre de Berulle

Not all saints are, as it were, Saints. Pierre de Berulle was precociously holy, some of those who were around him have been beatified or canonized but he, rather surprisingly, remains without an official halo, perhaps because he was, to the taste of those who regulate these things, far too involved in politics.

He was born on 4 February 1575 at the chateau of Sérilly, near Troyes, to the south-east of Paris. His family was wealthy, part of the legal upper class in France, and his parents wished him to study law. He attended the University of Paris, first at the college of Boncourt, then at that of Burgundy, but finally, at his mother's insistence, he went to the Jesuit-run college of Clermont. There he had a Carthusian monk as his spiritual guide, and under his influence, at the age of only seventeen he wrote his first book on the spiritual life, a *Brief Discourse of Abnegation in the Interior Life*, which appeared in 1597. Though the Carthusian may have encouraged him, the little book reflects a Jesuit heritage. The inspiration for the book was *A Short Compendium of Christian Perfection*, supposedly by a Milanese mystic, Elizabeth Berinzaga, but in practice the work of her Jesuit spiritual director Achille Gagliardi. It appeared in a French translation in 1596, though not in its original Italian until more than a decade later. Maybe Berulle's work was less an original treatise than a new version of Gagliardi's book, and his own spirituality was yet to develop, but it was nonetheless indicative of the way Berulle's career would progress. His next book, only two years later, was, however, a deviation. It was on demonic possession.

He moved now among the devout, rather than among lawyers. One of those he visited often was his cousin Madame Acarie. She had been born Barbara Avrillot, and had married Pierre Acarie. After some years together her husband had come across her reading romantic literature and had introduced her to devotional writings. Her life changed, and to the moderate distress of her husband she turned their Paris house into an meeting place for some of the most distinguished clergy of the day. When King Henry IV succeeded to the French throne, necessarily becoming a Catholic in the process, he banished Pierre Acarie from Paris as one of those most active in the Catholic League which had opposed him. This left Madame Acarie free to entertain as she willed. Much later, after Pierre's death, she became a Carmelite nun as Sister Marie of the Incarnation and, not quite two centuries after her death, was beatified. Meanwhile she had been the instigator of one of Berulle's major undertakings, the introduction to France of the Carmelites of the reform instituted by St Teresa of Avila.

Berulle was ordained priest on 5 June 1599. Soon afterwards he came to the attention of Cardinal Duperron, a convert to Catholicism, who had in turn instructed Henry IV when he decided to abandon his Protestant faith in return for the French throne. When the leading Protestant Philippe de Mornay published a treatise on the Eucharist in the early Church, Duperron accused him of misquoting the fathers some five hundred times. On 14 May 1600 there was a conference at Fontainebleau at which the disputed quotations were to be debated. De Mornay retired hurt after the first nine quotations presented had been decided in the cardinal's favour: Berulle had been the cardinal's researcher, and the debate helped to bring him to prominence. He became a chaplain to the King.

He was now in a position to put Madame Acarie's plan into operation. Under the pretext of negotiating on behalf of the King the marriage of the Dauphin to a Spanish princess he travelled to Spain to persuade the Carmelites to make a foundation in France. The Carmelite general was opposed to the idea, but the pope was in favour, and a small group, led by Anne of St Bartholomew and Anne of Jesus, close collaborators with Teresa of Avila herself, travelled back to Paris where they found that Madame Acarie had already collected in her house a group of women who wanted to join the order. Berulle was one of those who was designated a superior over the newly arrived nuns.

His next project was to establish in France the Oratory founded in Rome by St Philip Neri. The Council of Trent had insisted, to improve the education of the clergy, that seminaries be set up for their training. France had resisted many of the innovations of the Council, including this one. Berulle, seeing clearly the need for a better-informed priesthood, hoped his variety of Oratorians would be able in time to provide the colleges needed. This was perhaps a departure from Philip Neri's original vision for his congregation, giving it a greater emphasis than the Roman saint had intended on an apostolic mission, but it worked, and a network of colleges of different types emerged with remarkable speed. Not only that, but a number of other Congregations with a similar missionary purpose were founded in quick succession by men who were close to Berulle and inspired by him.

Berulle was not a natural courtier, but he was close to Henry IV, as has been noted, and also to his successor, Louis XII. He was sent on diplomatic missions, most particularly to Rome to negotiate the granting of a dispensation to permit the Catholic Henrietta Maria, sister of the King, to marry the future Charles I of England, a Protestant. He then travelled to England with the Queen to be. She was received coldly, both by her husband and the people. After Berulle returned to France he kept in correspondence, encouraging the despondent bride. (The relationship between Charles and his Queen, it should perhaps be remarked, later became very close and Charles showed increasing sympathy for his wife's religion. But that was not in Berulle's lifetime.)

The last decade of his life was overshadowed by his conflict with Richelieu. Richelieu was a decade younger than Berulle, and by inclination a politician rather than a churchman. Both he and Berulle were involved in brokering a reconciliation between Louis and his mother, Marie de' Medici, but in their vision of the role of France they were completely at odds. Berulle wanted a treaty with the Catholic powers of Spain and Austria while Richelieu sought to control the rise of Spain and Austria by allying France with Protestant Germany. The King requested Pope Urban VIII to make Berulle a cardinal, and the rank of cardinal priest was conferred on him on 30 August 1627, but Richelieu, also a cardinal, was the man whose advice the King followed.

For Berulle the final blow came in September 1628. In July 1627 the English had invaded the Huguenot stronghold of La Rochelle, which they held for almost a year and a half. Berulle refused to put his signature to the treaty with the English which followed the reoccupation of La Rochelle by the French because it contained no clauses guaranteeing freedom of religion for English Catholics. He left the royal court in disgust, intending to resign all his titles. He did not live to do so. The cardinal, who had never received his red hat, died in Paris while saying mass on 2 October 1628. He was buried in the church of the Oratory he had founded.

Gregorio Barbarigo

The family of Barbarigo was ancient and noble: two of Gregorio's ancestors had been successive doges of Venice at the end of the fifteenth century, and his father, Gianfrancesco, was a senator of the city. He was born in Venice on 16 September 1625, but his mother, Lucrezia Lion, died in an outbreak of the plague in 1630 and his father brought to the house his cousin, Franchesina Lippomano, to look after him when he was small. It was his father, however, who educated him and the two remained very close, Gregorio frequently writing home to tell his father what he had been doing and to ask advice: Gianfrancesco died only a decade before his son. It was a devout family, but its religious loyalty to Rome had been somewhat suspect: Gregorio's grandfather had supported the Venetian Republic in the schism from Rome in the early years of the seventeenth century. Gianfrancesco did not envisage an ecclesiastical career for his son but rather a diplomatic or political one. As a step on the way he found for Gregorio a place in the mission of Alvise Contarini, who in 1643 the Republic sent to negotiate what, five years later, became the Treaty of Westphalia marking the end of the Thirty Years' War.

The papal mission arrived in Munster a year later. It was headed by Bishop Fabio Chigi, to whom at first Contarini refused to speak given the tension between the papacy and the Republic. They eventually agreed to meet and after a long discussion became allies. The greater impact, however, was upon the young Barbarigo, who became very close to Chigi to the extent of the bishop becoming his unofficial spiritual guide. The papal emissary introduced Barbarigo to the writings of the recently deceased Francis de Sales, and gave him a copy of de Sales's *Introduction to the Devout Life*. He also introduced him to *The Imitation of Christ*.

Barbarigo kept in touch with Chigi after the embassy was over and he had returned to Venice. He was considering whether to become a priest, and if so, whether to offer his services to the diocesan priest or to join a religious order and, if the latter, which kind of religious order, an active one or one which was more contemplative. Chigi, who had by this time become a cardinal and was Secretary of State to Innocent X, advised him to continue his university studies, then become a diocesan priest. This he did. He received minor orders on 5 April 1655, received his doctorate in canon and civil law at the University of Padua the following September, and on 21 December was ordained priest.

Also in April 1655 Fabio Chigi was elected Pope as Alexander VII, and the new Pope summoned his protégé to Rome. He went in obedience to the papal request, but never settled in the city. He discovered his colleagues in the papal service were in pursuit of wealth and of fame: Barbarigo, who was already comfortably off and from a distinguished family, was in pursuit of neither. He performed his duties punctiliously at the tribunals to which he was attached, but attracted attention only when the plague struck Rome in July 1656 and he was given charge of the care of the sick in Trastevere, the poor region of the city near the Vatican. On 4 December 1656, without having any form of pastoral experience other than dealing with the infirm, he was despatched to Bergamo as its bishop. He was consecrated bishop in Rome on 29 July 1657. It was typical of him that, before he received episcopal orders, he retired to Rome's Jesuit novice house of Sant'Andrea and made a retreat.

He may not have had experience, but he certainly had a blueprint. He was a fervent advocate of the reforms introduced by the Council of Trent a century before, and he took as his model the ideal of a Tridentine bishop, Charles Borromeo (see p. 112), who had already been declared a saint. The first thing he did was to summon a diocesan synod. He did so, he said, in direct obedience to the canons of Trent. He then embarked on a thorough visitation of his diocese, making rural parishes his first priority. It took two years, and at the end of it he again summoned a diocesan synod. The purpose of the synod was not to issue reforming decrees or to discipline the clergy so much as to encourage them in their duties and to assure them that they were engaged with him on a common enterprise. He wanted above all to have a better instructed clergy and set in train improvements to the seminary, where each new candidate for the priesthood was given a copy of *An Introduction to the Devout Life*: he was as much concerned for the spiritual development of his clergy as he was for their academic instruction. But the last was not forgotten. He organized monthly meetings of clergy on a local basis where they might discuss problems both theological and moral. He encouraged them to buy books. He gave them each, as he had the seminarians, a copy of *An Introduction to the Devout Life* and urged them to spend some time each day in meditation.

On 5 April 1660 he was created a cardinal priest with the title, later bestowed, of S. Tommaso in Parione: he later opted for the title of San Marco. His friend Alexander VII wanted him in Rome, but Barbarigo had not got over his distaste for the city. Though he travelled there for an *ad limina* (a visit to the 'threshold' [*ad limina*] of the apostles which bishops are required to make every so often) and attended four of the five conclaves (not that of 1669–70) at which he was eligible to vote, he never stayed longer than was absolutely necessary, always returning to his diocese at the first opportunity. Only after the two-month conclave of 1676 which elected Innocent XI did he remain in the city at the Pope's request to advise him, and on this occasion stayed three years.

On 24 March 1664 he was transferred to the diocese of Padua, where he employed the same plan of reform both in the parishes and the seminary that he had implemented in Bergamo. This time he had the advantage of experience, but he also took some of those upon whom he had relied in Bergamo to assist him in the diocese and particularly in the seminary. He established a new seminary in Padua close to his palace and drew up both rules for the conduct of the students, and guidance as to what they were to be taught. He had personally always been interested in science (mathematics had been a particular interest in his youth, and he had studied it at the university), and science was added to the curriculum as well as astronomy. But students were also required to learn languages and the history both of Church and State, and to pay special attention to biblical scholarship. He gave great attention to the library of the seminary – he had built up an impressive one of his own – and he also started a printing press for the publication of scholarly works as well as textbooks.

The parishes were also included in his eagerness to raise the standard of learning. He encouraged the teaching of Christian doctrine in Sunday schools, and produced guidelines for what was to be taught. The devolved structures that he had put in place in Bergamo, dividing the diocese into what might now be called deaneries, he repeated again in Padua, giving each 'dean' responsibility for the intellectual and spiritual wellbeing of the clergy in his area.

He was personally very generous to the poor, donating vast amounts of money to charitable causes. He had a particular interest in the Eastern Churches (at great expense he acquired oriental fonts for his printing press) and welcomed Orthodox clergy to his house. He was also interested in Judaism, and similarly entertained Jewish visitors.

He died in Padua on 18 June 1697, and was interred in the cathedral. He was beatified by Clement XIV in 1771, and declared a saint by John XXIII, who had once been secretary to a bishop of Bergamo, on 26 May 1960. His feast is celebrated on 18 June.

Jean Louis Lefebvre de Cheverus

Cheverus has some claim to be considered the first American cardinal, though he was neither born, nor did he die, in the United States. He was born on 28 January 1768 in Mayenne in France, the eldest son of a magistrate: his very pious mother came from a noble family and it was her influence that persuaded him to become a priest. He attended the college of Louis-le-Grand in Paris, then the seminary of S. Magloire, being ordained priest on 18 December 1790. He also studied at the Sorbonne. After ordination he went to assist his mother's brother, the parish priest at Mayenne, who had been struck by paralysis. These were the years of Revolution, and of a tense relationship between Church and State in France. Both Louis and his uncle refused to take the oath to the new regime, and were removed from office, though Louis continued clandestinely to tend his flock. He was discovered, arrested and imprisoned in Dol. He managed to escape, and make his way to Paris: on 11 September 1791 he became one of the many French priests who made their way to England.

He had little money but some English. Though the government in London was prepared to assist the émigré clergy he refused their offer, and found himself a job teaching French and mathematics in a school in Wallingford, serving also as a chaplain to local Catholic families. He soon moved on, opening a chapel in Tottenham with the approval of the Vicar Apostolic for the London District. He was for a time attracted by the idea of a royalist invasion of Brittany, backed by the Bishop of Dol, who had made him his vicar general, but in the end he stayed in London. That was just as well: the landing at Quiberon in 1795 was a disaster. The royalist force was swiftly overwhelmed, and the Bishop of Dol was captured and executed by a firing squad. Cheverus now reverted to an earlier proposal from the Abbé Matignon, who had taught him at the Sorbonne. Matignon had gone to America where, based in Boston, he looked after such Catholics as were to be found in New England, a geographically enormous 'parish'.

Cheverus arrived in Boston in October 1796, and worked there, among the settlers – mainly Protestant – and the Native American tribes, whose languages he learned, for more than two decades. He remained there despite efforts by his father to entice him back to the parish of Mayenne. He and Matignon won particular credit for the way, during two epidemics of yellow fever, they looked after the sick and buried the dead. They built the first Catholic church in Boston, consecrated in September 1803. Rome decided that a bishopric should be established in Boston, and proposed Matignon, but he demurred, insisting that Cheverus was the more obvious candidate. Rome agreed, and he was ordained bishop in Baltimore, on 1 November 1810. But episcopacy caused little change: Cheverus still walked the region from settlement to settlement, still worked with the Native Americans (though by this time he had another priest colleague whose specific task this was), and was still at everyone's beck and call whatever time of day or night.

Matignon died in 1818, and shortly afterwards the priest who worked with Native Americans returned to France, worn out by his labours. There were moreover problems between the bishops who originally came from France, and those who were Irish by birth. Cheverus was himself becoming worn out, as the French government's representative in the United States observed. There was increased pressure upon him to return home, which he resisted until, at the behest of King Louis XVIII, Pope Pius VII named him Bishop of Montauban. The appointment came as a complete surprise, but he sold off his goods for the benefit of the church in Boston (his books he gave to the Boston Athenaeum), and left the United States in October 1823, arriving back in France, where he was greeted as if he were returning in triumph, a month later. It was not until the end of July 1824 that he formally took possession of his new see.

Once again he won the affection of Protestants and Catholics alike, especially after his efforts to help those displaced by a great flood over the winter of 1825–26. But he did not stay long at Montauban. In 1826 he was offered the post of Minister of Ecclesiastical Affairs by King Charles X, which he turned down, but he was nevertheless made a peer of France. In October of that year the Pope appointed him Archbishop of Bordeaux. There he reorganized the seminary (he had built a seminary at Montauban), set up a retirement home for the clergy, and improved the spiritual life of clergy and laity alike. Again it was a plague, this time of cholera, that brought him most respect from the people of his city: he turned his episcopal palace into a hospital.

As much as possible he avoided political entanglements, and rarely took his seat in the house of peers, though in 1828 he was named a councillor of state. The overthrow of Charles X and the coming to the throne of Louis-Philippe ('the citizen king') in 1830 freed him from state duties, but he played a considerable part in winning over hesitant Catholics to the new monarch. Louis-Philippe was suitably grateful. He petitioned Pope Gregory XVI to grant the Archbishop of Bordeaux a cardinal's hat. He was created cardinal priest in the consistory of 1 February 1836, and he travelled to Paris to receive the red biretta, as was customary in France, from the hands of the French King. But he was already seriously ill. He died in Bordeaux shortly after his return, on 19 July 1836.

Ciriaco María Sancha y Hervás

Ciriaco was born on 18 June 1833, the seventh child of Ambrosio Sancha and Baltasará Hervás, a peasant family from Quintana del Pidio in the province of Burgos: he was so ill at his birth that his family had him immediately baptized. He attended the village school, and the catechism classes. The parish priest noticed his intelligence and willingness to study, and gave him extra classes, including classes in Latin and in the humanities as a preparation for entering the seminary. That he did indeed decide to become a priest was not surprising. Every Catholic family in Spain at the time wanted to have a son a priest or a daughter a nun, and the number of vocations was astonishing: between fifteen hundred and two thousand young men entered the seminary each year in the province of Burgos alone.

Ciriaco offered himself to his own diocese of Osma, and went to the seminary of Osma in September 1852. He did well in his studies. He had been entered on the 'short course', one which would have trained him to serve as a priest in some rural parish, but his ability was spotted and, with a scholarship from the bishop, he was translated to the 'long course' – in which he was both student and, occasionally, lecturer. He was ordained priest on 27 February 1858, and acquired his degree of bachelor of theology in June of the following year. He continued studying for another three years while lecturing in philosophy and serving as secretary to the bishop. He was proposed for a canonry in the cathedral of Osma, but was not elected.

In July 1861 the Archbishop of Santiago de Cuba died. As his successor the Holy See appointed Primo Feliciano Calvo Lope, who like Ciriaco was from the diocese of Osma. He in turn proposed Ciriaco as his secretary. The offer was accepted, and the young priest left for Cuba in May 1862. Cuba was still a Spanish possession, but the situation in the country was fraught: a ten-year war of independence broke out in 1868 which, though unsuccessful, at least won a greater degree of self-determination, at least in theory. But the war brought with it a great deal of suffering, and it was against this background that Ciriaco carried out his pastoral ministry, working especially with the poor. Just after the war broke out he founded the Sisters of Charity (now known as the Sisters of Charity of Cardinal Sancha) to work with the poor, the sick, and particularly with children.

Meanwhile the Archbishop had unexpectedly died. For two years the diocese of Santiago was without an Ordinary, and then the anticlerical Spanish government appointed a wholly unsuitable candidate to the post, a nomination rejected by Rome. The Spanish government's action divided the diocese, the pro-Rome faction being led by the administrator of the see and Ciriaco. The schism broke out in 1873 and was settled in 1874, but both Ciriaco and the administrator of the diocese spent the year in prison.

It may have been thought wiser to remove him from Cuba, but for whatever reason, almost as soon as he was released he was appointed as assistant bishop to the primatial see of Toledo. Toledo then encompassed Madrid, and after consecration in March 1876 he lived in Madrid and served the church there, preparing for the Spanish capital to become an independent diocese. He also organized the construction of a church dedicated to Our Lady 'Almudena'. His work was appreciated, and in 1882 Rome entrusted the diocese of Avila to him, although there was still, technically, a bishop of Avila who was the diocesan Ordinary. In the few years he was there he carried out a visitation of the diocese, improved both the morale and the educational standards of the clergy, and founded a convent of Trappist nuns. It was the first in Spain, and the bishop had to draw up a constitution suitable to the situation in the country.

In 1885 Madrid became a diocese. The first bishop nominated to the post was assassinated after only a few months, such was the tension between Church and State. Ciriaco became Bishop of Madrid and Alcalá de Henares the following year and lived in Alcalá. He had (at, it is said, the behest of the Spanish Queen) been proposed for the diocese of Santiago de Compostella, but the situation in the capital was difficult for the Church, and Ciriaco's prudence was much admired – though it is true that even in Avila he had run into trouble with the government. As in Avila so now in Madrid, he worked to raise the morale of clergy and to provide new churches and parishes – there were twenty when he arrived, thirty when he left – and complete the new cathedral, Santa Maria de la Almudena.

The conflict with the government had revealed the deep divisions within Spanish Catholicism. He decided to address this problem by holding a series of annual Catholic congresses, each in a different city, to bring people together to study the major questions of the time. While Ciriaco was in Madrid, Pope Leo XIII produced his famous encyclical on the condition of workers, *Rerum Novarum*, and Ciriaco was to the fore in giving it publicity in Spain. He founded the Central Committee of Catholic Action to coordinate Catholic responses to the politics of the day, and established organizations for lay people to educate them in their faith.

In 1892 he was again moved, this time to the Archbishopric of Valencia. One of his first acts was to organize a national Eucharistic Congress, which took place in 1893, then he set up an organization of Catholic workers and, in 1894, led a pilgrimage to Rome of some eighteen thousand workers from all over Spain. That was in April. The following month he was created cardinal, receiving the title of Cardinal Priest of San Pietro in Montorio the following December.

He spent only a little over five years in Valencia. He adopted the same tactics which he had used elsewhere, to move the Church to a position of political neutrality. It was a time of financial crisis and political instability and – just as Ciriaco was again moved – the four-month war with the United States over Cuba. But before he was transferred, he had, as in Madrid and elsewhere, started organizations to foster the faith of the laity, and improved the stand-ard of teaching in the seminary. Indeed, he managed to convert the seminary into a pontifical university. He was particularly concerned about the welfare of the clergy, many of whom were living on the breadline or below. He started a savings bank for priests which had an outreach into their personal and spir-itual lives. He also made a mark with the intellectuals of Valencia, traditionally anticlerical, inviting them into the bishop's residence for discussions. He even began a magazine aimed at the intellectual elite of the city.

Rome appointed him Archbishop of Toledo and Primate of Spain in March 1898. Once more his first concern was to improve the quality of priestly for-mation. But he had an equal concern for the people in the pews and set up an organization of 'Lady Catechists' as they were called (*Damas Catequistas*) to teach the faith all over his, and neighbouring, dioceses among the working classes, in prisons. He set up Catholic newspapers and magazines and pro-moted Catholic trade unions. He also brought back the Jesuits, who had been intermittently exiled from Spain during the nineteenth century. But one of the most serious problems he had to resolve was division among the bishops of Spain. In 1907 he brought them together in a conference with the aim of establishing projects right across the country upon which they could all work together.

He died in Toledo on 25 February 1909. It had been a particularly bitter winter, and he caught a chill while he was out in the city distributing food and clothes to the poor. 'He lived in poverty, and he died in great poverty', says his memorial tablet in his cathedral. He was beatified in the same cathedral on 18 October 2009.

Andreas Carlo Ferrari

It is unusual to find among the saints someone who was at odds with the pope of the day, still odder to discover one such among the ranks of the cardinals. However, Andreas Carol Ferrari did not relate easily to Pope Pius X, himself declared a saint, despite the fact that, in the conclave of 1903, he had helped to elect him.

Ferrari was born on 30 August 1850 in Lalatta, a village within the commune of Prato Piano in the diocese of Parma. His parents were of fairly modest means, but sent him to school in Parma, and he then entered the diocesan seminary. There was nothing remarkable in his training, and he was ordained priest on 20 December 1873. The following February he received his first posting as a pastor in Mariano, then in July he went as assistant priest to Fornovo di Taro, and the year after to San Leonardo. After only a year of work in parishes he was called back to the seminary in 1875 to serve as vice rector while teaching physics and mathematics. Two years later he became rector, teaching theology and ecclesiastical history. He published in 1885 a frequently reprinted summary of dogmatic theology.

From seminary rector to bishop is a common enough progression in the Catholic Church. In May 1890 he was elected Bishop of Guastalla, travelling to Rome the following month for his episcopal consecration. He did not stay long in Guastalla, being transferred exactly a year later to the see of Como. On 21 May 1894 he was made cardinal priest of Santa Anastasia by Pope Leo XIII: his appointment to the archdiocese of Milan, where he was to remain for the rest of his life, was announced the same day. Milan is commonly the see of a cardinal, but his rise to the rank, after only four years as a bishop, was unusual. Even more unusual was his promotion to the cardinalate before the announcement of his move to Milan. Clearly he had made a considerable impression.

Perhaps an explanation can be found in his personal commitment to the ideas of a just society which Pope Leo had outlined in his 1891 encyclical *Rerum Novarum*. He was one of the most socially committed bishops of his day. He created in his seminary a chair of economics which he entrusted to Giuseppe Toniolo, one of Italy's leading Catholic economists. Directors of companies, Ferrari wrote, should come to see their workers not as slaves but as brothers, treating them with the dignity due to someone created in the image of God, and paying them a just recompense for their labour. He set about creating unions for workers both in industry and in agriculture, he helped to set up friendly societies, he even founded a magazine, *L'Unione*, which later became a daily paper under the name *L'Italia*.

His disagreement with Pope Leo's successor, Pius X, arose during the Modernist crisis when the Vatican took up opposition to some strands of the scholarship of the day concerning historical issues, but more importantly the interpretation of the Scriptures. A network of spies was set up to report back to the Vatican any deviations which they claimed to have discovered from traditional Catholic teaching. Ferrari was a cultured man, and though he was no radical in his thinking he objected to the measures which were being taken and tried to prevent Modernist thought affecting the clergy and laity of his archdiocese. It lead to a distancing between himself and the Pope: the Pope, he reflected, thought him too tepid in the campaign against Modernism. In 1914 he took part in the conclave to elect a successor to Pius X. The man they chose, who became Pope Benedict XV, though being careful not to condemn the anti-Modernist crusade of his predecessor, immediately put a stop to it. Pope Benedict's relations with Ferrari, whom he much admired, were far warmer than Ferrari had enjoyed with the previous Pope.

During the First World War Ferrari was occupied with taking care of prisoners of war and others caught up in the fighting, for which, in 1919, he was awarded the Grand Cross of SS Maurizio e Lazaro. Meanwhile he built churches for the growing population of his city. He also provided for their education. He set up the Catholic University of the Sacred Heart, and one of his last acts was to approve its constitution. He did so as he lay dying. He developed cancer of the throat, which made him first sound hoarse then made it next to impossible for him to speak. It was not something that could be kept hidden, and he did not attempt to do so. People of all stations in life came to his room to talk to him. Towards the end he wrote a farewell letter to the people of his diocese.

He died of cancer on 2 February 1921, and was buried, as he requested, near the tomb of St Charles Borromeo, to whom he had a great devotion: he had adopted 'Carlo' as one of his names. He was beatified by Pope John Paul II in May 1987, and his feast day is kept on 2 February.

The Pastors

If the origins of the office of cardinal are indeed as described in the Introduction – and given all the unknowns that is a big if – then the earliest cardinals in Rome were all pastors. They were either the parish priests of the titular churches, or the bishops of suburbicarian dioceses, or the deacons who looked after the welfare services provided by the Church. The cardinals, according to that account, were the senior clergymen of the city of Rome. Rather oddly it was very largely the eleventh-century reform movement that began the rupture between a pope's closest advisors and the Roman clergy.

The Gregorian (or Hildebrandine) reform had begun long before Hildbebrand was himself elected to the papacy in 1073. It was instigated from outside Rome, by the German emperors who in the first half of the eleventh century placed four German-born reforming pontiffs on the papal throne. Not all popes up to that point had been Roman in origin, but most, if perhaps not quite all, had been members of the Roman clergy. But when protagonists of the reform movement gained control they sought out from around Europe clerics who would support them in their enterprise. They thus broke the link between the life of the city's basilicas and churches and the men who served them as cardinal bishops, priests and deacons. The cardinals, however, continued to have pastoral responsibility because they accumulated benefices. It was the way that the papacy, or ruling monarchs, rewarded them for their services, but they did not personally, or only very rarely in person, oversee the pastoral care of the living from which they drew their income, whether a parish, canonry, abbacy or bishopric. The theory was that out of the revenue of the benefices they paid other clerics as vicars to perform their duties for them.

This situation continued until well after the Council of Trent. Trent insisted on residence for bishops and other holders of benefices in an effort to reform the Church. But cardinals, as the advisors to the pope of the day and senior officials in the papal curia, still needed to be in Rome. For these, and for other bishops who were engaged full-time on Vatican business, the notion of 'titular' churches was invented in a form rather different from the way the term 'titular' had been used of Roman churches. Bishops were consecrated to serve churches *in partibus infidelium* as the phrase was, 'in the regions of the unbelievers'. These were, in other words, made bishops of ancient dioceses, mainly in the East or in North Africa, which had long since been abandoned.

A small number of cardinals, however, even in the middle ages, were resident bishops. One example was Stephen Langton (c. 1150–1228), who was called to Rome in 1206 by his old friend Pope Innocent III, made a cardinal, and then, by dint of the Pope leaning on the monks of the Canterbury Cathedral chapter, elected Archbishop of Canterbury also in 1206. It was not uncommon for bishops of major sees to be made cardinals: it was a means by which the papacy could exercise a modicum of control over Churches which were distant from Rome.

It was not, however, until the nineteenth century with the increasing concentration of power at the Roman centre, that it became usual to have a cardinal in each country with a significant Catholic population. Of the cardinals whose lives are recorded below, Charles Borromeo was raised to the purple long before he was able to exercise active pastoral care for his diocese of Milan, originally bestowed on him to provide him with income. The others are much more recent, and are examples of the trend just mentioned, to internationalize the College of Cardinals and have a cardinal in major dioceses such as Milan, Chicago (Cardinals Cody and Bernardin) or Lyons (de Bonald), while Baltimore was the only archdiocese in the whole of the United States when James Gibbons was made a cardinal. Bartolomeo d'Avanzo is an example of another Roman practice. His diocese was small and relatively insignificant. He was rewarded with a red hat for his support for Pius IX's desire to have himself and his successors formally declared to be infallible. He has not been included here for his role at the First Vatican Council, but rather for the strange story of the attempt on his life.

Charles Borromeo

Among his collection of studies on early modern Italy, Professor Peter Burke of the University of Cambridge includes an essay entitled 'How to be a Counter-Reformation saint'. The essay was first published in 1984, and since then questions have been raised about the appropriateness of the term 'Counter-Reformation': the preferred form now appears to be 'the Catholic Reformation'. But whether one uses the term Counter Reformation or Catholic Reformation, one of the heroes of this movement in the last decades of the sixteenth century is, as Burke points out, Cardinal Charles (Carlo) Borromeo, Archbishop of Milan.

He was born in the castle of Arona, which stands on Lake Maggiore, on 2 October 1538. The room in which he was born was called 'the room of the three lakes', but was later named after him. There were six children in the family and he was the second son and third child of Count Ghiberto II Borromeo. His mother, Margherita de'Medici, was sister to Giovanni Angelo de'Medici, already at the time of Charles's birth in the papal service, but not yet a cardinal. Charles was baptized in the church at Arona, and spent his childhood either there or in the family palazzo in Milan. As the second son he was destined for a clerical career, something which, as a devout youth, he wholeheartedly embraced. He was financed by the revenue of an abbey in Arona, passed on to him by an uncle who had held the abbacy before him, but he gave much of the money to the poor, and often found it difficult to make ends meet during his studies.

He studied first in Milan, then attended the University of Pavia, where he graduated a doctor in civil and canon law on 6 December 1559. On Christmas Day 1559 his uncle Giovanni Angelo became Pope Pius IV. The election changed Charles's life. He immediately took the road to Rome and in the consistory of 31 January 1560 he was made a cardinal deacon with the title of SS Vito e Modesto. He became the 'Cardinal Nephew' when he was not much more than twenty-one years old and still only in minor orders. (He later became cardinal priest of S. Martino ai Monti, and later still of Santa Prassede.) He was then appointed to be administrator of the archdiocese of Milan, and given the office of legate in Bologna and in the Romagna, and governor successively of a number of cities of the Papal States.

Not long after his election, Pius IV determined, under Charles's prompting, to reopen the Council of Trent, suspended for a decade, and in 1562–63 Charles became heavily involved in the Council's proceedings. When it was ended he presided over a commission to produce the *Catechism of the Council of Trent*, and was also on the commission for the reform of Church music: Charles was a patron of musicians, and it was he who commissioned Palestrina to compose the *Missa Papae Marcelli*. He also worked on the revision of the Church's liturgical books, the missal and the breviary.

During the Council his elder brother died, leaving Charles as head of the family and heir to the title. He could still at that point have chosen to leave the clerical state and once more become a layman, but he did not choose to do so. He was ordained priest on 4 September 1563, and was consecrated a bishop on 7 December of the same year. He had been administrator of the diocese of Milan, and could now become its Ordinary. He wanted to return to his home city, but his uncle the Pope would not allow it. Eventually he was given permission simply to return to Milan and hold a synod, the purpose of which was to implement in the diocese the reforming decrees of Trent, then being obliged to return to Rome. On his way to Milan, however, he learned that Pius IV was dying. Charles arrived back in Rome just in time: the Pope breathed his last on 9 December 1565. His successor, Pius V, was elected on 7 January. In April Charles was allowed to return permanently to his diocese.

He had already held one reforming synod in his diocese: in all there were eleven, and five more provincial ones – his jurisdiction extended beyond Milan and into Switzerland. His reforms were far from welcome among some of his clergy. The canons of the collegiate church of Santa Maria della Scala refused to accept his authority, and turned to the civil power in Milan for support. When he attempted a visitation of their church they refused him entry, and one of their supporters fired on the cardinal, hitting the cross he was carrying. They were excommunicated, but some months later they asked for forgiveness. There was a second attack on him a couple of years later when a lay brother belonging to the Humiliati, a religious order suppressed shortly afterwards by Pius V, was hired as an assassin. Again the bullet missed him.

Charles Borromeo's chief concern was the improvement of education in his diocese, both for the clergy and the laity. The establishment of seminaries was one of the most important of Tridentine reforms, but Charles also established the Confraternity of Christian Doctrine to teach catechism, especially in Sunday schools. Huge numbers of children were enrolled. In 1576 he began his own religious order of priests to assist him in his work of reform, the Oblates of St Ambrose: Archbishop Manning in Westminster nearly three hundred years later used his model for his own order of priests, whom he named the Oblates of St Charles.

His concern was, however, as much for the material as for the spiritual well-being of those in Milan. During the famine of 1570 he provided food from his own resources for three months. He was away from home in 1576 when the plague struck, and he hurried back to the city to care for the sick: the civil authorities had in the meantime fled. In gratitude the people of Milan erected a huge statue of him in his birthplace. In his will he left his personal fortune to the city's main hospital.

In his episcopal palace he lived simply, but was a generous host. He was also generous to those who served him, paying them well but at the same time forbidding them to receive gifts, which might be interpreted as bribes. He went on retreat twice a year, and required his clergy to do likewise. He preached regularly and movingly, though he suffered from an impediment in his speech. He went to confession every morning before mass. His confessor was a priest from Wales, and another Welshman was one of his vicar generals.

He died at the age of only forty-six, on 3 November 1584. He was interred in the cathedral, though his body was moved in the middle of the eighteenth century to a specially constructed chapel. He was immediately after his death regarded as a saint by the people of Milan, and the process for his canonization began there, as well as in Pavia and Bologna. He was declared a saint by Pope

Paul V on 1 November 1610. His feast is celebrated on 1 November, as well as on the anniversary of his death.

Louis de Bonald

The Cardinal Louis de Bonald was the fourth son of the Vicomte Louis de Bonald (1754–1840), and to understand the cardinal one has to turn to the Vicomte, soldier, statesman, even on occasion a journalist, but above all a philosopher and political theorist. The first of his many writings was a three-volume work entitled *A Theory of the Role of Political and Religious Power in Civil Society, Demonstrated by Reason and by History* which appeared in 1796. In it he argued that society was based on two principles, monarchy and religion – specifically the Catholic faith – and the foundation of both of those was tradition. They should sustain each other when under attack. He was the guru of French conservative political thinking, and a major theoretician of what came to be known as 'integrisme', the symbiotic union of throne and altar. His son the cardinal was much in the same mould.

He was born at Millau, in the Départment of Midi-Pyrénées on 30 October 1787, and travelled north to Lyons for his early education, then to Amiens and finally to the seminary of Saint Sulpice on Paris, where he was ordained on 21 December 1811. His father refused to work for the government of the Emperor Napoleon, but the son was not quite so squeamish, and became a clerk of the imperial chapel and a chaplain at the Salpétrière, the former gunpowder factory which by this time had become the world's largest hospital (it is also the hospital where, in 1997, Diana Princess of Wales died). That, however, was pretty much the extent of his collaboration with the regime of Napoleon. At the restoration of the monarchy he began to play a larger role, travelling with the French ambassador to Rome as his secretary. In 1817 he became the vicar general of the Bishop of Chartres, and spent the next few years in pastoral work. In 1823 he became a very active Bishop of Le-Puy-en-Velay, being ordained to the episcopate in the church of Saint Sulpice in Paris. In 1840 he was named Archbishop of Lyons, and on 1 March 1841 he was created cardinal priest of SS. Trinità al Monte Pincio.

As Cardinal Archbishop he was a loyal supporter of Pope Pius IX, taking up a special 'Peter's Pence' collection to defray his expenses when after the revolution of 1848 the Pope had to flee Rome. He was a vigorous opponent of the nationalistic French Catholicism called Gallicanism, and abetted the centralizing tendency of Pio Nono when he attempted against stiff resistance to replace the local Lyonnais liturgy with that of Rome. He played a small part in the political life of France: he was named a senator in 1852, but his chief work was in his diocese, where he fostered devotion and built a hospital for incurables.

He had also inherited some of his father's political convictions, in particular his concern for the urban poor. The modern city (such as Lyons, of course) served the interests of the bourgeoisie, rather than those of the workers, argued Bonald *père*. It was a sentiment shared by Bonald *fils*. There had been a great deal of unrest among the workers of the city before his arrival, and the clergy had been criticized for failing to maintain order. But it was the cardinal's conviction that responsibility for the unrest lay more with the employers than with the put-upon workers. He was also active on behalf of those without jobs. Learning from his father, Cardinal de Bonald was an early exponent of nineteenth-century Catholic social activism, though it was of course in the interest of the upper classes, such as the de Bonalds, whose wealth lay primarily in land, to complain of the harsh treatment the newly arrived entrepreneurs meted out upon their employees.

The cardinal died in Lyons on 25 February 1850.

Bartolomeo D'Avanzo

D'Avanzo was the son of a doctor, born at Avella in the diocese of Nola, Italy, on 3 July 1811, the youngest of three children. His father died when he was still very small, leaving the three children – Bartolomeo was the youngest – to be brought up by their mother Caterina assisted by her devout sister Patrizia. He entered the seminary at Nola, then regarded as one of the better ones in Italy. He was ordained priest on 20 September 1834. After his ordination he attended the University of Naples, becoming a doctor of theology in September 1842.

He was sent back to his seminary at Nola to teach theology and Hebrew, and became a canon of the cathedral chapter, also serving as censor of books, an advisor on ethics, and secretary of the Academy of the Catholic Religion which had been established by his bishop. Early in 1851 he was appointed Bishop of Castellanetta and Mottola, being consecrated on 28 March of that year. In his cathedral at Castellanetta he built a marble chapel in honour of the Immaculate Conception – a teaching about the Virgin Mary which was declared an article of the Catholic faith by Pope Pius IX in 1854 – set up a distinguished library, and purchased and restored the Dominican convent. He brought in nuns to educate the poor, and purchased medicine for the sick during an outbreak of cholera. For all of this Ferdinand II, King of Naples and the Two Sicilies, awarded him the Grand Cross of a Commander of the Order of Francis I.

Not everyone, however, was quite so enamoured of the bishop who, in July 1860, was transferred to the fairly recently created diocese of Calvi and Treano, while remaining administrator of Castellanetta and Mottola. Ferdinand II had been succeeded by Francis II, but Ferdinand's tyrannical rule had fostered the growth of secret societies plotting the overthrow of the monarchy in favour of establishing a united Kingdom of Italy. This movement was opposed by the Pope. There was in consequence a great deal of ill-feeling in the region towards the Church, and on 13 August 1860, while D'Avanzo was en route in his carriage from Castellanetta to his home town of Avella, he was attacked by two men as he came out of a forest. Four shots were fired. One ricocheted harmlessly in the carriage, but he was hit by the other three – one in the right hand, one in the ribs, and the last squarely in the chest.

It might very well have killed him – but for his pectoral cross, the ornate cross which bishops wear on their chest. The bullet hit the cross, twisting it out of shape, but did no further damage: the cross and the bullet are still to be seen displayed in a church in Avella. He was driven off to hospital in Sorrento, and even after he had recovered from the assassination attempt it was decided that, such was the anticlerical feeling in the region, it would be better if he remained away from his see: he only went back there in 1867.

As in Castellanetta, so too in Treano he began a series of works to improve the cathedral, decorating the dome with a mosaic of the triumph of Mary Immaculate – it was destroyed during the Second World War. He also restored the episcopal palace.

In 1869 he was, as were all Catholic bishops, summoned to the First Vatican Council. He had a reputation for theological expertise, and was made a member of the controversial *De Fide* Commission – controversial because the Constitution 'On the Catholic Faith' dealt with the hotly debated topic of papal infallibility. On 20 June 1870 D'Avanzo made an impassioned speech in favour of the doctrine of papal infallibility, dealing one by one with objections: it was reckoned to have swayed at least some of the doubters. The Constitution *Pastor Aeternus*, defining papal infallibility, was passed just a month later, on 18 July 1870.

His reward came on 3 April 1876 when he was created cardinal priest of Santa Susanna. It must have been a reward: a cardinal's hat rarely followed appointment to such modest dioceses as D'Avanzo had governed. The populace was delighted. He did not, however, long remain in the diocese after his elevation. A bout of ill-health persuaded him to retire to Avella, whence he continued to govern his diocese at a distance. He left Avella to take part in the conclave of 1876, but Avella is where he died, on 20 October 1884. His funeral took place not in his cathedral but in a church in Avella, and he was buried in his family's tomb in the town's cemetery.

James Gibbons

Biographers of Cardinal Gibbons struggle to explain it, but he seems to have been one of the most popular, if not *the* most popular, prelates in the United States of his day. He was a man of an easy-going nature and a ready smile, which no doubt accounts for a good deal, but he was also a lackadaisical administrator who at his death on 24 March 1921 left his diocese much less flourishing than it was when he first came to it in May 1877 as a coadjutor bishop with right of succession to the see. He retained his popularity until the end of his life – though it may be, as the history of the archdiocese of Baltimore suggests, that he was so pleased with his fame that he avoided doing anything which might have put it at risk.

He was born in Baltimore on 23 July 1834, and was baptized in the cathedral, though his parents, Thomas Gibbons and Bridget Walsh, were in 1829 immigrants from Ireland via a spell in Canada. The family returned to Ireland in 1837 to live in Ballinrobe, Country Mayo, where Thomas ran a grocery store until his death in 1847. In 1853 Bridget and her five children returned to the United States to settle in New Orleans where James took, like his father, a job in a grocery store. Inspired by a retreat he heard preached by Redemptorists he decided to become a priest. In 1855 he entered St Charles's College in Baltimore, a minor seminary, and two years later went to St Mary's Seminary. He was ordained for the archdiocese of Baltimore, the only archdiocese in the country at the time, on 30 June 1861. He was given his first posting, to St Patrick's parish, but after only six weeks there was assigned as pastor to St Brigid's, an offshoot of St Patrick's. As pastor of St Brigid's, he was also chaplain to Fort McHenry, the fort whose exploits during the battle of Chesapeake Bay in 1812 had inspired the words to the 'Star Spangled Banner'. But by Gibbons's time, the period of the American Civil War, it had become a prison for Confederate prisoners of war and for Confederate sympathizers – who included many Baltimore notables, not least the mayor.

In 1865 James Gibbons became secretary to Archbishop Spalding of Baltimore, a common enough step on the ladder to ecclesiastical preferment. That came soon enough. In 1868 he was appointed vicar apostolic of North Carolina, which necessitated his being consecrated a bishop. This happened on 16 August 1868, when he became the youngest bishop not just in the United States but throughout the Catholic world. He was at the First Vatican Council of 1869 to 1870, but he seems to have made little impact on it, or it on him. Back in the United States he was promoted to the see of Richmond in 1872. Archbishop Bayley of Baltimore asked that he be appointed his coadjutor archbishop. This happened in May 1877, but before he could arrive back in Baltimore, Bayley died, and he therefore automatically succeeded to the premier see in the

United States, the first diocese to be founded, in October of that year.

Although it was the premier see, it was not technically a primatial see. Nonetheless it fell to Gibbons to convene and, as Apostolic Delegate, preside at the Third Plenary Council of the American Bishops, held at St Mary's Seminary in Baltimore from 9 November to 7 December 1884. It was the last such Council ever to have been held, and is perhaps most famous for the Baltimore Catechism. The idea of having a uniform catechism in the United States had a long history, and Gibbons appointed a committee to discuss the matter in the run-up to the Council. The first draft was written in the course of the Council, and presented to a session on 6 December, though it received little attention. The final version, 'Prepared and Enjoined by the Order of the Third Plenary Council of Baltimore', as it said on the title page, received the imprimatur for its seventy-two pages and four hundred and twenty-one questions in April the following year. Though immediately much criticized – with the result that some bishops continued to produce their own – it was not revised until 1936, and remained widely in use until the mid 1960s.

Another topic of debate at the Plenary Council was the attitude of Catholics towards secret societies, the main ones under discussion being the Grand Army of the Republic, the Ancient Order of Hibernians, and the Knights of Labour. Uniformed 'knighthoods' of one sort and another – such as the still flourishing Knights of Columbus – were very much a part of American Catholic life at the end of the nineteenth century. The official Church, as ever drawing its notions of such organizations from continental Europe, was highly suspicious. Whether they were secret societies in the sense understood in the Vatican was a matter of debate. The Vatican had, however, at the request of a Canadian bishop, banned the Knights of Labour in that country shortly before the Plenary Council. The problem for Gibbons and his fellow bishops was complicated by the fact that the 'Grand Master Workman' of the Knights, Terence Pownderly, was a Catholic, and many Catholics had joined as he rid the Knighthood's constitution of provisions that might have been objectionable to Catholics. Gibbons was against banning the Knighthood, though other archbishops were in favour. Gibbons argued that to prohibit Catholic working men from joining would simply alienate the working class, and the ban would in any case not be observed. 'To lose the heart of the people', he said, 'would be a misfortune for which the friendship of the rich and powerful would be no compensation.' Over in England, the Archbishop of Westminster, Henry Edward Manning, who was of a similar mind, thought Gibbons's arguments irresistible. It was possibly Gibbons's robust defence of the Knights of Labour which won him much of his popularity.

That popularity, with Catholics and non-Catholics alike, was much on display when he returned to the States from Rome after receiving the cardinatial red hat, and the title of cardinal priest of Santa Maria in Trastevere, on 17 March 1887. It had been announced almost a year earlier. A cable to another US Archbishop had been misunderstood by the recipient, who let it be known that Gibbons was about to be elevated to the purple when the cable had said nothing of the sort. Hence the Vatican was obliged to make the announcement a good while before the event. But if Rome was to create an American cardinal, it had to be the Archbishop of Baltimore; to do anything else would have been a major snub. As it was, Gibbons felt not a little put out when, a few years later, the Archbishop of New York was similarly raised in rank.

Not that Rome was wholly pleased with the Archbishop of Baltimore. He was a firm defender of the US Constitution, and regarded the separation of Church and State enshrined in it as an undisguised blessing. That was not the Vatican's view. In an encyclical entitled *Longinqua Oceani* of June 1895, Pope Leo XIII said that the American model was no doubt admirable because of the freedom to practise their religion it granted to Catholics, but it was not a model which had universal application. Gibbons's influence in Rome was declining. He had managed to have a priest sympathetic to his views appointed as rector of the North American College. The rector had acted as Gibbons's agent in trying to explain both to the Pope and to the Congregatio de Propaganda Fide, which at this point still controlled the US Church, the US way of doing things. But this priest was sacked for, among other things, an inappropriate friendship between him and a Miss Virginia McTavish of Baltimore. Miss McTavish, a lady of irreproachable morals, had upset the Vatican establishment by going from an audience with Pope Leo to a meeting with the Queen of Italy, whom the Pope did not recognize as such. Matters were made worse by the French who, much to the annoyance of the monarchists whom Pope Leo had been cultivating, claimed that the Americans had shown it was entirely possible for the Catholic Church to live in harmony with a secular state. So *Longinqua Oceani* was followed in January 1899 by a letter addressed to Gibbons, *Testem benevolentiae*, in which the US bishops were accused of creating a Church which was distinct from that elsewhere in the Catholic world. Pope Leo had invented the heresy of 'Americanism'. There was no such thing, the bishops responded – and the cardinal told the Pope so to his face, while publicly refraining from comment.

Problems about the 'American model' had arisen for various reasons, not least the existence in the States of 'national' parishes which served, and were served by, nationals of a particular European country – Germans, Italians, even Bohemians. In the early years of his episcopate Gibbons tried to integrate them into the diocese, and though as time went on he grew more tolerant of them, the fact that so many Catholics in the United States were immigrants remained a problem for him. He wanted them to assimilate, and they were unwilling to do so. He even preached the virtues of the American model at the installation of the Austrian-born Frederick Katzer as Archbishop of Milwaukee, an appointment made against the advice of the US bishops. Gibbons regarded that particular sermon as one of the most audacious things he had ever done.

Another audacious thing that he attempted, but that he eventually failed to achieve, was to integrate the Catholic parochial schools within the US public school system. Had the plan succeeded, the history of the Catholic schools in the United States would have been very different, but few shared his conviction that it would be a good thing to do, and the plan made very little progress. He might thus seem to have been on the liberal wing of US Catholicism, but judged by modern standards he was conservative. He was not an active opponent of racial discrimination – there continued to be specifically black parishes in his archdiocese – nor of votes for women – though when they were enfranchised he urged them to use their vote. A friend of (almost) every US President during his time at Baltimore, he was a Republican sympathizer in national politics, though a Democrat in local affairs. But his devotion to both the American Church and the American State was never in doubt. The diocese of Baltimore had been founded in 1784, and raised to the rank of a metropolitan see in 1808. When the centenary of its elevation came around, Cardinal Gibbons had erected over his residence, and illuminated, an enormous gilt eagle, holding the US flag in its beak.

He died in that same residence on 24 March 1921, and was buried near John Carroll (see p. 228) in the crypt of the cathedral.

John Cody

Bishops and their clergy do not always see eye to eye. It is difficult to imagine, however, any conflict more public and more rancorous than that between Cardinal John Cody and the Chicago clergy over whom he ruled in the last couple of decades of his life. It was a regular topic in the city's newspapers and on its radio stations. The fault was perhaps not all on his side. He took over the diocese just as the Second Vatican Council was drawing to a close. In the light of all the discussion of collegiality among bishops, the priests' expectations of greater involvement in the decision-making processes of the Chicago diocese were high, perhaps unrealistically so. On the other hand, though he had attended the the Second Vatican Council, Cody's understanding of the office of bishop was far more autocratic. A clash was inevitable.

John Patrick Cody was born in St Louis, Missouri, on Christmas Eve 1907. His father was an Irish immigrant, who rose through the ranks of the fire service to become its deputy chief. He attended the local parish school, the St Louis High, which melded seamlessly into a minor seminary for the diocese. Cody's parish priest was a close friend of the Archbishop, John Glennon, and Glennon came to know the young man, and liked him. He selected him in 1926 to go to Rome, where he became a student at the North American College. Though some tutoring may be, and usually is, carried on within their walls, Roman colleges are generally halls of residence rather than teaching institutions. Those attending them go to classes elsewhere. Oddly, perhaps, Cody was sent to the college of Propaganda Fide, which specialized in training men from, or destined to be sent to, missionary countries. He became doctor of philosophy in 1928 then doctor in theology in 1932 (Roman doctorates were not then quite what they have since become, and it was not unusual to emerge with two of them). He was ordained in Rome in December 1931, but did not return to parish life in his home diocese. Instead he stayed on as a staff member of the North American College, and took a doctorate in Canon Law at the St Apollinaire Institute in 1938. During this time he also worked in the Vatican's Secretariat of State, for which he was rewarded with a Bene Merenti (= 'Well done') medal. It was only then that he finally moved back to the United States.

But not to parish work, not at least as a regular posting. Instead he became private secretary to Archbishop Glennon for two years, then chancellor of the archdiocese. In February 1946 Glennon was made a cardinal, and he set off for Rome with some trepidation, considering himself too old to make the journey. He was right as it turned out, because when he stopped off in his native Ireland he was taken ill, and died in Dublin. He had taken Cody with him, and Cody was with the newly appointed cardinal when he died. The following year he was made auxiliary bishop to the see of St Louis, where the new Archbishop, who had hitherto served all his life in Indianapolis, needed someone with local knowledge. In 1954 he was named coadjutor (or assistant bishop with the right of succession to the see) of St Joseph Missouri. Two years later it was united with the diocese of Kansas City and he became bishop of the combined dioceses. Five years later he was sent to New Orleans, again as coadjutor bishop – though he had been personally raised to the rank of Archbishop – and in 1964 he became Archbishop of New Orleans.

It was in New Orleans that he began to make his mark. His decision to desegregate the parochial schools hit the national headlines, and was met with some resistance, but he went ahead nonetheless. It was an expensive business, however, and it left the diocese with a considerable burden of debt. He was also very unpopular among many of the clergy, who threw a party and sang a solemn *Te Deum* on his departure.

His departure was announced in June 1965, and he arrived in Chicago on 24 August. He came by train into the main station, accompanied by the mayor of Chicago and the governor of Illinois. It was a carefully planned, ostentatious entry into the largest diocese in the United States, and one of the largest in the world if measured in population. It had some 3,000 priests. People wondered how it was that Cody came to be ordinary of a diocese which was second only in prestige to that of New York. The fact that the papal nuncio in Washington had been a classmate of Cody's in Rome, they decided, might have had something to do with it.

As has been remarked, priests had begun to expect something different from their bishops after the Second Vatican Council. But consultation and collaboration was not Cody's style. From the start he acted in an authoritarian manner, sacking priests, moving them, demanding their retirement without providing for their future accommodation or sustenance. He had not been in his new post for a year when the clergy of the diocese, or many of them, decided that they would have to band together if they had any chance of opening a dialogue with their bishop. They set up the Association of Chicago Priests to represent them in the hope that they might be able to discuss with Cody issues of personnel – moves, retirement and salaries. The salaries of the Chicago clergy were among the lowest in the country. They asked for a rise. Cody objected on the grounds that a rise in salary would not be welcomed by all, especially not by those who were trying to identify with the poor of the city. He had a point. There was a number of clergy who felt that way, and the cardinal (he became a cardinal priest with the title of Santa Cecilia in June 1967) was adept at exploiting divisions among those who opposed him. At first he cooperated with the Association, but stopped doing so entirely when the senate of priests had been established – and then he began increasingly to ignore the senate likewise.

With the demographic changes in the city it was unavoidable that some parishes should be amalgamated and parochial schools closed because there was no longer a sufficiently large Catholic population to support them. But with the closing of the schools some of the clergy wanted to hand the property over to the city for public schools. Cody refused. He cut subsidies to poor parishes, making them no long viable. He sold off Church property in a way that seemed to canon lawyers contrary to the Church's own Code. When challenged, he flew off to Rome to get retrospective approval for his actions from the Vatican. He pleaded poverty, saying that the diocese needed the money – and then, without consultation, spent $4 million establishing a diocesan television service. The atmosphere among the clergy and religious became so bad that one congregation of nuns circulated a form letter for their members to send to the papal nuncio requesting that the cardinal be promoted – to a job in Rome.

It was not only the clergy of the diocese who found Cardinal John Cody difficult. From the end of the 1970s a Chicago newspaper, the *Sun-Times*, began an investigation into his financial dealings. He had the reputation for being something of a financial wizard, and had for a time been treasurer of the National Conference of Catholic Bishops. The fact that he occasionally made some very bad investments he waved away, saying that people even more financially astute than he had made similar mistakes. What, however, the newspaper was investigating was his alleged diversion of $1 million or so of tax-exempt Church funds to a private individual, a Mrs Helen Dolan Wilson.

Helen Wilson was distantly related to the cardinal, and they had known each other from childhood. While he was in Rome she had married and borne two children, but divorced her husband about the time Cody returned. He had found work for her in St Louis diocese, and she had followed him from place to place, eventually buying a lakefront apartment in Chicago, though in 1975 she moved back to St Louis. He had made loans to her, she was the beneficiary of his life insurance policy, and her son David, an insurance salesman, benefited from diocesan policies being put through his hands. The US Attorney demanded to see diocesan papers, but the cardinal's lawyers stalled, and they were never produced. Then a Grand Jury investigation was begun, and again the cardinal stalled.

By this time he was ill with heart trouble, and spent a long time in hospital. Soon after his release from hospital, on 25 April 1982, he died in his home, and all investigations ceased. There was never any question of sexual impropriety with Mrs Wilson, only the misappropriation of Church funds, but there were certainly those who believed him guilty of that. 'I have forgiven my enemies', he said in a letter written not long before his death, and released after it. 'But God will not so forgive.' 'The Cardinal is answerable to Rome and to God, not to the *Sun-Times*', said his lawyer on one occasion. And as his clergy well knew, he was certainly not answerable to the diocese of Chicago.

Tomás Ó Fiaich

When Thomas James Fee was born, on 3 November 1923, at Annamore, Cullyhanna, Co. Armagh, just two years after the treaty between Westminster and Dublin which separated the British north of Ireland from the Irish south, the area was socially and culturally English. Many of the young men had fought in the British army during the First World War: the Britishness is reflected in the name by which in the early years he was known. His father's father had been a landless labourer, who spoke Gaelic fluently, but his own father and mother – who died when he was only eight – both schoolteachers, gave him an English form of name. His father, eventually headteacher at the school in Creganduff attended by both Tom and his brother Paddy, was always known as 'Master Fee'. From the 1950s, however, Ó Fiaich began to use the Irish Tomás Seamus alongside the English version. After it was announced that he was to become Archbishop of Armagh and Primate of All Ireland, he declared that henceforward the Irish version alone was to be used in official communiqués. It was indicative of the way in which culturally he understood himself.

It was the Irish sports which attracted him. He and Paddy were enthusiastic followers both of hurling and Gaelic football. When in September 1940 he began his studies for the priesthood, it was in the Republic, at the Irish national seminary of St Patrick's College, Maynooth near Dublin (the Irish Church operated as a unity across the political boundaries). Apart from his philosophical and theological studies he opted for a special course in Gaelic studies, and when he took a degree with first class honours at University College, Dublin, it was in Early and Medieval Irish History. His 1950 MA dissertation was on the tribes of Armagh.

By this time he was a priest, ordained on 6 June 1948 not at Maynooth but at St Peter's College, Wexford: he had been sent there because, after a serious illness, it was decided he needed a less pressured environment. The pressure, however, was scarcely removed before he was off first to UCD but then for further studies to the University of Louvain, where in 1952 he received a 'licence' in historical sciences, the minimum essential degree required if he was to teach in a seminary. He did not at first return to Maynooth, but spent a year in parish work – his only experience of the everyday work of a priest – as a curate at Clonfeakle. In 1953, however, he returned to the seminary, as lecturer in modern history, an odd title for someone whose abiding interest, and area of scholarly research, was early medieval history, and especially the impact of the Irish monks on continental Europe. In 1959 he became professor of modern history. In his spare time he edited the Armagh history journal, and served as president of an association of Irish-speaking priests, as well as editing their magazine.

His involvement with the Irish language movement had not gone unnoticed. He was approached by the Irish government to chair a commission on the restoration of the Irish language, and then, after its report was published in 1964, to chair the committee tasked with implementing the report. He was an effective and energetic chairman. Meanwhile, in addition to an interest in the poetry of Ulster, he translated the writings of St Columbanus, and for the canonization of Oliver Plunkett wrote two studies of the saint who had been Archbishop of Armagh from 1669 to his martyrdom in 1681. One of the books was for English readers, the other for Irish: they were noticeably different.

Maynooth had been founded at the end of the eighteenth century, just before the Act of Union of Britain and Ireland, as a college for the training of clergy. But in common with other similar institutions, in the 1960s it began to expand its remit. In 1966 it was opened to lay people, which required some reorganization. Ó'Fiaich was appointed registrar, then later vice president and, in 1974, president of the College. It was an uneasy time for the clergy, and it was a particularly difficult time for institutions which bridged the divide between the clerical and the lay life. When two of the staff of Maynooth returned from a sabbatical wearing – as has now become much more common – lay attire rather than the dress of clergymen, Ó'Fiaich felt obliged to dismiss them. It became something of a *cause célèbre*, with demonstrations by students in Maynooth itself and in Dublin. The priests took the College to court but by the time the case was finally over (the Irish Supreme Court ruled in favour of the College), Ó'Fiaich had been made Archbishop of Armagh.

It was unusual for a priest to be raised directly to the rank of Archbishop of Armagh and Primate of all Ireland: it was generally a post for someone already in episcopal orders. The genial, pipe-smoking Ó'Fiaich took it in his stride. He was consecrated bishop on 2 October 1977, and created cardinal priest of San Patrizio in the first consistory of John Paul II, 30 June 1979.

He took over the office of Primate when the situation in Northern Ireland was at its most problematic. His role straddled the border, but his commitment to all things Gaelic made it rather too clear, at least for the British government, where his sympathies lay. He spent a day visiting Republican prisoners in Northern Ireland, and afterwards appeared to sympathize with their 'dirty protest'. Similarly he made something on an apologia for one of the hunger strikers who died. In January 1984, in the course of a radio interview, he refused to condemn Sinn Féin, the political wing of the militant IRA. People could join it, he said, so long as they did so for the right reasons, and so long as they believed that Sinn Féin councillors were working for the benefit of the local community. As British troops and the (very largely) Protestant Royal Ulster Constabulary were battling the IRA, not least in the region in which Ó'Fiaich had grown up, his words were taken by some as condoning violence, and criticizing the government in Westminster. It did not help when he claimed in defence of the IRA that it was killing Protestants not because they were Protestants, but because they were members of the security forces. It may have been unfair to call him 'the Provo Prelate', but that is how he came to be dubbed. But it was indeed unfair. Long before the broadcast that caused all the trouble (it was as unwelcome in government circles in Dublin as it was at Westminster) he had unequivocally condemned the violence of the IRA. It was a mortal sin, he insisted, to indulge in violence – and it was also a mortal sin to cooperate with violence in any way: a warning to those who sheltered or aided members of the IRA.

The violence, however, did not abate during his period of office. It adversely affected him when, after the murder of Lord Louis Mountbatten and eighteen

British soldiers at the end of August 1979, it was decided that Pope John Paul II would not visit Northern Ireland, instead making his plea for peace on the Republic's side of the border. Ó'Fiaich nonetheless made the most of the occasion. The excitement at a papal visit, he said, was akin to the excitement of an All-Ireland hurling final at Croke Park.

On 7 May 1990 the cardinal set off, as he regularly did, on a pilgrimage to Lourdes. While in Lourdes he suffered a heart attack. He was taken by helicopter to a hospital in Toulouse, but died there on 8 May. Ó'Fiaich's successor, like his predecessor in the see of Armagh, was far more outspoken in his condemnation of the IRA's violence.

Joseph Bernardin

In the middle of the sixteenth century the great reforming Church Council, the Council of Trent, was held in Trento in northern Italy. Its influence on the Church was immense, and for the good. But the adjective which has been derived from Trento – Tridentine – has for many Catholics come to mean out of date, conservative, even reactionary. That is perhaps a pity, but it is nonetheless true. In that sense there was little that was 'Tridentine' about Joseph Bernardin, so it is something of an irony that his stone-cutter father Joseph (his mother Maria was a seamstress) had been baptized Giuseppe in the province, if not the actual city, of Trento. He had then emigrated to Columbia, South Carolina, where his children were born. There were two: Joseph being the elder. He was born on 2 April 1928.

His education was unremarkable, but he was an able student and decided to train as a doctor. He had spent only one year at the University of South Carolina before he decided to become a priest in his home diocese of Charleston. Again his education was unremarkable. He was sent to St Mary's College, Kentucky, followed by St Mary's Seminary in Baltimore – where he received his bachelor of arts degree – then to Catholic University in Washington DC, where he received both a master of arts degree in education, and a doctorate in theology. He was ordained in his home parish of St Joseph in Columbia on 26 April 1952, and then did a couple of years of pastoral work in the diocese before holding a succession of offices including that of administrator of the diocese of Charleston from 1964 to 1965. Over the course of these years he became first a privy chamberlain and then a domestic prelate to the Pope, customary honours for diocesan officials, granting him the title of Monsignor.

He was clearly on his way to a bishopric, and in March 1966 he became assistant bishop of Atlanta: he was the youngest bishop in the United States. His role in Atlanta was to serve as parish priest of the cathedral, thus acquiring more pastoral experience. Though the US bishops had met regularly to discuss common problems, they were not formally constituted as an episcopal conference in the form envisaged by the Second Vatican Council. Bernardin was placed – elected by his fellow bishops – in charge of the process to produce a national episcopal conference. This was a full-time job, and he resigned his office in Atlanta. But his role in the bishops' conference was fairly short-lived. In December 1972 Pope Paul VI appointed him Archbishop of Cincinnati. This was a post he held for ten years, during which time he played host to, and obviously impressed, the Cardinal Archbishop of Kraków, one Karol Wojtyła, who, as Pope John Paul II, appointed him to the Archbishopric of Chicago in August 1982 and created him cardinal priest with the title of Jesus the Divine Workman in the consistory of February 1983.

As Archbishop of Cincinnati, Bernardin had served on a number of Vatican bodies, and had regularly attended the Synod of Bishops as an elected representative of the American episcopacy. Under John Paul II these Roman duties increased, and he served, under both Pope Paul VI and Pope John Paul, on the organizing committee of the Synod of Bishops. But despite the confidence that Rome appeared to place in him, he was not afraid to take a stand when he thought Rome had behaved irregularly. After complaints by conservative Catholics, Rome instituted a visitation of Archbishop Raymond Hunthausen's diocese of Seattle, and the Archbishop was effectively removed from the day-to-day administration of his see. The whole affair, which caused considerable scandal and not just in the United States, dragged on for five years, and it was partly through Bernardin, who thought Hunthausen had been unjustly treated, that an accommodation which restored the Archbishop's authority was finally agreed.

He promoted many causes, but that of peace was perhaps closest to his heart. When he had been assistant bishop in Atlanta he and the diocesan bishop together drafted an encyclical on this issue, and it was Bernardin who was the prime mover in the pastoral letter, *The Challenge of Peace: God's Promise and Our Response*, which was published by the American bishops in 1983. He chaired the committee, he presided at the public hearings on the text (like the bishops' pastoral on *Economic Justice for All* of 1986 it was produced in consultation with the laity, a practice which the Vatican was not too happy about, and which failed when they tried it a third time with a document on the role of women in the Church). As a consequence of his commitment, he was awarded the Albert Einstein International Peace Prize.

But perhaps he was best known throughout the Catholic world for what came to be called, in his phrase first used in 1984 in a lecture at St Louis University, 'the seamless garment'. He had hitherto talked of a 'consistent ethic of life' as central to Catholic moral teaching. By that he meant that he upheld the Church's position on contraception and abortion but, he argued, this defence of life must be extended to all issues concerned with human beings, in particular the death penalty – which he opposed. Many of those who applauded his stance on abortion and contraception were at odds with him over the death penalty. Traditionalists could and did argue that the right to impose the death penalty was upheld by the *Catechism of the Catholic Church* published in English in 1994. It was removed from the second edition published in 1999.

By that time Joseph Bernardin was dead. He died on 14 November 1996, and was buried in the Bishops' Chapel in Mount Carmel Cemetery, not far from the tomb of his predecessor, Cardinal Cody. In June 1995 he was told he had inoperable liver and pancreatic cancer. His first act was to tell his clergy, and then the people of his diocese. He quite consciously then developed a personal ministry towards others who were dying of the same disease. His acceptance, and courage in the face of, the onset of death impressed not just those who knew him but many more besides. Pope John Paul spoke of his 'witness of dignity and hope'.

His final years were blighted by two things: by the accusation that he had sexually abused a former seminarian named Steven Cook, and by the divisions within the American Catholic Church. The first was resolved when Cook dropped the claim, which Bernardin had strenuously denied: he had only come to think he had a memory of the alleged abuse, Cook admitted, when under hypnosis. In his last book, *The Gift of Peace*, which became something of a bestseller, Bernardin hinted that Cook had been encouraged to bring the charge by a Catholic priest – he did not name him – who was at odds with the cardinal. At the start of his governance of the Chicago diocese there were many clergy who were at odds with the diocesan administration, in the aftermath of the governance of Cardinal Cody, and Bernardin had won them round. But divisions within the American Catholic Church he found harder to deal with. He began an initiative to find a 'common ground' among the diverse tendencies within the Church. The initiative survives, even though it did not find much favour among the American bishops. But like 'the seamless garment', 'the common ground' became a phrase, and a programme, which has endured. President Obama made reference to it in his address at the University of Notre Dame on 17 May 2009 – itself a highly controversial occasion, the President's presence at a Catholic University being opposed by many, including influential members of the US hierarchy. Obama went out of his way to praise the late cardinal. 'He was congenial and gentle in his persuasion,' said the President, 'always trying to bring people together, always trying to find common ground.'

That was undoubtedly true, but he did not compromise on his principles. In September 1996, shortly after announcing that he was dying of cancer,

President Bill Clinton invested him with the Presidential Medal of Freedom. Shortly after the investiture Bernardin joined other bishops in a vigil protesting against Clinton's approval of partial-birth abortions.

Men of War

This is not the place to rehearse the Church's attitude to war as it developed in the middle ages. It was understood very early on that the clergy ought not to fight, and certainly ought not to draw blood. In the late fourth or early fifth century a document was drawn up which laid down that a Christian ought not voluntarily become a soldier, and if he did join the army, then he must not shed blood (which seems an odd provision for a soldier), and if he did shed blood then he should stay away from the Eucharist until he had done penance. With the development of a warrior class whom we nowadays call knights, the Church authorities became even more alarmed, and attempted to limit warfare through 'the truce of God', confining it to particular seasons and defining groups of people (naturally including the clergy, but certainly not only the clergy) who should not be molested. In almost any film that purports to be set in the middle ages there will be a sequence showing a tournament, and there is no doubt that, among the warrior class, tournaments were popular both as a sport and as a means of training for war. But the Church was opposed to tournaments as well, banning them in 1130 at the Council of Clermont. Which makes it all the more strange that exactly at this period the Knights Templar came into existence, a religious order of warriors committed to defending the Holy Land. But that is another story.

The Knights Templar and other military religious orders apart, there is no doubt about the hostility of the Church to war. So why then were there not just warrior monks like the Templars but warrior cardinals and other prelates? Even popes had led armies into battle, Leo IX for one in the early middle ages, and Julius II in the renaissance. There are all kinds of different answers to that question, but at the root of the problem was property. At the time of St Gregory the Great, at the end of the sixth and the beginning of the seventh century, the Roman Church needed estates to enable it to feed the population of the city of Rome, and to finance the papacy, already a very considerable enterprise. What came to be known as the Papal States did not precisely begin then, but when they eventually came into being not all that long afterwards, they had to be defended against the depredations sometimes of the Byzantines, sometimes of

131

the Lombards, sometimes of Muslim armies from North Africa and later on against the Normans.

Italy was, during the middle ages and renaissance, and down indeed into modern times, a patchwork of duchies and tiny city-states, sometimes falling within, sometimes without the patrimony of St Peter, as the Papal States were often called. The situation was not stable. These small states were prey to the ambitions of the French King, of the German Emperor, even at times of the Spanish monarchs. The popes believed they had to defend their inheritance. They probably did not give it much thought: this was what one did. They did not have major armies to fight their battles. Instead they used local militias and, very frequently, mercenary forces. The highly decorative Swiss Guard which performs security duties in the Vatican is exactly that, a mercenary army, albeit a very small one. It has been in existence, though not quite continuously, since 1506.

Mercenary troops under the command of their captains, or *condottieri*, are all very well, but in the prolonged struggles in which popes were frequently involved, they needed their own commanders. Which is where the cardinals whose lives are related below come in. Most were soldiers, but particularly in the struggle against the Turks, sailors were also required, as the lives of Pierre d'Aubusson, Grand Master of the Knights Hospitaller (the Knights of Malta as they are now known) and Oliviero Carafa indicate.

There was often, it should be added, another aspect to the wars conducted by popes. They were sometimes wars conducted not in defence of the patrimony of St Peter, but wars of aggrandisement for the pope's family. The office of cardinal and of the papacy itself was seen in the later middle ages and the renaissance, and indeed into the early modern period, as a means of enriching one's relatives. No one saw this more clearly, perhaps, than Pope Alexander VI. His army commander was his son Cesare Borgia. His story is recounted elsewhere in this book (p. 206).

Gil Álvarez de Albornoz

For most of the first two-thirds of the fourteenth century the official residence of the Pope was not in Rome but in Avignon. There were many reasons for this. The popes of the day, and the majority of the cardinals, were French, and Avignon, though not then strictly speaking in French territory, was certainly within easy reach of the French monarchs. But what kept successive popes in Avignon was not simply the allure of France, it was also the unrest not just in Rome itself but in the city-states of the Italian peninsula which had once recognized the suzerainty of the papacy. Before the popes could set out to return to Rome, the city, and the peninsula, had to be brought back under papal control. Happily for Pope Clement VI and his successors Innocent VI and Urban V they could rely on the military expertise of Cardinal Gil Albornoz, abetted, and sometimes hindered, by the English soldier of fortune Sir John Hawkwood.

Gil (Giles, or in Latin Aegidius) was born at Carrascosa del Campo in 1310, the son of García Álvarez, Lord of Albornoz in the (Spanish) province of Cuenca. His mother, Teresa de Luna, belonged to the royal house of Aragón and was the aunt of Pedro de Luna, who became the antipope Benedict XIII. More significantly for Gil, however, she was the sister of Jimeno de Luna who, as Archbishop of Toledo from 1328 until his death in 1337, was the most important churchman in a Spain which had not yet rid itself of its Muslim invaders. Toledo was almost at the frontier: Jimeno's predecessor as Archbishop of Toledo had been killed in battle. Before he transferred to Toledo, Jimeno had been Archbishop of Zaragoza, and it was there, under the watchful eye of his uncle, that Gil began his studies. From Zaragoza he went to the university in Toulouse where, like all ambitious clerics, he studied not theology but law, obtaining his doctorate about 1325.

From Toulouse he returned to Castile, to the court of Alfonso XI. He was not, it seems, yet ordained a priest. He was a deacon, the archdeacon of Calatrava, a frontier fortress town, and chaplain and counsellor to the King to whom he was very close. In 1335 Alfonso sent him as part of the embassy to the King of Aragón. Three years later, when he was probably not yet twenty-eight, the King had him elected to the Archbishopric of Toledo in succession to his uncle Jimeno. He was a conscientious churchman – he had earlier become a canon regular of St Augustine – and held reforming synods in his diocese, but it was still as a soldier that he was best known. He accompanied the King at the battle of Rio Salado, where the most recent Muslim invasion was turned back. He was one of the commanders of the Castilian troops and took part in the battle on horseback, surrounded by a bodyguard of clergy and wielding a sword – though, as a good canonist he was careful to say, without drawing blood, something the Church's law forbade. He was also present at the battle for Algeciras (a battle in which Geoffrey Chaucer's Knight took part) and in 1350 at the unsuccessful siege of Gibraltar.

The siege was unsuccessful because, in the course of it, Alfonso died, carried off not by wounds he had received but by the plague. Though he had been nicknamed 'the Implacable' because of the severity with which he put down the rebellion of the nobles who had attempted to assert their independence during his long minority, on the whole he had been an admirable ruler. The same could not be said for his son and successor, Pedro, who was nicknamed 'the Cruel'. Gil was annoyed by Pedro's meddling in Church affairs; Pedro was angered by Gil's criticism of his extra-marital affairs: his father's, seemingly tolerated by Gil, had been even more blatant. Pedro the Cruel was not a man to cross: Gil fled the kingdom for the safety of the court of Pope Clement VI at Avignon. Clement promptly (17 December 1350) named him cardinal priest of San Clemente.

The Pope's first campaign to re-establish his suzerainty in Italy had been launched before Gil was made a cardinal, and had resulted in abject failure. The Pope's great enemy was Giovanni Visconti, Archbishop of Milan, and because of the failure of the papal army Clement was obliged to hand him Bologna as his fief for a period of twelve years. It was Clement's successor, Pope Innocent VI, who recognized Gil's potential as a pontifical warrior. At the end of July 1350 he was named papal vicar in Italy, with the job of restoring papal governance there: his letter of appointment described him an 'an angel of peace'. He was, however, despatched with only a small military force, mainly to serve as a bodyguard. When going to war he had to depend upon mercenary troops, such as the English 'White Company' to which Hawkwood was attached and whose highly burnished armour and military skill was a matter for much Italian comment.

The first campaign was just north of Rome; the enemy was Giovanni di Vico. Albornoz's ability was as much diplomatic as military. He was able to win back support for the papacy from its erstwhile vassals, and to persuade them into battle on the pope's side. So Giordano Orsini was tempted out of his fastness of Montefiascone to help defeat Vico at the battle of Orvieto, after which Viterbo fell to the papal forces. The cardinal entered the city in triumph on 14 July 1354. Now town after town fell. By 1357 almost the whole of the Papal States had been recovered. Gil set about restructuring them, producing the *Constitutiones Aegidianae* ('The Constitutions of Giles') for the governance of the territories, which he presented for approval at a parliament he held in Fano at the very end of April 1357. This Constitution, which among other things divided the Papal States into five provinces, remained in force until 1816, and even then was not formally abolished for another century.

He also provided for the future security of papal territory by building castles – at Viterbo he is said to have laid the foundation stone of the castle himself – creating a naval base at Ancona and, also at Ancona, building a particularly huge castle which was intended as a place of refuge for the Pope. Innocent VI might have been expected to be grateful. He wasn't. In 1357 Albornoz was replaced by the abbot of Cluny as the papal legate in Italy. The abbot, however, did not prove capable of the office. A year later Albornoz was back. Once again he campaigned, dealing brutally with those who opposed him and, especially, with those who betrayed his trust. When Forlimpopoli rose against him he had the town destroyed, its bishopric transferred, and a new castle, Salvaterra, built on its site. In March 1360 the people of Bologna placed the city under his control but Bernabó Visconti rallied its citizens against Albornoz. He hurried there with his mercenaries and camped outside its walls until the city surrendered.

The cardinal took part in the conclave which elected Urban V: it was said that Albornoz had been offered the papacy but refused it. He did not have a high opinion of the new Pope, who once again replaced him as legate in Italy by the abbot of Cluny. On this occasion, however, the Pope left him as legate in Naples, where once again he found himself at war with the Visconti, whom he defeated near Faenza in April 1363. One of his last acts was to form a pact among the city-states of Italy to defend the peninsula from the marauding bands whom he had been partially responsible for recruiting during the earlier wars. But at this point the Pope withdrew the office of legate from Albornoz, and two years after that, on 24 August 1367, he died at Viterbo. The previous June he had been able to welcome Pope Urban as he disembarked at Corneto on his way back from Avignon to Rome. The cardinal left money to endow a Spanish college at the University of Bologna. He was buried at Assisi, in the basilica of St Francis, but in 1372 he body was taken back to be interred in the cathedral at Toledo. The bier on which his body was returned to Spain has ever since been used to carry the bodies of the Archbishops of Toledo to their final resting place in their cathedral.

Giovanni Vitelleschi

The date of Vitelleschi's birth is unknown, but the place was Corneto. Now known as Tarquinia – it has reverted to a form of its original Etruscan name – it is a coastal town some fifty miles north-east of Rome. Little or nothing is known of his youth except that he was a member of the nobility and received training as a soldier of fortune, or *condottiere*, in the service of Tartaglia di Lavello, Lord of Tuscania. Despite this military background he entered the service of the papacy under Martin V (1417–31) and by 1420 was castellan of Bologna. Shortly after the election of Martin's successor, on 16 April 1431 Pope Eugenius IV appointed him Bishop of Recanati and Macerata. It was a tactical move. Eugenius was about to reassert papal control over lands that had been over-generously bestowed on his relatives by the Colonna Pope Martin, and the Colonnas were not going to submit without a battle or two: Eugenius needed soldiers around him, albeit with the rank of bishop.

Eugenius put him in charge of Rome as his deputy, then of other papal territories. He was made governor of Bologna. When the Colonna-fomented revolt eventually broke out in Rome in 1434 and a commune was declared, forcing

Eugenius to flee the city for Florence, Vitelleschi was called upon to restore it to papal obedience. This he did with great speed and even greater severity, demanding as a reward that the supposedly grateful, but cowed, citizens of Rome should bestow on him the title of *pater patriae*, 'father of the country'. There was even talk of erecting an equestrian statue to him in Rome. Although the proposal came to nothing there is a supposed representation of what it would have looked like in a fresco in Tarquinia's Palazzo Comunale.

He next turned his attention to the Colonnas, destroying their stronghold of Palestrina in April 1437. Among his victims was Jacopo di Vico, whose family had traditionally dominated Corneto. A more complicated task faced Vitelleschi in the struggle for control of the Kingdom of Naples. Succession to the throne was disputed between the Aragonese and the Angevins. Eugenius needed the support of France, and therefore backed René of Anjou. But there was a further complication. The Angevin cause was also being upheld by the *condottieri* Francesco Sforza of Pesaro, but Sforza was himself a threat to the integrity of the Papal States, and Eugenius did not want to depend upon him for the States' security. In this instance, despite Vitelleschi's customary brutal campaign and almost capturing Alfonso of Aragón, he was not successful and eventually, though only after Vitelleschi's death, the Pope had to accept Alfonso as the new King of Naples.

Vitelleschi had meanwhile been rising up through the ecclesiastic honours system. In February 1435 he was appointed nominal Patriarch of Alexandria – and in consequence was commonly referred to as 'the Patriarch', and on 9 August 1437 he was made cardinal priest of San Lorenzo in Lucina: there is no record of him ever receiving episcopal, or even priestly, ordination. He was known thereafter as 'the Cardinal of Florence', but he was never, it seems, the Archbishop of that See. He built himself an appropriate palace still to be seen in modern Tarquinia, where he collected a fine library. He was, after all, very well paid. As a cardinal and papal general his stipend was raised from 400 to 500 ducats a month. He was worth the money. In May 1438 Niccolò Piccinino had taken the papal city of Bologna, acting on behalf of the Visconti of Milan. This was a threat to the security of the Council which Eugenius was assembling at Ferrara – it was moved for safety to Florence – and the Pope asked Vitelleschi to take it back, which he did with his usual efficiency. He was still in pursuit of the Colonna and their allies. He sacked Zagarolo, a Colonna township, and defeated and beheaded the Lord of Foligno, taking Spoleto and executing the governor of the city.

The danger for Cardinal Vitelleschi was that he was both too powerful for the Pope, and had created too many enemies. In his *History of Florence* Machiavelli wrote of him: 'He acquired so much power over the pontiff and the papal troops that the former was afraid of commanding him, and the latter obeyed no one else.' On somebody's orders – and the chief suspect must be Pope Eugenius – he was lured into Castel Sant'Angelo by the governor and shortly afterwards, on 2 April 1440, he died. How he died is not clear. One story has it that he died of wounds: he had drawn his sword to defend himself on his arrest, and was seriously hurt in the scuffle which followed. According to another version, however, he died in prison of poison. A decade later his remains were transferred to the cathedral in Corneto.

Lodovico Trevisan

Trevisan was born in November 1401. His father was a doctor. His mother's maiden name was Mezzarota, and in later life the cardinal used a half wheel as his emblem as a pun on the name. His birthplace is a touch uncertain. It is commonly given as Padua, which was then part of the Venetian Republic, but some sources suggest Venice itself, where apparently he first went to the university. Then he attended the University of Padua where he obtained his doctorate in medicine in July 1425. For a time he seems either to have practised medicine in Padua, or to have taught it, but in 1430 he became the personal physician to the Venetian Cardinal Gabriele Condulmaro.

This was a wise career-move because at the beginning of March 1431 Cardinal Condulmaro became Pope Eugenius IV, and Trevisan began to be rewarded with benefices, including a canonry at the cathedral of Padua. In October 1435 he became Bishop of Trau, an office he exercised through a vicar, the abbot of a local monastery. He was himself otherwise engaged, effortlessly transferring his skills from medicine to warfare. He was, however, with Pope Eugenius at the Council of Florence-Ferrara: his signature was appended to the bull of union with the Greeks that Eugenius issued in July 1439.

Shortly afterwards he was named Patriarch of Aquileia, so he, like his great rival Giovanni Vitelleschi (p. 135), was known as 'the Patriarch'. He was, indeed, suspected of having a hand in the downfall of Vitelleschi: Antonio Rido, the governor of Castel Sant'Angelo, who may well have played an active part in Vitelleschi's demise, was a loyal supporter of Trevisan. Certainly he promptly succeeded Vitelleschi as the general commanding Eugenius's troops. Some of them, however, remained loyal to their previous commander so that one of his first tasks was to bring them back under control, as well as to subdue the regions of Viterbo and Civitavecchia. In June 1440 he was invested with his own military standard, and given a force of 3,000 horsemen and 500 foot soldiers to command. On 29 June 1440 he took part in the decisive battle of Anghiari alongside the *condottiere* Francesco Sforza against Niccolò Piccinino in which he personally took charge of the right flank of the victorious papal forces. For this triumph he was rewarded on 1 July 1440 with the title of cardinal priest of San Lorenzo in Damaso. A commemorative medal was ordered to be struck in his honour.

He was then appointed legate in the Romagna with the objective of recovering Church lands, especially Bologna. The campaign had to be called off in November but began again the following spring. Bologna was recaptured, but lost again shortly afterwards because of a revolt among the citizenry. By that time, however, Trevisan had other tasks. The Florentines and the Visconti of Milan now turned against their former ally Francesco Sforza, who had even planned, with the encouragement of at least one cardinal in the papal curia, to march on Rome, and Trevisan was given the task of invading the Sforza territory of the March of Ancona. By July 1446 the March of Ancona had been returned to its former subjugation to the papacy.

He had, meanwhile, risen further through the clerical ranks. In 1437 he became Archbishop of Florence, and was also for a time administrator of the diocese of Bologna. He moreover became Bishop of Cava and abbot of a Cistercian monastery in the diocese of Rieti. All these benefices contributed handsomely to his already considerable wealth. He built himself a palace beside his titular church of San Lorenzo, a palace so grand one contemporary described it as paradise. It was an enviable residence, and the young Cardinal Francesco Gonzaga, when he arrived in Rome, coveted it: he was told that if he needed to know how a cardinal should live he ought to attach himself to Trevisan. After Trevisan's death Gonzaga did indeed acquire the palace. He also acquired Trevisan's cook, Maestro Martino of Milan, perhaps the world's first celebrity chef and the author of the modern world's first cookbook. Soldier though he often was, the cardinal was also a gourmet, and someone who loved to entertain guests at San Lorenzo to sumptuous banquets (a painting completed c. 1455 by Mantegna shows him to be a somewhat rotund individual). To provide for his table he cultivated exotic fruits in his garden, and to amuse his guests he kept a menagerie of exotic animals.

This of course was while he was in Rome. He had responsibility for the city's security, and for the free passage of traffic along its major roads. He improved the area around the Campo dei Fiori, and in front of the Pantheon, from which he cleared away the stalls of all the small traders, and built an aqueduct. But he was often out of Rome – rarely attending to the needs of his various benefices, though he repaired the basilica in Aquileia, much more frequently on diplomatic missions for the pope of the day. He took part in three conclaves, the last one of which (1464) elected Pietro Barbo as Paul II. He was also a Venetian, but no friend of Trevisan's, and the election marked the end of his major role in Church affairs, though under Pope Paul he became the Cardinal Bishop of Albano, a town in which he sought refuge from the plague.

Perhaps his most remarkable exploits were under Pope Callistus III, who launched a naval crusade against the Turks with Trevisan appointed in 1455 as admiral of the papal fleet. Callistus had even made him responsible for building the galleys. There were ten of them, and they left Naples for the Aegean in August 1455. The Pope's navy fairly easily freed some of the smaller islands from the Turks, and then went on to set up a naval base in Rhodes. In 1457 he beat off an attack on Mytilene, in the course of which he captured several Turkish vessels, earning much gratitude from the Pope for his exploits. Despite his various triumphs, when Callistus's successor Pius II called a conference at Mantua in June 1459 to discuss another crusade, Trevisan opposed the plan, which in the end came to nothing.

Lodovico Trevisan died in Rome on 22 March 1465, and was buried in his titular church of San Lorenzo in Damaso. His grand monument, still to be seen, was, however, erected not by himself or his family but by a canon of San Lorenzo who had been in his entourage. He had left his great wealth for the most part to his two brothers, but his possessions, his collection of jewels and cameos and other objects he had collected in his years of travel around the Mediterranean were seized by Paul II ostensibly to pay for a crusade. The Pope eventually compensated Trevisan's family for some at least of the *objets d'art* he had confiscated. He used the collection as a surety against a loan from Lorenzo de' Medici, and so much of this collection, some of which had originally come from Florence, finally found its way back to Trevisan's one-time archiepiscopal see.

Pierre d'Aubusson

It is, perhaps, a touch unfair to include d'Aubusson among the warrior cardinals. That he was a warrior there is no doubt, but he became a cardinal for a piece of political, rather than military, chicanery, and he received the red hat long after his fighting days were over. He may be best remembered for the politics, but he deserves to be remembered for his successful defence of the island of Rhodes from Turkish attack in one of the most ferocious battles of the late middle ages.

Pierre was born in 1423 at Monteil-le Vicomte, near Bourganeuf in the diocese of Limoges. A relative brought him to the court of Charles VII, and he became a close friend of the Dauphin, the future Louis XI, whom he accompanied into battle on several occasions. He might have had a successful career as a courtier-soldier, but instead he chose, around the year 1445, to join the Knights Hospitallers of St John of Jerusalem. The Knights seem odd to modern susceptibilities. They were at the same time soldiers and monks. There were several military religious orders during the middle ages, of which the Templars are the best known, though for all the wrong reasons. But there were others, such as the orders of Santiago and Calatrava founded to fight the Muslims in Spain, or the Teutonic Knights who, after a period in the Holy Land, went to fight – literally – paganism in the Baltic. But the Templars and the Knights Hospitallers, the latter so called because they had originally been brought into existence to look after sick pilgrims, were the most powerful. And after the Templars were suppressed early in the fourteenth century the Hospitallers were the main, sometimes the only, Christian force committed to holding back the advance in the Levant of the Ottoman Turks.

After the fall of the Holy Land the Knights had settled first on Cyprus and later on Rhodes, and it was to Rhodes that Pierre was eventually summoned after serving in several important roles in France itself. By 1471 he had become superintendent of the fortifications of Rhodes, and effectively second-in-command to the grand master. At the death of grand master Orsini he was elected in his place. He was well aware of how exposed was Rhodes to the Ottoman threat, a threat that became all the greater after the Venetians, who had been vying with the galleys of the Turks for control of the Mediterranean and its lucrative trade, concluded a peace treaty with the Sultan. The way lay open for an attack on the Hospitallers' citadel.

Pierre had prepared for their coming. The Knights' council had wanted him to pay tribute to the Turks to buy off their hostility, but d'Aubusson had refused. Instead he played for time. He entered a commercial arrangement with the Turks. He signed treaties with Egypt and with Tunis so as to reduce the number of potential enemies. But he also fortified Rhodes itself. He strengthened the towers which guarded entrance to the harbour; he put a strong chain across the harbour to make it impossible for ships to enter; he had ditches dug, and those already existing made deeper; he laid in a large supply of munitions, and waited. The army of Mehemet II, under the command of Mezih Pasha, arrived on 23 May 1480.

Contemporary sources claim they arrived in 160 ships, carrying upwards of 70,000 men. Against them Pierre's forces numbered less than three thousand, knights, sergeants-at-arms, foot soldiers, backed by the civilian population of the island. The odds seemed overwhelming, but Mezih Pasha had reckoned without the military competence of the grand master. The first wave, launched against the apparently vulnerable – and isolated – tower of St Nicholas, was thrown back, and fire ships sent amid the Muslim fleet. When a floating bridge was built under the cover of darkness to allow the attacker to storm the city, the stratagem was spotted, artillery turned on the advancing enemy, and there was nowhere for them to flee. The following morning their corpses floated in the harbour. After some six weeks of bombardment the Turkish guns reduced one tower to rubble and troops rushed in, but d'Aubusson, already wounded in the thigh by an arrow, led a successful counter-attack in the course of which he was again wounded, this time by a spear to the chest, and had to be carried to the Hospitallers' hospital. But by that time the Knights of St John were victorious, capturing the banner of Mehemet. After a siege of eighty-nine days Mezih Pasha withdrew, leaving d'Aubusson the toast of Europe. It was not, however, for his military triumph that he gained his cardinatial title, but for the bizarre events which followed.

A few months after the Muslim retreat, Mehemet II died. His throne was disputed between his two sons, Bajazet II and Djem, also called Zizim. Djem was defeated in the power struggle, and fled for asylum to Rhodes. He was at first received hospitably, and granted the freedom of the island, but then Bajazet demanded that he be handed over. D'Aubusson engaged in careful diplomacy. He would not deliver him over to his brother, but he undertook to keep him under careful guard on the understanding that Bajazet would pay handsomely for his upkeep. It was effectively a pension from the Sultan to the grand master: the sum agreed was 45,000 ducats. The Sultan also presented the Knights with a thorn from the crown of thorns, and part of the arm of John the Baptist, relics which had fallen into Ottoman hands after their capture of Constantinople. There was, between Constantinople and Rhodes, only a relatively short distance, and the danger remained that Bajazet would attempt to recover his brother. D'Aubusson therefore sent him to one of the Hospitaller properties in the Auvergne, and he remained in France for the next seven years, being moved from castle to castle.

A number of European powers would have liked to have had Djem in their safekeeping. In the end it was Pope Innocent VIII who persuaded the grand master to transfer custody of the Muslim prince. Djem arrived in Rome on 13 March 1489, where he was received with great honour, but was nonetheless a prisoner. The 45,000 ducats 'pension' was divided between the Knights Hospitallers and the Pope, so effectively Innocent VIII became a pensioner of the Sultan. In the meantime d'Aubusson had let it be known to the ruler of Egypt and to Djem's mother that, in return for a ransom of 20,000 ducats, the prince could be released: the money was paid, but as by this time d'Abusson was in no position to hand Djem over, the Pope made him pay it back.

For his agreement to place Djem in the custody of Pope Innocent VIII, Pierre d'Aubusson was in March 1489 created a cardinal deacon of the title of S. Adriano al Forno. He had never, as far as is known, received any sacred orders, which would in any case have been alien to the customs of the Knights Hospitallers. He was also made papal legate for Asia. The order itself also benefited. In return for gaining custody of Djem the Pope amalgamated with the Hospitallers several other smaller orders of knighthood, thus endowing the

Hospitallers with the property belonging to these orders, as well as granting them a number of other privileges.

Cardinal d'Aubusson returned to Rhodes. He started to rebuild it after the depredations of the siege, and once more to improve its fortifications. He fostered the commerce of the city of Rhodes, which prospered – at the expense of the Jews, whom he drove out. He drew up a new version of the statutes of his order, and tightened discipline, which was said to have become lax. He died on 3 July 1503, they said of anger at the failure to launch another crusade. Djem, his one-time hostage, had died in 1494, still in Rome.

Not twenty years later, in July 1522, Suleiman brought the Ottoman army back to Rhodes. The Knights, a smaller force than in 1480, held out for five months, but at the end of that time the people of Rhodes felt they had suffered enough. Suleiman offered to let the Knights depart honourably, and the inhabitants of the city begged that the Knights take up the offer. Reluctantly the grand master of the day agreed, and the Knights sailed from Rhodes on 1 January 1523.

Oliviero Carafa

Of the several warrior cardinals included in this collection, most were soldiers. Oliviero, on the other hand, was a sailor. Although born in Rome – on 10 March 1430 – his father Francesco, Lord of Torre del Greco and elsewhere, was a member of one of the patrician families of Naples, and it was as a Neapolitan that he thought of himself: after he had been set upon an ecclesiastical career his first benefice, a canonry granted him when he was seven years old, was of the cathedral church of Naples. His mother, Maria Origlia, was said to be distantly related to the thirteenth-century theologian, Thomas Aquinas. Oliviero studied at Naples, Perugia and Ferrara, and obtained the customary doctorate in canon and civil law requisite at the time for high ecclesiastical office. That office came soon enough. On 18 November 1458, at the request of Ferdinand I of Aragón, the King of Naples, he was created Archbishop of that city. No record survives of his ordination to the priesthood that must have preceded his consecration as bishop, but consecrated he was, at the Torre del Greco on 29 December of that year.

His administration of the diocese – if any – was overshadowed by his political commitments, and he was by 1465 president of the King's Privy Council. The King urged Pope Paul II to make him a cardinal, which he did on 18 September 1467. Oliviero was still in Naples, so it was only on 3 December that he received the red hat, and the title of SS Pietro e Marcellino: he subsequently swapped this title for S. Eugenio, then for that of Cardinal Bishop of Albano, later, of Sabina and finally of Ostia. Once in Rome he rapidly established himself as a patron of the arts, a collector of antiquities and a protagonist of the printing press, which had just arrived in the city.

He also became involved in papal plans for a crusade against the Turks. The matter had become more urgent after 1470 when the Venetians' last outpost in the East, which they called Negroponte (it is Euboea in Greece), fell to the conqueror of Constantinople, the Sultan Mehmet II. Pope Paul tried to form a pact among the Italian states to take the battle to the Turks, but all he achieved before his sudden death in 1471 was a defensive alliance. His successor, Sixtus IV, shared Paul's enthusiasm for a crusade, and won support from both Venice and Naples. A papal fleet of some eighty craft was assembled remarkably quickly, Venice providing half, Naples over twenty vessels. Sixtus placed Oliviero in command. On 28 May 1472 Oliviero said mass in St Peter's, received a papal blessing, and shortly afterwards set off for Naples – where he was still Archbishop – and joined the fleet. The ships set off for Rhodes, where they were joined by two further galleys, then by way of Cephalonia and Samos made their way to the coast of Asia Minor. They launched an attack on Setalia (now Adalia) where, clearing the chains from across the mouth of the port, they bombarded the town, though without doing it any lasting damage. The Neapolitan fleet then returned home but the remaining galleys attacked Smyrna. After that the Venetians went home, and so did Cardinal Carafa, by way of Rhodes and Naples, arriving in Rome with twenty-five Turkish prisoners, twelve camels, and part of the chains from Setalia. The last were for a time displayed in St Peter's.

His Neapolitan connections were very important to Carafa, though he did not visit the city very often. He was there, however, in September 1476 to celebrate the marriage of Beatrice of Aragón to Matthias Corvinus of Hungary, followed by the crowning of Beatrice as Queen of Hungary. His links with Naples became problematic when Pope Sixtus launched a war against the Kingdom, then spurred the Venetians to attack Ferrara, then turned against Venice. Naples sided with Florence, and the King of Naples sent his son Alfonso of Aragón to assist the Florentines. Alfonso turned up with his army outside the walls of Rome, and Carafa undertook to broker a peace, for which he received public thanks from the Senate of Rome.

At the death of Sixtus in August 1484 Ferdinand of Aragón naturally favoured Carafa as the next Pope, but he was not unhappy with the choice of Giovanni Battista Cibò, who had spent his youth at the court of Naples and was therefore presumed to be sympathetic. He took the name Innocent VIII. When Alfonso of Aragón turned up at Rome's Porta del Popolo on his way back to Naples from Ferrara he was given a warm welcome by the new pontiff. But then Innocent, persuaded by Giuliano della Rovere, the future Julius II and the cardinal largely responsible for his election, decided to back Neapolitan nobles who were in rebellion against their King. This led to a disastrous war, which put Oliviero in a very difficult position. He continued, however, to act as representative at the papal court of Ferdinand of Naples. A tenuous settlement was reached in 1486. By that time he was no longer Archbishop of Naples. He had continued to collect benefices and other offices – in 1478, for example, he became cardinal protector of the Dominican Order – and in 1484 he gave up the see of Naples to his brother Alessandro, though he reserved to himself the right of succession to the bishopric in the event of his brother's death.

Relations between the papacy and Naples again deteriorated when Ferdinand failed to fulfil the settlement of 1486, or to pay the tribute owed to the Pope. On 29 June 1489 Innocent declared Ferdinand excommunicate and deposed him. In January 1492 Oliviero helped to patch up a new peace, the papacy in the process losing part of its territory to Ferdinand. Oliviero was a significant figure in the Roman curia by this time, and he was the cardinal to whom the King of Spain turned if he needed something from the Pope. So it is no surprise that when Innocent died on 25 July 1492 he should have been the cardinal to gain most votes, though not quite enough to elect him, in the conclave which followed. It was therefore not Carafa who was elected on 11 August but Rodrigo Borgia, who took the name Alexander VI. It was an openly simoniacal election, and Cardinal Carafa showed his disgust – and hid his disappointment – by withdrawing from Rome. By the following summer, however, the two contenders for the papacy had been reconciled, not least, perhaps, because part of Alexander's plan for his family's advancement was to marry his son Joffré to Sancia, the illegitimate daughter of King Ferdinand. For that he needed Oliviero's help. Much to his disappointment, however, Carafa was not sent to crown Alfonso when he succeeded to the throne on his father's death. The then Cardinal Cesare Borgia went instead (see p. 207)

Pope Alexander's support for the Spanish ruling house of Naples angered King Charles VIII of France, who believed he also had a claim to the Neapolitan throne. Encouraged by Giuliano della Rovere he marched south, and when he arrived with his army in Rome, Cardinal Carafa was one of those who took shelter with the Pope in Castel Sant'Angelo. When he emerged he handed over a large sum to Charles to ensure the safety of his family when the French attacked Naples. Charles did indeed capture Naples, and without difficulty. His problem was holding on to it, becoming particularly vulnerable after Alexander had joined a league against him which threatened his rear. He withdrew, and the Aragonese returned to the Kingdom.

While it is true that Alexander VI enjoys a reputation of being perhaps the most dissolute pontiff of the millennium, it is also the case that after the mysterious death of his eldest son Pedro Luis he had a temporary change of heart and decided to reform the Church from top to bottom. To draw up proposals for such a reform he appointed a commission of six cardinals and a number of others. Cardinal Carafa was a member of the commission. A good number of reforms were suggested, including banning relatives, and women, from the Vatican precincts. There was also an attack on the widespread practice of simony, without which practice Alexander would not have been Pope, and on the over-luxurious lives of cardinals. Carafa did not, on the other hand, suggest, as some had done, that the accumulation of benefices should be prohibited. Over the years he had himself collected a large number of very profitable ones, so much so that he could divest some of them on his relatives, such as Naples to his brother, the administration of the diocese of Rimini to one nephew, and the abbacy of the monastery of Pulsano to another. Yet despite this amassing of wealth, he was a devout man, serious both about his faith and about his responsibilities as a cardinal. As Cardinal Protector of the Dominicans he became involved in the controversy in Florence over the fiery Fra Girolamo Savonarola, and for some time supported him in his denunciation of abuses. Unfortunately for Carafa, when the Florentine government turned against Savanarola, the friar, under torture, said that the cardinal had been behind his call for a general council of the Church to address the Church's, and especially the papacy's, failings. After the events of the Council of Constance (see the life of Baldassare Cossa, p. 40), the thought of another general council which might again proclaim its superiority over the Pope was something every fifteenth-century pontiff dreaded, not least Alexander VI. Carafa thought it wise to withdraw from the curia and make his way to Naples.

He arrived by sea in Naples in April 1498, and was warmly received. He spent just under a year in the city and then returned to Rome, where he was also warmly received, and once more took up his role in the curia. In the two conclaves of 1503 he was again a candidate, but despite his links with Spain was thought to be too pro-French to be elected. It is also possible that he was thought to be too old. He took little part in the politics of the reign of Julius II. In any case, he did not think it proper that the Pope should engage directly in warfare, as Julius did, and was excused from accompanying him. The only major role he played was in entertaining in his rented palace – it belonged to the Orsinis – the ambassadors from Venice when they came to Rome in 1509 to discuss peace terms with the papacy.

This Orsini palace was on the corner of the Piazza Navona, where the Palazzo Braschi now stands. Outside it he placed in 1503 an ancient – said to date from the third century BC – and much mutilated statue of Menelaus that had been discovered when some road works were being undertaken nearby. It became known as 'Pasquino', from which 'pasquinade' is derived, though the origin of the name is uncertain. Oliviero built churches, monasteries and hospitals and was a considerable patron of scholarship and the arts. (The often-repeated charge that it was he who started the campaign to cover Michelangelo's naked torsos in his Last Judgement fresco in the Sistine chapel with loincloths is completely mistaken. That was another, and much later, Carafa.)

Oliviero employed Bramante in his first significant Roman commission, the cloister of Santa Maria della Pace, but his most striking contribution to the renaissance in Rome was undoubtedly the altarpiece in the Carafa chapel in the Dominican church of Santa Maria sopra Minerva, for which the cardinal commissioned Filippino Lippi. It shows the cardinal, as protector of the Dominicans, being introduced to the Virgin Mary by the Dominican saint Thomas Aquinas. Carafa was responsible for commissioning not just the frescoes but the chapel itself, which he conceived of as a mortuary chapel, and for the upkeep of which he bequeathed the rents from numerous proper-ties. He did not, however, wish to be laid to rest there but in the chapel of St Januarius (San Gennaro) in the cathedral at Naples. This, too, at least in its design, may have been the work of Bramante, and is one of the outstanding renaissance works in that city.

And it was to this chapel that Oliviero Carafa's remains were taken after they had first been interred on the day of his death, 22 January 1511, in Santa Maria sopra Minerva. His monument in Naples still displays the chains which his fleet had broken through at the siege of Setalia.

Francesco Alidosi

Very little is known of the early life of Alidosi beyond the fact that he was born in Castel Del Rio in the diocese of Imola, the third son of Giovanni Alidosi, Lord of Castel del Rio, and Cipriana Franceschi. Even the year of his birth is uncertain: it is thought to have been about 1460, though it may have been a decade earlier. Likewise nothing is known about his education beyond the fact that he was judged bright and quite handsome. Whatever his qualities, he was taken up by Pope Sixtus IV, who gave him a position in the papal curia before passing him on to his nephew, Cardinal Giuliano della Rovere. When, in 1494, the cardinal fled to France to escape from his arch enemy, the newly elected Pope Alexander VI, della Rovere took Alidosi with him, and made him his secretary.

The cardinal had been in France before, as Pope Sixtus's legate from 1480 to 1482, and felt comfortable there. But even though he arranged the marriage of Pope Alexander's son Cesare (see p. 206) to a French princess, he remained effectively in hiding throughout Alexander's pontificate. He did, however, join the French King in a campaign to conquer Naples between 1494 and 1495, an enterprise which he had himself encouraged. He was not elected Pope in the first conclave of 1503, but was chosen in the second, which lasted only one day, when Pius II died after a reign of only three weeks. Giuliano della Rovere took the title of Julius II.

Alidosi's rise thereafter was swift. He was almost immediately made a privy chamberlain, and before the end of 1503 he had been put in charge of papal finances. He was so close to the Pope that he was allowed to combine the della Rovere arms with those of his own Alidosi family. Somewhere along the way he must have collected minor orders, presumably also the priesthood, because in April 1504 he was consecrated Bishop of Mileto, the main officiant in the ceremony being Pope Julius II himself (another della Rovere was consecrated bishop on the same occasion). The title of cardinal priest of SS Nereo e Achilleo was conferred upon him in December 1505: he exchanged that title for Santa Cecilia just under a year later. He had already been appointed Bishop of Pavia in March 1505, with the approval of Louis XII of France, Pavia being then under French control. He retained the title of bishop of Pavia, and enjoyed its revenues along with those of numerous other benefices, until his death.

He was not a popular figure in Rome and several of the cardinals had protested at his appointment to the Sacred College, but as a protégé of Pope Julius his position was well nigh unassailable, and his rise was continuous. It was Alidosi, for instance, who negotiated with Michelangelo for the painting of the Sistine Chapel, and signed the contract with the artist on behalf of Pope Julius, and it was he who later commissioned the bronze statue of the Pope that Julius ordered to be erected in Bologna after he had captured it. He was even for a short time, and ineffectively, cardinal protector of England. But he is chiefly remembered for his rapacious and bloodthirsty governance of the papal city of Bologna.

He rose by stages. In March 1507 he became legate, or papal governor, in Viterbo, as well as legate in the patrimony of St Peter. Bologna was handed to him the following year, and in 1509 he was made legate of the Romagna and the Marches – though after taking possession of Ravenna he handed it over to his brother to administer. But Bologna was the real prize. From 1463 to 1506 it had been ruled by Giovanni II Bentivoglio, whose family had long been powerful in the city. In 1506, however, Julius II excommunicated Giovanni and placed the city under an interdict, then proceeded to capture the city with the assistance of King Louis XII: Giovanni spent his last couple of years as a prisoner of the French in Milan. Meanwhile Pope Julius had entered the city in triumph, and for a time it remained in papal control despite efforts by the Bentivoglios to recover it. When Alidosi was appointed legate to the city he proceeded to rid it of the leading supporters of the Bentivoglios: he had them strangled. Whether because of the complaints of the people of Bologna about his cruelty or possibly to retain the loyalty of Ferrara, which was allied with France, Julius summoned him to Viterbo in September 1508 and transferred the Legation to Cardinal Ippolito d'Este of the ruling dynasty in Ferrara (see p. 149), but later reinstated Alidosi. Julius then sent him to Milan as an intermediary with the French King, who had entered Italy at the head of an army: Louis made him Bishop of Cremona, without consulting the Pope.

After the capture of Bologna the issue now for Julius was Venice. The Republic had failed to hand back, as agreed by an earlier treaty, several cities which it had taken from the Pope. Julius put the army in charge of his nephew Francesco Maria della Rovere who was, by adoption, Duke of Urbino. He was to share command with Alidosi. It was a difficult situation. The two did not get on, the Duke accusing the cardinal of keeping him short of munitions, and the army was something of rag-bag of murderous Spanish infantry and Swiss mercenaries. The campaign was nonetheless a success, the cardinal bribing some garrisons into submission, the Spanish soldiers massacring others. Alidosi was proud of his military achievements, and returned to Bologna to ride down streets spanned by triumphal arches and decorated with wooden depictions of the defeated towns. He had a medal struck to commemorate his prowess.

But then the Pope turned against Venice, against the French and against their ally Ferrara – the city had given refuge to the Bentivoglio family. Julius personally led the campaign and did so with considerable panache. At first all went well, but eventually the offensive began to falter. Alidosi meanwhile had been having problems of his own. He again had to travel to the papal court to answer to the Pope against complaints of the Bolognese, but to the distress of its citizens had been returned to his post by Julius. The citizens now claimed that he was treacherously dealing with the French. When he went to the papal army then camped at Modena, his old enemy, the Duke of Urbino, arrested him and took him off as a prisoner under armed escort back to Bologna, where the Pope was in residence. To everyone's astonishment Julius not only reinstated him as legate, but also made him apostolic administrator of the see of Bologna.

It was a mistake. The people of the city had suffered enough from Alidosi and, fomented by supporters of the Bentivoglios, they rose against him, and against the Pope, whose colossal bronze statue they toppled to the ground and melted down to make cannons. Julius, who at the time was elsewhere, had to transfer his residence to Ravenna, while Alidosi on 20 May 1511 fled the city with as much of his accumulated treasure as he could carry. He took refuge in Castel del Rio. The Duke of Urbino abandoned the defence of Bologna and the city into which Julius had once ridden in triumph fell to the French and their allies, who included the Bentivoglios.

Julius was furious. The Duke said the cardinal had behaved treacherously, the cardinal blamed the Duke. Both went to Ravenna to explain themselves to the Pope, della Rovere arriving first. Julius received the Duke coldly. As he was leaving the city della Rovere encountered Alidosi and his armed escort making their way to the papal residence – Julius had invited his old friend to dinner. The cardinal made some sort of friendly greeting to the Duke, but della Rovere was so angry he drew his sword and struck the cardinal, knocking him off his mule: Alidosi was then promptly attacked and mortally wounded by Filippo Doria, one of della Rovere's men, before his own bodyguards could come to his defence. He died an hour later, confessing that what had happened to him was the consequence of his own sins. The murderers were tried but acquitted. The cardinal died at ten in the evening of 24 May 1511. He was buried in Ravenna cathedral after a service conducted by his old friend the Pope, though he was later reinterred in the abbey of San Vitale. When his tomb was opened three hundred and fifty years later the blow to the head, which had been the cause of his death, could still clearly be seen.

Ippolito d'Este

One becomes accustomed to the extraordinarily swift rise through the clerical ranks of renaissance grandees, but that of Ippolito d'Este was faster than most. At the age of three he was endowed with his first abbacy, at six he received the tonsure and his second abbey, and at seven he became the archbishop-in-waiting of the rich and important Hungarian diocese of Esztergom. He was born in Ferrara on 20 March 1479, the third child of Ercole I, Duke of Ferrara, and his wife Eleonora of Aragón, daughter of the King of Naples. He owed his spectacular rise to his mother's sister, Beatrice of Aragón, who was the second wife of Matthias Corvinus, the much-admired King of Hungary. Unhappily for Ippolito, Corvinus died in April 1490, and his death was followed by a period of political instability in Hungary. So turbulent was the country that Ippolito's father decided to bring him back to Italy, though for some years afterwards he continued to visit. He was compensated by yet another abbacy, which was followed on 20 September 1493 by promotion by Pope Alexander VI to the rank of cardinal deacon with the title of Santa Lucia in Silice. He was still only fourteen years old and still, technically, Archbishop of Esztergom. He asked Pope Alexander's permission to swap it for the extremely rich diocese of Eger, which he was able to hold without being resident in the see.

He arrived in Rome for the first time in December 1497, turning up at the Santa Maria del Popolo gate with a great train of retainers and an impressive display of his already considerable wealth. A month later he was named as Archbishop of Milan. Milan was the Sforza dukedom, ruled over at the time of Ippolito's appointment by his brother-in-law Ludovico, known as Ludovico il Moro. When Ippolito arrived in Milan, however, Ludovico was absent, and he took over the running of the city, a task which he found beyond him, and he found it politic to withdraw for the good of his health. When Ludovico returned he instructed the young Archbishop-to-be to set about the uncongenial task of reforming the monasteries. But Il Moro's days were numbered. The French under their new King, Louis XII, attacked the city and in September 1499 the Duke had to flee, to end his days a prisoner of the French. Ippolito fled with him, but relations between the d'Este family and the French were good: Ercole d'Este was in attendance when the French King entered Milan, and Ippolito, abandoning his brother-in-law, who died a few years later still in custody, returned in February 1500.

The great excitement for the d'Este family was Ippolito's brother's second marriage. Alfonso's first bride, Anna Sforza, died in 1497. In December 1501 he married the daughter of Pope Alexander VI, Lucrezia Borgia. Ippolito went off to Rome to escort his soon to be sister-in-law back to Ferrara. It was all very splendid. The d'Estes were received in Rome with great splendour and ceremonial, for which the papacy footed the bill. In the meantime, as well as becoming legate in Bologna, Ippolito was appointed archpriest of St Peter's, which meant that he could have a palace in Rome. The cardinal's friendship with the Borgia family cooled, however, when he developed too great an interest in Cesare Borgia's mistress. It may well have been this which kept him out of Rome after the death of Alexander VI, because for the moment Cesare was still very much in evidence. The pontificate of Alexander's successor Pius III lasted less than a month – in which time Ippolito got himself nominated as Bishop of Ferrara – and he arrived for the next conclave of 1503, which elected Giuliano della Rovere as Julius II.

There was then a proposal to tie the d'Este family to that of Julius II by marrying Ippolito's half brother, Ferrante, to the daughter of the Pope, but that came to nothing because of worsening relations between Ippolito and Julius – relations not helped by the requisitioning of Ippolito's archpriest's palace during the reconstruction of St Peter's. He also found himself raising an army first to defend Modena from the papacy, and then to recover territory which his father had ceded to Venice in 1484. He also sent reinforcements to the imperial army which was besieging Padua. But then the Emperor suddenly abandoned him, leaving him to face the Venetians alone. Fearing the consequences he dispatched an emissary to the Pope to seek his help, but the very day that his emissary, Lodovico Ariosto, was granted an audience with Julius, troops commanded by Ippolito defeated the Venetians. It was a particularly spectacular victory for Ferrara, celebrated in Ariosto's *Orlando Furioso*. With Ippolito in command, first the majority of the Venetian galleys (it was in part a river battle) were destroyed, and then its land forces. A *Te Deum* was sung,

Venetian banners were hung in Ferrara's cathedral, and Ippolito ordered for himself a new suit of armour.

Duke Alfonso now entered an alliance with the French against the Venetians, but this was a step too far for Pope Julius. He showed his displeasure by excommunicating the Duke, and by annulling Ippolito's election to yet another abbacy, and giving it to someone else. When he summoned all the cardinals to return to Rome in 1510 Ippolito would not come, and the Pope had to issue a bull instructing him to do so. It did not help matters that when, in January 1511, Pope Julius personally led the charge when capturing the city of Mirandola, the widow of whose lord had put herself under the protection of the French, it was soon after retaken by Ferrara. The forces of Ferrara then came to the aid of the French in taking Bologna. Pope Julius himself only narrowly avoided capture.

Shortly after this Ippolito went to France to ensure the support of the French King in defence of Ferrara, but when Louis XII, supported by a group of dissident cardinals, called a council at Pisa to depose the Pope, Ippolito held back. He signed the document summoning the council but did not attend it. But neither did he attend the Lateran Council called by Julius as a riposte. His hostility to Julius was well known: a Roman agent reported that the cardinal had spat at Michelangelo's statue of the Pope in Bologna. Julius was nonetheless attempting to reach some sort of understanding with Ferrara. He summoned Alfonso to Rome for talks, but though the Duke went he rejected the Pope's overtures and put himself under the protection of the Colonnas. Ippolito was then summoned to Rome. He set off, but claimed he had at Florence broken his leg in a fall from his horse, and was consequently forced to take to his bed. Apparently thinking that Italy was no longer safe, he returned to his old haunts in Hungary, arriving at Eger in February 1513, shortly before the death of Pope Julius. When he heard of Julius's death he returned to Italy, but still thought it safer to stay away from the conclave which elected Leo X.

Back in the duchy Ippolito dedicated himself to re-establishing the d'Este family, constantly under threat from the Medici Pope's efforts to reward his family with territory. In order to safeguard their possessions they were again obliged to ally themselves with the new King of France, Francis I. With Ferrara reasonably secure he went off again to Hungary in October 1517, and the following year attended the marriage in Kraków of Bona Sforza to Sigismund I of Poland, then returned to Hungary where he oversaw the construction of fortifications against the Turks. He was also able to take part in the election of the new Emperor: his vote was for Charles Habsburg, the Emperor Charles V.

He was still holding numerous abbacies, was Bishop of Eger, of Ferrara and Modena, as well as Archbishop of Capua. He had also been Archbishop of Milan, but in May 1519 he made the see over to his nephew, also called

Ippolito d'Este. Much of his immense wealth he spent on his palaces, and he was a patron of musicians, but apart from war his chief delight seems to have been hunting. His mistress Dalida de Putti bore him two children, Ippolito and Elisabetta.

He died in Ferrara on 3 September 1520, and was interred in the sacristy of the cathedral of which, at least in name, he had been bishop. As far as is known he had never received episcopal orders, nor indeed priestly ones.

The Politicos

At least from the turn of the sixth and seventh centuries when Pope Gregory the Great had to take over the running of the city of Rome in the absence of any effective imperial authority, clerics have been politicians. In the middle ages they were commonly among the high officers of state. The reason was simple enough: they were the best-educated members of society. They had studied at university – once universities had come into being – and although at first they may have graduated in theology, for very many of them their highest qualification was in law, or rather in laws, because they were doctors *in utroque iure*, in both laws, the laws of the State and the laws of the Church (canon law). They wrote and spoke Latin, the common language of Christendom, and very often they had travelled to Paris, to Bologna, to Salamanca or Alcalá de Henares in search of learning. They knew Europe, and they knew its scholars. As royal emissaries, or as chancellors of the kingdom, they were indispensable.

There were several such prelates around Europe in the middle ages, one of the most distinguished being England's Stephen Langton (*c.* 1150–1228). Langton never held political office, but as Archbishop of Canterbury he was heavily involved in the struggles of the barons against King John, and it was possibly Langton who caused the barons' demands to be put down in writing in what has become known as the Magna Carta, much to the Pope's displeasure, King John having rather niftily made himself a vassal of the papacy. Politics was not all domestic. The little-known Adam Easton, created a cardinal by the notorious unstable Pope Urban VI in 1381, represented the English King at the papal court at the start of the Great Western Schism. In 1385 Urban turned against him and other cardinals, had him and them imprisoned and tortured, and the English crown had to plead for Easton's safety. On his arrest on the charge of conspiring against the Pope he was stripped of his cardinalate by Urban but was reinstated and released from prison by Urban's successor, Boniface IX. Holding high office was all too often a dangerous game, as Thomas Wolsey (*c.* 1470–1530), Cardinal Archbishop of York, discovered to his cost when his ministry ceased to satisfy Henry VIII. Wolsey, who never went to Rome, even had hopes of the papacy in the two conclaves of the 1520s.

There are two chapters devoted to political cardinals. The one which follows recounts the lives of some of the cardinal secretaries of state. They were concerned with the internal management and external relations of the Papal States, when they existed, and after they had disappeared the relationship of the Holy See, as the papacy is formally known in international law, to other sovereign states. This chapter, on the other hand, contains biographies of political cardinals who were involved one way or another in the government of Spain, Scotland and France, though Giuseppe Doria Pamphilj Landi has been added for good measure. He was briefly Cardinal Secretary of State, but spent most of his life as a papal diplomat.

Perhaps most famous of any of these 'political' cardinals were Armand Jean du Plessis de Richelieu (1585–1642 and a cardinal from 1622) and Jules Mazarin (1602–61, a cardinal from 1641), who successively served as chief ministers of France from 1624 to Mazarin's death, but their careers, rather too complex for summary treatment, are in any case already well known. It is, however, perhaps just worth noting that Mazarin was born in Naples as Giulio Raimondo Mazarino, and brought up in Rome where his father was chamberlain to the Colonna household, and he was a close friend Girolamo Colonna, himself a future cardinal.

Francisco Ximénez de Cisneros

To addicts of crossword puzzles the name Ximénez is the pseudonym of Derrick Somerset MacNutt, the classics teacher who from 1939 to his death in 1971 compiled the weekly crossword in the Sunday newspaper *The Observer* – his puzzles indeed outlasted him, the final one appearing long after his death. MacNutt took his pseudonym partly in homage to his predecessor at *The Observer*, who had used the name Torquemada. Both Torquemada and Ximénez (sometimes spelled Jiménez) were Grand Inquisitors in late-medieval Spain. The puzzles were, no doubt, intended to be torture of an intellectual variety, in contrast to the physical suffering inflicted by the Spanish Inquisition – especially in English folklore.

Gonzalo Ximénez was born in 1436 to a noble but impoverished family of Torrelaguna in the Kingdom of Castile: his parents had originally come from the village of Cisneros in the province of Palencia, hence the name. Under the patronage of an uncle he studied first at Roa, and then at the college in Alcalá de Henares attached to the Franciscan house there. He then went on to study law at Salamanca, preparing himself for a career in administration, either of the Church or of the State. It was more than likely this ambition which took him to Rome in 1459. The death of his father brought him back to Spain in 1471, where by a brief of Paul II he had been allocated the vacant benefice of Uceda. Unfortunately for Gonzalo, the Archbishop of Toledo had already promised the benefice to someone else. There followed a bitter dispute with Gonzalo, who refused to give way and was sent to prison. The prison term was indefinite: Gonzalo could be free whenever he abandoned his claim to the benefice, but this he refused to do. For six years he was in gaol, and was only freed after the Archbishop gave in and granted him the benefice. Gonzalo did not hold it long. Rather than live under a hostile prelate he joined the diocese of the Cardinal Archbishop of Sigüenza, who made him a vicar general.

He did not stay long. In 1484 he suddenly decided to become a Franciscan, a member of the Observant branch of the order, entering the friary of San Juan de Reyes, founded by Ferdinand and Isabella at Toledo. For a while he lived as a solitary until in 1494 he was recommended by his old patron, the Cardinal of Sigüenza now become the Cardinal of Toledo and Primate of Spain, as confessor to Queen Isabella. He agreed to accept the post, which was as counsellor as much as spiritual director, only if he did not have to appear at court too often. Two years later he became Provincial of his order in Spain. Three years after that he was appointed at the request of Queen Isabella as Archbishop of Toledo. He did not want the position, and tried to refuse, but was ordered to accept by the Pope: he was consecrated on 11 October 1495 in the presence of Ferdinand and Isabella – no information survives on when he had been ordained priest.

He now began a long and rigorous reform of his diocese, holding synods in Alcalá and Talavera. He also undertook a thorough reform, first of all of his own order, then of all Franciscans in Spain, and finally of all the Mendicant orders. Even the Minister General of the Franciscans thought he was too severe, and came to tell him so, but Ximénez held firm to his principles. It was claimed that three hundred friars had fled to Morocco and converted to Islam rather than live under the regime he imposed. He applied the same vigour to the conversion of the Moors. Granada had been conquered by the Catholic Kings in 1492, but there still remained a great number of Moors in the city and in the surrounding countryside, in the Alpujarras, the mountainous region to the south of the city. His method was simply the carrot and stick approach: first try bribes and if those failed, then threats. The result was an uprising in Granada and the Alpujarras, and the Archbishop's house was surrounded by rioting Moors. But in the end the Moors lost. They were given the choice of baptism or exile, and by 1500 Ximénez could claim to the Catholic Kings that there were no longer any Muslims in Granada, and that all the mosques had been converted into churches. It was such actions against the Moors that made him a figure of hate.

He carried his campaign into North Africa. At his own expense he launched a successful attack on Mazalquivir in 1505, and four years later he led in person an attack on Oran. He discovered, however, that Ferdinand's interests lay in Europe rather than across the Mediterranean, and no further conquests were possible – and towards the end of his life the Spanish coast was again being menaced by corsairs. His missionary endeavours were not limited to Spain and Africa. From 1500 onwards he sent out missionaries, mainly Franciscan friars, to the New World. He was sympathetic to the complaints of Bartolomé de las Casas about the conduct of the *conquistadores* towards the indigenous population of the Americas and attempted to ameliorate the situation by having villages constructed, and he saw to the structures of the Church across the Atlantic.

Isabella had died in November 1504, and the claimant to the throne of Castile was Ferdinand's son-in-law Philip. Ximénez brokered an agreement, the Concord of Salamanca, which left Philip with the throne. But he died soon afterwards, when by chance Ferdinand was in Naples. Ximénez immediately constituted a council of regency, and averted a plot to unseat Ferdinand who should now have inherited the throne. In gratitude Ferdinand prevailed upon Pope Julius II to create the Archbishop a cardinal, becoming cardinal priest of Santa Balbina. Shortly afterwards the King made him Inquisitor General.

He was now a central figure in the government of Spain. After the death of Ferdinand in January 1516, and in accord with the late King's will, Ximénez became regent for the young Prince Charles, the future Emperor Charles V, who was at the time in the Spanish Netherlands under the tutelage of Adrian of Utrecht, the future Pope Hadrian VI. There were those at court who wanted the cardinal to have advisors from the Netherlands, but he succeeded in governing on his own while the Prince was out of the country. Ximénez moved the royal court to Madrid, the strategic centre of the country, and created a standing army. After Charles had arrived in Asturias in September 1517 he did not show himself particularly grateful for the cardinal's efforts on his behalf. He thanked him, but told him to return to his diocese. By this time Ximénez was ill. He had set out to meet Charles, but never reached him. He died at Roa, where he had been born, on 8 November 1517. There were rumours that he had been poisoned.

Although he is remembered as the most significant Inquisitor General after Torquemada, Ximénez was heart and soul a humanist. He petitioned Pope Alexander VI that his former college in Alcalá should become a full-scale university, a petition which was granted in 1499. This was – is – the Universidad Complutense – 'Complutense' being the Latin name for Alcalá – now Spain's major university, and no longer in Alcalá but Madrid. He invited to the university some of the best renaissance biblical scholars and provided them with manuscripts he had collected to produce the Complutensian Polyglot Bible which, in its five volumes, contains the text of the Old and New Testaments in different languages in parallel columns. This massive work of scholarship began in 1502 and ended about the time of Ximénez's death. He never saw in print the work he had commissioned.

David Beaton

There have been few Scottish cardinals. Before Beaton the only Scottish cleric elevated to the purple was Walter Wardlaw (*c.* 1320–87), Bishop of Glasgow. He, however, was named as a cardinal in 1383 by an antipope, Clement VII, the Kingdom of Scotland having backed during the Great Western Schism the popes of Avignon because the Kingdom of England, the historic enemy, was supporting the popes in Rome. He is therefore frequently referred to as a 'pseudo-cardinal', though contemporaries on either side of the schism would have accepted his status. And after Beaton there was no other cardinal from Scotland until William Heard, a curial official made a cardinal in 1959. But he was a priest of an English diocese, and lived in Rome's English college: it was another decade before an Archbishop of Edinburgh joined the Sacred College. So Beaton was a rare figure.

He was born *c.* 1494 in the parish of Markinch in Fife. His father and mother, John Beaton, laird of Balfour, and Isobel Moneypenny, are thought to have had fourteen children, though only nine can be identified with certainty. David was the fifth son. His early education was possibly at a neighbouring school, but nothing is known of him until in 1508 he became a student at the nearby University of St Andrews. He presumably graduated as master of arts before moving, probably with the advice and support of his uncle James Beaton, the Archbishop of Glasgow, first to Glasgow then to the University of Paris and then, in 1519, to the law school at Orleans. He was supported financially by the revenues of the canonry of Cambuslang and the rather more lucrative chancellorship of Glasgow cathedral. More significant still was the abbacy of Arbroath, transferred to him by James Beaton when James moved from Glasgow to St Andrews in 1524.

As a nobly born Scotsman, a country allied with France, while in that country he frequented the court of Francis I: he was, a near contemporary remarked, indistinguishable from a Frenchman. He had a friend at court in the person of John Stuart, Duke of Albany, 'governor' of Scotland between 1515 and 1524, who himself had a claim to the Scottish crown, but whose visits to Scotland were determined less by his desire for the throne than by the French King's fluctuating policy towards England. When he came in 1521 Beaton travelled with him, and spent some time on diplomatic missions to France and to England – and one to Rome was also contemplated. He was in France again in

1524 with the Duke of Albany to negotiate a marriage alliance between France and Scotland, together with the hope that France might provide troops for the defence of Scotland. He returned to Scotland at the end of the year with the marriage alliance still in abeyance.

Not only was Beaton a nobleman but as abbot of Arbroath he was entitled to a seat in the Scottish parliament. Over the next few years he consolidated his position in the government of the young King James V – he was one of his guardians and, from 1529, keeper of the privy seal. He favoured an alliance with France, but for a time his influence was eclipsed by the return to Scotland of Archibald Douglas, the Earl of Angus and estranged second husband of Queen Margaret Tudor, the mother of the King (by her first marriage) and the elder sister of England's King Henry VIII. Though Margaret had come to loathe the Douglases, both she and the Earl favoured an English alliance rather than a French one. In 1527, however, Pope Clement VII granted Margaret a divorce (which he was later to deny to her brother Henry), and she married Henry Stewart. In the midst of all this the young King, having escaped the tutelage of the Earl of Angus – who after the divorce once again fled Scotland – was decreed able to govern, and the Francophile party led by Beaton was back as the dominant force in Scottish politics.

It was about this time that Beaton met Marion Ogilvie, with whom he lived for the rest of his life though as a cleric he could never marry her. Together they had eight children, all born in the decade or so before he was ordained priest. Marion, a distant relative of her lover, was the daughter of Sir James, later Lord, Ogilvie, and had been brought up in Airlie Castle. She was not well provided for after the death of her father and mother and, when she established her relationship with Beaton, was about thirty years old, beyond the normal age for a first marriage. In 1542 Beaton purchased Melgund Castle, east of Aberlemno in Angus, and Marion lived there until her death in 1575.

Meanwhile, as a councillor to the King and someone experienced in the ways of the French court, Beaton was the obvious man to negotiate what had long been intended: a royal marriage between Scotland and France. In September 1536 he accompanied James to France where, on 1 January the following year, the Scottish King married Madeleine de Valois, daughter of Francis I. Madeleine did not, however, long survive, dying only half a year later, and once again Beaton was back in France negotiating on behalf of King James. James was next married by proxy in the cathedral of Notre Dame in May 1538 to Mary of Guise, daughter of the Duke of Guise and a widow. She had borne her first child shortly after her first husband had died, and she bore three children to James. The first two, both boys, died in infancy. The third, a girl, was born six days after James's death. She survived as Mary Stuart. Beaton was rather better rewarded in France than in Scotland for his diplomatic endeavours. Francis I named him Bishop of Mirepoix in December 1537, a particularly profitable benefice, but one which required him at last to take orders. The date of his ordination as a priest is not known, nor that of his consecration as bishop, though this latter was towards the end of July or in early August 1538. In the consistory of 20 December that year, and again at the behest of the French King, Pope Paul III created him a cardinal priest and he received the red hat and the title of San Stefano in Monte Celio the following September.

His uncle James Beaton was aging, and David was appointed to assist him as coadjutor archbishop with right of succession: he automatically became Archbishop of St Andrews on his uncle's death in February 1539. He began his episcopate vigorously, putting to death seven people convicted of heresy. He wanted to pursue more, including members of the nobility, but King James refused to let him do so. The cardinal's concern for the purity of the Catholic faith probably weighed rather less in his mind than the political implications of heresy. It had spread, he believed, up from England: several of those he wanted to charge with heresy were supporters of an English, rather than a French, alliance. And the danger of the growth of heresy in Scotland constituted a threat to ecclesiastical revenues, as the policy of Henry VIII, abetted by Thomas Cromwell, had so clearly demonstrated south of the border.

In 1542 relations with England had so far deteriorated that war broke out, urged on by Beaton who presented the case for war to the Pope as a crusade against heresy. It was a disaster for the Scots. They were completely defeated at the battle of Solway Moss in November and less than a week later James died, not of wounds but – probably – of a fever. A regency council was established of which the cardinal was a member along with the Protestant Earl of Arran, who emerged as governor of the Kingdom, and who appointed Beaton as chancellor. Henry VIII was now attempting to arrange a marriage between his son Prince Edward, the future Edward VI, and Mary Stuart. This proposal was encouraged by Arran but opposed by the cardinal. Arran had Beaton arrested and for three months held under house arrest in St Andrews. A treaty with England was signed in his absence, but it did not last. Anti-English feeling was running high in Scotland, especially after some Scottish merchant ships were seized, and the governor changed his mind. He reached an agreement with the cardinal, publicly recanted his Protestantism, and received absolution from Beaton. Then in December 1543 the parliament annulled the English treaty.

Cardinal Beaton was now in the ascendant, but his dominance was shaky. Divisions between the pro-French and the pro-English parties were exacerbated and there was a short-lived rebellion. Then Henry invaded the Scottish borders. The Scots proved unable to withstand him, and the French sent an inadequate force to assist them. Henry's propaganda portrayed Beaton as the cause of an unnecessary war, and people believed him. He also plotted to have him assassinated. In the end there was no need. Beaton's show of force in his persecution of heretics had made him many enemies, and the burning at the stake of the itinerant Protestant preacher George Wishart at St Andrews on 1 March 1546 proved the cardinal's nemesis. A group of local lairds conspired to kill him. This they achieved in his castle at St Andrews on the morning of 29 May. He was stabbed to death in his room by three men, one of whom paused in the act to make it clear to the cardinal that it was in revenge for the death of Wishart. 'I am a priest', were the last words David Beaton was heard to say. As the conspirators entered the castle they had seen Marion Ogilvie slipping out. She had spent the night with the Cardinal.

Ippolito II d'Este

The younger son of Alfonso d'Este, Duke of Ferrara, and Lucrezia Borgia was born on 25 August 1509. The name Ippolito ran in the d'Este family, but it is very likely that the choice of his uncle's name, Cardinal Ippolito d'Este, was intentional. As a younger son he was destined for a career in the Church, in pursuit of which his extremely rich relative could be of immense assistance. As indeed he was. The cardinal, who died in 1520, in 1519 bequeathed his nephew the wealthy diocese of Milan. He was named the administrator only, because he was below the canonical age and obviously was not in, and indeed never received, episcopal orders nor even priestly ones. He did not visit his diocese for thirty years. He was, however, in minor orders and when Ferrara was put under an interdict by Pope Leo X it was felt proper that he should be sent away. He returned when the interdict was lifted, and was then educated at the d'Este palace by leading humanist scholars. To complete his schooling he attended the University of Padua.

While he was removed from personal involvement in the Italian politics of the period, they nonetheless significantly impinged upon his life. Traditionally the d'Este family had been pro-imperial in the power struggles in northern Italy, but Duke Alfonso's father had made his peace with France after Louis XII captured Milan. As indeed did Pope Clement VII, who entered an alliance with France and the Republic of Venice against the Emperor Charles V. The alliance proved a costly mistake which led, after the defeat of Francis I by Charles at the battle of Pavia in 1526, to the horrific sack of Rome the following year by Charles's Lutheran troops, abetted by several thousand Spaniards. Duke Alfonso, however, had decisively switched sides after the defeat at Pavia and had allied himself with Charles against France and the Pope. This enabled him to recover territories which Ferrara had earlier been forced to cede – including Modena – but it was a problematic alliance to maintain and Alfonso determined to make his peace both with the papacy and with France. To achieve the former he sought a cardinal's hat for Ippolito who was, after all, as the offspring of Lucrezia Borgia, the grandson of a pope. It was not forthcoming. To achieve reconciliation with France a marriage was arranged between Ercole d'Este, Alfonso's eldest son, and Renata de Valois. Ippolito threw a party.

He also proposed to his brother that he should take advantage of the recovery of Modena by becoming its bishop. Unfortunately for him Clement VII had already decided to bestow the bishopric on (the future cardinal) Giovanni Morone and threatened that, if the d'Este family did not give up their claim he would prevent Ippolito receiving Milan. Ippolito was forced to give way, but nevertheless managed to extract a reasonable pension from Morone's revenues.

Links with France were steadily increasing, and Francis I several times pressed Ippolito to visit his court but just as often the political situation was thought too problematic. An opportunity arose in July 1535. It proved profitable. Francis I bestowed on him valuable abbacies and other benefices. He stayed there three years, creating a reputation for himself as a distinguished patron of the arts. What, however, he had really set his heart on was a cardinal's hat, for which it was clear he was ready – and able – to pay whatever price was asked. In the consistory of 1536 Paul III created two cardinals *in petto* and there were hopes among the d'Estes that Ippolito was one of them. That proved not to be the case, despite the strong representations of the French King. The new Duke of Ferrara, Ercole d'Este (Alfonso had died in 1534), said he was prepared to put up even more money.

The hat did not arrive until December 1538, and even then it was reserved *in petto*, only to be revealed some three months later when Ferrara and the papacy had settled their differences. Ippolito became cardinal deacon of Santa Maria in Aquiro. It was neither Ercole's nor Ippolito's money that had made the difference, but the earnest request of Francis I of France. More French benefices now came the new cardinal's way, including the diocese of Lyons. There were great celebrations in Ferrara to mark his promotion, and he then left for Rome for the ceremonial installation. But he did not delay in the city longer than necessary. He visited Naples, made his way back to Ferrara and then on to Paris to rejoin the court of the French King. There he had considerable influence, and was able to negotiate several important dynastic marriages, both for his own family and for the Farnese, the family of Pope Paul III. Francis used him as an ambassador, to the Republic of Venice and to Rome.

Francis I died in March 1547 and Ippolito organized grandiose funeral ceremonies at Ferrara and in Milan. He had been close to the King, but remained on good terms with his successor, Henry II, and with the Guise family. Henry named him Cardinal Protector of France in April 1548, and the following year he set off for Rome, buying as his residence in the city the palace of Monte Giordano belonging to the Orsini family. He was therefore well ensconced in Rome when, in November 1549, Pope Paul III died. In the conclave which followed Ippolito played an important part in delaying the opening of the voting to allow more French cardinals to arrive – which they did with a considerable amount of money from Henry II to be dispensed in bribes. The election lasted the whole of December and January and into February. Two cardinals retired sick and one died: poison was suspected. Pope Paul had kept a delicate balance between pro-French and pro-imperial cardinals, with only a handful who were neutral. It was in this conclave that the English Reginald Pole (see p. 43) was nearly elected, but because he was thought to be pro-imperial, and because of ancient antagonisms between France and England, the French would not support him. For a time Ippolito fancied his own chances.

It was not to be, but the new Pope, Julius III, was grateful for the support which, after the failure of his own candidacy and that of any of the pro-French cardinals, Ippolito had eventually shown him: he made him governor of Tivoli. There, inspired by the nearby Villa Adriana – the palace of the Emperor Hadrian – and on the site of a former Benedictine monastery, he built the famous Villa d'Este, with its gardens, cascades and fountains tumbling down the hillside. The house itself may have been spectacular, but it was the garden which attracted more attention, and which had a significant influence on gardens across Europe.

Ippolito was not able to spend much time at the villa because, as representative of the French King, the political situation in Italy demanded all his attention. Julius III attempted to eject Ottavio Farnese, grandson of Pope Paul III, from the duchy of Parma, which the Emperor Charles V claimed as his. War broke out between the Emperor and France, and Spanish troops occupied one of Ippolito's own benefices, that of Brescello. The French made him governor of Siena, which was under threat from the Empire until the Turkish advance made the Emperor turn eastwards. Ippolito was now hesitant about tying himself too firmly to the French. This would, he believed, weigh against him in any future conclave at which he might be a candidate, and in May 1554, after less than two years in Siena, he resigned. Leaving Siena proved to be a problem because it was under siege from the army of Cosimo de'Medici, who refused him a safe conduct, but when he managed to get out he made his way to Ferrara instead of going to Rome as the Pope had demanded. Rome, he complained, was too hot, and bad for his health. When he eventually went to Rome in December it was once again as the representative of France.

Ippolito took part in both the elections of spring 1555. Marcellus was elected at the first conclave because the two parties, French and imperial, were so finely balanced that the reformers managed to get one of their own chosen. Ippolito had pushed hard for the papacy for himself: Cardinal Gianpietro Carafa said that he had behaved like Simon Magus, which was unfortunate for Ippolito because at the second conclave the anti-imperial, but not expressly pro-French, Carafa was himself elected, taking the name Paul IV. Pope Paul promptly banished Ippolito from Rome, accusing him of simony and licentiousness, and stripping him of the governorship of Tivoli. He could not return to Rome until after Pope Paul's death in August 1559.

The Cardinal of Ferrara once again hoped for election to the papacy but his record was against him. There was the accusation of simony to contend with, and the fact that the late Pope had insisted on prelates holding only one bishopric at a time. Ippolito was Archbishop of Milan, of Ferrara, of Lyons and held a further four French sees. In the end Cardinal de'Medici became Pope Pius IV. Pius gave him back the governorship of Tivoli and made him legate for the patrimony of St Peter, which meant he lived in Rome once more. He even became a member of the commission discussing Church reform, alongside, among others, the saintly Charles Borromeo (see p. 112). Then, at the beginning of June 1561, he was named papal legate to France.

Queen Catharine de' Medici was regent for her son Charles IX, and the worry for Rome was that she was too sympathetic to the Huguenots. Ippolito's role was to detach her from the Huguenots, but also to attempt to persuade Queen Elizabeth of England to return to the Catholic fold. He was also to establish contact with Mary Stuart. He set off from Rome in grand style, accompanied by six hundred horsemen. A more surprising addition to his party was Diego Lainez, the outstanding theologian at the Council of Trent but since 1558 the General Superior of the Society of Jesus. His policy was one of moderation – in Paris he even attended a Calvinist sermon at the request of the Queen Regent, an action much disapproved of by the leaders of the Catholic party in France. But Ippolito was unable to dissuade the Queen from her readiness to allow Huguenots a degree of toleration. His influence with her was further damaged by the trial of Cardinal Odet de Coligny and his dismissal from the cardinalate (see p. 209). When one of Ippolito's benefices was torched by the Huguenots, many regarded it as an act of reprisal for the fate of the former French cardinal. Furthermore, the death in November 1562 of the King of Navarre, who under promptings from Ippolito among others had made a public profession of Catholicism, and the assassination of the Duke de Guise the following February, had deprived France of its Catholic leaders. Ippolito felt at risk and he returned to Rome by way of Ferrara.

He once again considered himself a candidate in the conclave of December to January 1565–66. Ippolito's nephew the Duke of Ferrara sent a letter saying that they ought to elect a candidate from one of Italy's princely families as popes chosen from the lower-born had proved disastrous. It did not help.

Nor did the fact that the reform-minded Charles Borromeo, one of the most powerful figures in the conclave, did not trust him, and also insisted that the election begin ten days after the late Pope's death, according to instructions he had left. It therefore opened without the presence of the French cardinals. Michele Ghislieri became Pope Pius V.

Although he still harboured forlorn hopes of the papacy at the death in 1572 of Pope Pius V, there was no chance of his election, especially after Queen Catherine de' Medici had instructed the French cardinals not to vote for him. Under Pius V he played no significant role and devoted himself to the ornamentation of his villa at Tivoli, to his antiquities of which he was a great collector as well being a patron of archaeologists, and to music: Giovanni Pierluigi, better known as Palestrina from the town of his birth, was in his employ. Ippolito was not wholly out of favour at Rome. Pius V's successor, Pope Gregory XIII, who was not of princely birth but the son of a merchant, came to visit him at the Tivoli villa in September 1572.

He died at Tivoli on 1 December 1572, and, dressed in purple vestments and wearing a mitre, he lay in state in his palace of Monte Giordano. He was, however, buried at his request in the church of Santa Maria Maggiore, which stood beside the villa.

François de Joyeuse

To understand the role played by Cardinal de Joyeuse he has to be put into the context of the murky world of the French religious wars of the second part of the sixteenth century. In its origins the struggle was between the French Protestants, the Huguenots and the Catholics, but the reality was more complicated. The Huguenots were entrenched in France, so much so that successive monarchs had to give them some freedom of worship – a fact which irritated the papacy otherwise ready to assist the King financially against the Protestants. When Catherine de' Medici occasioned the St Bartholomew's Day (24 August) Massacre in 1572 to protect her son, King Charles IX, from Protestant influences, the Pope of the time attended a service of thanksgiving in Rome's French church. Four years later, however, the Huguenots were able to exact from a weak King Henry III almost complete religious freedom.

The situation was further complicated by the death of the King's likely successor, leaving Henry of Navarre as next in line to the throne. He was recognized as such by the King. The problem with Henry of Navarre was that he was a Protestant, and the possibility of a Protestant succession was the occasion of the establishment of a Catholic League led by the Guise family and backed by the Pope, at least to the extent of barring Henry of Navarre from the throne.

The League, with which the family of François de Joyeuse allied itself, became extremely powerful and came to constitute a threat to King Henry himself. On 23 December 1588 the King had the Duke de Guise and his brother Cardinal Louis II de Guise assassinated when they were in the Castle of Blois supposedly attending a meeting with the King. It was a mistake. The Guise family was powerful, and the cardinal very popular. On 1 August 1589 when Henry was about to launch an attack on Paris, then held by the League, he was stabbed by a Dominican friar and died the following morning. The way was thus open for the succession of the excommunicate Henry of Navarre.

François de Joyeuse had been a privy councillor to King Henry III, a position he owed to his brother, the Duke Anne de Joyeuse, an admiral of the French navy and a favourite of the King. He had been born at Carcassonne – though the family title de Joyeuse came from a small town of that name in the Ardèche – on 24 June 1562. He was the second of seven sons of Guillaume II de Joyeuse, Marshal of France, and of his wife Marie de Batarnay. It was a very religious family: another of the sons, Henri, became a Capuchin friar, but possibly François's vocation was the traditional one of the second son entering the Church. Certainly his career was swift. After schooling at Toulouse and at the Collège de Navarre in Paris and a doctorate in canon and civil law at the University of Orléans, he was promoted to the archdiocese of Narbonne, although under the canonical age – a dispensation was required – and still only a deacon of the diocese of Carcassonne. He took possession of the diocese in March 1582. Only eighteen months later he was created a cardinal priest with the title, bestowed rather later, of San Silvestro in Capite. In December 1587 he swapped that title for that of SS Trinità al Monte Pincio. After resigning the see of Narbonne, he became Archbishop of Toulouse in November 1588, and in December 1604 he was transferred to the Archbishopric of Rouen, having become Cardinal Bishop of Santa Sabina earlier that year. In June 1605 the newly elected Pope Paul V bestowed on him the pallium, the white stole worn by archbishops as a sign of their links with Rome.

His meteoric career through the ranks of the French Church owed much to his closeness, first to Henry III and then to Henry IV, and though much of his time was inevitably spent on affairs of state and on papal politics, he proved to be an exemplary prelate. At Toulouse he held a reforming synod, he built a seminary for the clergy and entrusted it to the Society of Jesus and built schools both for boys and for girls. He carried out visitations of his dioceses, especially of Toulouse but also of Rouen, and in October 1614, although already ill, he presided at a meeting of the Estates General where he persuaded the Assembly of the Clergy to accept the reforming decrees of the Council of Trent which, appealing to their Gallican traditions, they had hitherto refused to implement in France.

Henry III had named him Cardinal Protector of France in September 1585. He advised Henry that he ought to ask the Pope for absolution for the murder of the Duke and the Cardinal of Guise, which, at François de Joyeuse's request, the Pope granted – though almost immediately regretted doing so, and threatened Henry III with renewed excommunication after his reconciliation with Henry of Navarre. After the assassination of Henry III he returned to France from Rome and played a significant part in reconciling the Catholic League to the accession of Henry of Navarre as Henry IV – now become, at least formally, a Catholic. François was by now the most important member of his family because two of his brothers, including Anne, the eldest, had been killed at the battle of Coutras in October 1585 when their army was unexpectedly overcome by a much smaller Huguenot force.

Henry IV renewed his role as cardinal protector after François had assured him of his loyalty – hardly necessary after he had persuaded the Pope to grant the former Protestant a divorce (Henry had abjured his old faith in July 1595). The new King needed François's diplomatic skills to get papal approval to annul his marriage to Marguerite de Valois so that he could marry Marie de' Medici, daughter of the Grand Duke of Tuscany. The Pope set up a tribunal to discuss the case, the cardinal being a member, and it was approved. François de Joyeuse was at Marseilles to receive the new queen-to-be in November 1600. It was he who, in 1606, baptized the future Louis XIII and, after the assassination of Henry IV in May 1610, crowned Marie de' Medici as queen and regent of France – a role which should have belonged to the Archbishop of Rheims, but the Archbishop was not yet in priestly orders – and he served as a member of the Council of Regency. It was also Joyeuse who brought about the election of the highly esteemed Cardinal Alessandro Ottaviano de' Medici as Pope Leo XI – a somewhat futile act, as it turned out, because the new Pope survived less than a month, dying of a chill caught during the ceremonial taking possession of the Lateran.

Leo's successor, Paul V, almost occasioned a major European war very shortly after his election when he imposed an interdict on the Republic of Venice. England seemed to promise Venice the backing of the Protestant powers were a war to break out between Rome and the Republic, and an alarmed French King, who regarded himself as an ally of Venice, instructed de Joyeuse to attempt to resolve the conflict amicably. He managed to persuade the Republic to hand over to the Church the two criminals who were at the heart of the dispute, and to convince the Pope to remove his interdict. Other clergy who had been exiled were allowed to return to Venice – though not the Jesuits, who had been very active in the pamphlet war on the side of the papacy. Given the intransigence which both sides had hitherto shown, it was an extremely skilful act of diplomacy.

In 1613 François suffered a minor stroke, from which he recovered, though not fully. His health went into decline. He died of dysentery at Avignon on 27 August 1615, and was buried in the Jesuit church at Pontoise. The cardinal had been returning home from a pilgrimage to the shrine of the Madonna at Montserrat.

Giulio Alberoni

Many cardinals, some mentioned in this book, came from humble origins. There was, and is, nothing unusual in such a career. But the life-story of Alberoni is remarkable by any standard. He was born in Piacenza on 21 March 1664, one of the six children of a gardener and a seamstress. His father died when he was only ten years old, and to help support the family Giulio had as soon as possible to find whatever work he could. He started as a bell ringer in the parish church where he had been baptized on the day of his birth, and rose to the relatively important post of sacristan. As will be seen, he was a person of quite extraordinary character, and won over the clergy of the church, who taught him to read and write and then sent him to the prestigious Jesuit college in the city: someone must have paid his fees and, as his family could not, it surely must have been the parish clergy.

Still eager to earn money, Giulio struck up an acquaintance with a lawyer named Ignazio Gardini and began to help him in the courts. He seems to have made himself indispensable because when in 1685 Gardini was banished from the duchy of Parma, in which Piacenza lay, and went to Ravenna, he took Giulio with him. He was no sooner in Ravenna than he came to know the vice-legate, went to work for him, and rose quickly to be head of his household. The vice-legate was appointed to the bishopric of Parma, and so Giulio returned to his home territory. He was now of an age to be ordained priest, which he was in the cathedral of Parma on a date which cannot now be discovered, and appointed parish priest. For some, also undiscoverable, reason he did not last more than a couple of weeks in the post before, it would appear, he was sacked by the parishioners, and was once more without a job. This situation did not last long. The Bishop of Parma suggested him as a tutor to his nephew, Count Gianbattista Barni. In 1696 he and the Count travelled to Rome, but after two years in Rome parted company. Giulio returned to Parma as a canon of the cathedral chapter.

In 1701 there broke out the War of the Spanish Succession. The year before King Charles II of Spain had died, and the crown of Spain passed to a somewhat reluctant Philip, Duke of Anjou, who became Philip V of Spain. He was the son of the Dauphin, Louis XIV's heir to the throne of France, and therefore stood in line of succession to the French crown as well as being in possession of the Spanish one. This caused consternation among the major European powers, because a union of the two crowns would irreparably damage the delicate balance of power on the continent. As the war gathered momentum a Spanish–French army commanded by Louis-Joseph de Vendôme invaded northern Italy, including the duchy of Parma. The Bishop of Parma was sent to negotiate with the victorious Duke, and he took Giulio Alberoni with him as his secretary. The bishop served in this post of intermediary for two years before retiring back to his diocese and leaving Alberoni in his place.

Alberoni had considerable sympathy with the Franco–Spanish alliance. The alliance's major enemy was the Empire, and the Archduke of Austria, as Emperor, ruled over the Kingdom of Naples. Many Italians, Alberoni among them, were eager to see the 'Germans', as they tended to be called, driven out of the peninsula. He somehow attached himself to Vendôme's staff. Presumably he still radiated the charm which had already won over so many in his past, but he was also able to organize supplies, especially of food. Alberoni had an unassailable conviction in the superior merits of Parmesan cuisine. He not only provided cheese, pasta, sausages and sauces from his home territory, he was also highly skilled in cooking it. He became a general factotum to Vendôme, and Vendôme rewarded him with a small pension from the French government. When the general was summoned back to France, Alberoni went too. When Vendôme was sent to rescue the situation in Flanders, along went the abbé.

All this time he was also serving as the emissary of Parma. When Philip V added another pension to that provided by Louis XIV, Alberoni wrote to the Duke that he no longer needed a salary, and would work for the duchy for nothing. Nonetheless his situation was precarious. In 1708 Vendôme was defeated by Marlborough at the battle of Oudenarde. This was not Vendôme's fault, as Alberoni never tired of telling anyone who would listen, but the fault of there being too many courtiers in the army and too few professional soldiers. But the general was in disgrace. Alberoni told him not to worry too much but to return home and cultivate his garden. The abbé's own position, however, was more difficult. He was in a foreign country, out of sorts with the Pope, Clement XI, whom he thought spineless for having allowed without a fight 'German' troops to march down Italy, and dependent on pensions which, apart from that of the duchy of Parma, were unreliable. Indeed, the one from Spain stopped entirely, and he went off to see the Spanish ambassador to the French court, the Duke of Alba. In the course of his conversations with the Duke he managed to persuade him that the best thing for Spain would be the appointment of Vendôme as commander of the Spanish army and of himself as the government's first minister. Madrid agreed, and in August 1710 he left for Spain, and Vendôme, placed in charge of Spanish forces, won two victories on successive days in December.

But then, quite suddenly in June 1712, Vendôme died, and was buried at El Escorial. Alberoni wanted to return home, resigning his post as the emissary of Parma, but he was told to stay, and loyally did so. The war petered out, and was formally declared over by the Treaty of Utrecht in 1713. Alberoni was distinctly unhappy with its terms because it left the Austrians in command of some of northern Italy and of Naples. Then Philip V's wife, who had been the abbé's greatest supporter at the Spanish court, died in February 1714. Philip had much doted upon his wife, but swiftly found another – or rather, Alberoni found one for him, Elizabeth Farnese, the stepdaughter of the Duke of Parma. She was married by proxy to Philip in Parma cathedral in September 1714, and then made a slow progress from Parma to Madrid. It was rather too slow for the uxorious Philip, and Alberoni worried that she might not be well received.

He need not have been concerned. Elizabeth and Philip got along extremely well together and, at least for a time, with Alberoni. His friendship with Elizabeth was more complicated than with her predecessor, but he kept her supplied with his customary sausages and pasta, to which he added horses from England. It was important to keep the monarchs happy because he was about to embark on a radical change of policy. Partly it was domestic. He improved the economy by bringing in new industries (he had four hundred nuns taught lace-making) and reorganizing the administration. He improved the standard of the army and greatly expanded the Spanish navy. It was partly this last which brought about the shift in foreign policy. As had been remarked, he wanted the 'Germans' out of Italy, and he also wanted to be able to trade freely without worrying about the English navy. He therefore negotiated an alliance with England, which was signed in December 1715.

Unfortunately it did not survive. Partly this was because English politicians had no great hopes of Spain. More significant as far as the English King was concerned, however, was the threat to Hanover. The Elector of Hanover had just become the King of England and regarded it as imperative to defend Hanover when it seemed about to be threatened by Russia and Sweden. England, France and Holland formed the Triple Alliance, and the balance of power in Europe was once again under threat: to redress the balance Spain and the Empire had to forget their earlier animosity.

There was a further complication. Philip and Elizabeth thought it only right that their first minister should have a cardinal's hat. Clement XI did not approve of Alberoni, nor vice versa as has been remarked. The Pope's chief complaint was that Spain had not supplied troops to the Empire to assist in the war against the Turks, and therefore he was not disposed to gratify the Spanish monarchs by raising Alberoni to the cardinalate. Philip retaliated by banning the papal nuncio from Spain unless the Pope gave way. This he did. Alberoni was created a cardinal deacon in the consistory of 12 July 1717 and later given the title, which he was afterwards to change several times, of S. Adriano al Forno. In December of the same year he was appointed Bishop of Malaga, an office from which he resigned, without apparently having exercised it, in 1725.

This happened just after he had passed the high-water mark of his influence. In 1717 Philip of Spain insisted on an attack on Austrian-held Sardinia after Spain's Grand Inquisitor had been arrested while journeying, with permission, through imperial territory. Alberoni was against the plan but the King and Queen, and the Duke of Parma, were firmly in favour. Alberoni knew that such action would alienate England and also the papacy, especially at a time when the Empire was heavily engaged with the Turks. Sardinia was, however, captured and Alberoni decided to make the most of it. He proposed that the Spanish forces should press on to Sicily, that in any settlement which followed Naples and Sicily should go to Spain, Sardinia to Amadeus of Savoy, and Parma and Tuscany to the heirs of Elizabeth Farnese, and that there should be a league to drive imperial forces out of Italy. One problem with this, as he well knew, was that England was by now allied with the Empire. In August 1718 the English fleet, under the command of Admiral Byng, routed that of Spain. At this point no war had been declared, but a declaration swiftly followed. The English could not contemplate Spanish ships controlling the Mediterranean.

A further problem was France, which invaded northern Spain. Still in gung-ho mood, Philip and his Queen went to the front with Alberoni in tow. But the better part of the Spanish army was by this time tied up in Sicily, and against superior forces Philip had to beat a retreat. Someone had to be blamed for the disasters. Alberoni was the obvious scapegoat for failure in a war which he had not wanted and advised against. The Duke of Parma was prevailed upon to dismiss the cardinal, and in December 1719 he was given eight days to leave Madrid and three weeks to leave the country. All manner of charges were laid against him in an effort to persuade the Pope, who had never wanted to make him cardinal, to strip him of his rank. He was accused of failures in chastity, of not wearing proper clerical dress, of not having said mass for years.

He had become a well-known figure in Europe, and when he arrived in Genoa on his way home large crowds turned up to see him. But then he vanished. He simply disappeared for more than a year. Then Clement XI died, and in April 1721 he turned up, somewhat theatrically, at the gates of Rome to take part in the conclave which elected Innocent XIII. He stayed on in Rome and hostility to him gradually abated. Pope Innocent XIII was a friend, and pronounced him innocent of the charges brought against him. When the Young Pretender fell out with his wife, Alberoni, who at one time had involved the

Stuarts in his schemes, was sent by the Pope to attempt a reconciliation. In 1735 Pope Clement XII made him legate (or governor) of the Romagna, and he found himself back in Ravenna. It was the occasion for one of his rare errors of judgement. When San Marino, an independent principality, arrested someone who tried to claim clerical immunity, Alberoni had it attacked and quickly reduced to a papal possession. But the Pope did not want San Marino, and quietly gave it back its independence. In 1740 he was made legate in the important city of Bologna, where he could indulge himself, as he had in Spain, in much-needed administrative reform. In 1743 he returned to Piacenza which, in 1745, fell to the Spanish army. He cooked omelettes for some of the officers he encountered.

He was by this time eighty-one years old and effectively retired. In Piacenza he had built a splendid seminary, S. Lazaro, and he spent his last years improving it. For much of the time he lived in his villa at Castelromano, where he continued to cook for his occasional guests. He died in Piacenza on 26 June 1752, and was buried in his college of S. Lazaro.

Giuseppe Doria Pamphilj Landi

The family trees of the Dorias and the Pamphiljs are unusually complicated, but Giuseppe, born in Genoa on 11 November 1751, was distantly related to the Camillo Pamphilj who had in 1647 resigned his cardinalate to marry for love – or money (see p. 215). Tracing the relationships is all the more difficult because the same names turn up time and again, in particular Andrea Doria. Giuseppe's father was a Prince Andrea Doria, with the first name Giovanni, his mother was Eleonora Carafa della Stradera, who was a daughter of the Duke d'Andria.

When Giuseppe was nearly ten years old the family moved to Rome, where he attended the College for Nobles then run by the Society of Jesus, but because the Prince was a Spanish grandee, when the Jesuits were suppressed in Spain he thought it politic to withdraw his sons (Giuseppe had a younger brother Antonio Maria) and send them elsewhere. They were partly taught at home, then at La Sapienza, Rome's university, where both studied law. Giuseppe entered the clerical state in 1768, and was ordained five years later, on 18 July 1773. By that time he had entered the diplomatic service of the papacy and had been sent to Spain, an obvious choice, given his family's close connections with the Spanish court, by Pope Clement XIV to carry papal greetings on the birth of the Spanish King's son. He was at the court in Madrid from October 1772 to October the following year. He was not only ordained priest in Spain but also consecrated bishop there, with the title of Archbishop of Seleucia, on

22 August because he had been named by the Pope as nuncio to the court of the King of France, a post that carried at least the rank of Archbishop.

It was a difficult time to be in Paris. Because Clement XIV's predecessor had refused to abolish the Jesuits the French King had ordered the seizure of Avignon and the surrounding countryside, which were parts of the Papal States. Clement XIV had ordered the suppression of the Society of Jesus only a little while earlier – the brief *Dominus ac Redemptor* had been issued on 21 July 1773 – which made life a little easier. But there were still problems, especially with Avignon, where the Archbishop busily set about removing all the changes introduced by the French government as soon as the city was restored to the papacy. Clement sent Giuseppe to sort matters out, which he did with some success. He was destined for higher things. On 14 February 1785 he was created a cardinal priest, with the title of San Pietro in Vincoli, and the following December was appointed legate in Urbino. It was a three-year appointment to govern the former duchy, now part of the Papal States, but it was extended until 1794 because of Giuseppe's success as an administrator. The States were notoriously badly run, but there had been efforts to improve their economies, and Giuseppe took this task seriously, fostering the woollen industry, improving buildings and roads, and proposing new laws for the better government in his Legation – efforts, however, which were not carried to completion because of the worrying events in France.

He was recalled to Rome to give advice to Pope Pius VI on the developing situation in France, a country he had come to know well as nuncio. In April 1797, under pressure from Spain he was appointed as Secretary of State because of what was seen to be his conciliatory approach to France. He remained Secretary of State theoretically until the death of Pius VI in August 1799, but in practice his office was in abeyance from the time France occupied Rome in February 1798. So conciliatory was he that, after the occupation and at the request of the French General Berthier, he celebrated mass with thirteen other cardinals and sang the *Te Deum* to give thanks for the Roman people's 'recovery of liberty'. It was not long, however, before Giuseppe and other cardinals had been put in prison, first in a hastily converted convent on the Corso, then in Civitavecchia, and then expelled entirely from the new Roman Republic.

After the death of Pius VI he made his way to Venice for the conclave, and after the election he made his way back to Rome with the newly elected Pope Pius VII: he and another cardinal rode with the Pope into the city, the future Cardinal Ercole Consalvi (see p. 179)following on behind in a separate carriage. He was now no longer Secretary of State, that role having gone to Consalvi, but he was part of the special committee set up to examine the proposed concordat with Napoleon's France – he being in favour of a quick settlement. When Consalvi left for Paris for a month he temporarily took over the role of

Secretary of State. He then became pro-Camerlengo, and served on a committee concerned with economic problems. In September 1803 he became cardinal bishop, succeeding to the diocese of Frascati when Henry Stuart, as dean of the College of Cardinals, went the bishopric of Ostia-Velletri (p. 222).

When French troops again occupied Rome in February 1808 he once more took over as Secretary of State after Cardinal Casoni had resigned. He was chosen for his alleged understanding of France, and readiness to compromise. But compromise was pointless. The French ordered all cardinals who were not Romans by birth to return to their home towns, and Giuseppe made his way back to Genoa. He was not there long. In September 1809 all cardinals were ordered to report to Paris. This was no great hardship. He lived with the other cardinals, all of whom were rewarded with a reasonable monthly pension – until, that is, the wedding of Napoleon to the Archduchess Marie Louise of Austria. The cardinals were instructed to attend. Half refused to do so, and were deprived of their stipend, and of the right to wear their cardinatial purple: they were therefore the 'black' cardinals. Giuseppe, who had always enjoyed good relations with the Emperor (but then, hitherto, so had Consalvi), was naturally among those who went to the marriage ceremonies. He kept his pension, and was allowed to continue to wear his robes: one of the 'red' cardinals.

Napoleon had a problem with Pius VII, held in custody at Savona. The Emperor was embarrassed by the number of vacant sees in France, which the Pope steadfastly refused to fill. Giuseppe was despatched to try to persuade the Pope to appoint bishops, and after Pius was moved to Fontainebleau he went to see the pontiff to try – for a time successfully – to persuade him to sign a new accord between France and the Vatican, which Consalvi then persuaded the Pope to retract. In the meantime, however, the Emperor was so delighted with Cardinal Doria Pamphilj that he decorated him with the Legion of Honour. When the Pope was finally released and made his way back to Rome, Giuseppe met him at Foligno in May 1814 and offered his resignation from his Vatican offices. The reason he gave was his state of health: the real reason was his behaviour while in Paris, which was not unreasonably regarded as being less than loyal to the needs of the Church. He was, however, accepted as sub-dean of the College of Cardinals, and he changed his titular see from Frascati to that of Porto e San Rufino in September of the same year.

He had spent his life in Vatican diplomacy, too often following what with hindsight was a mistaken policy, one usually dictated by his Francophile sentiments. But there was another side to his life, much less well recorded. He had funded, for instance, a school for children who were both deaf and dumb, the first of its kind in Rome. Also first of its kind in the city was the garden he had planted in the English style, just outside the city's Porta Pinciana.

He died in Rome on 9 February 1816, and was buried in the church of Santa Cecilia in Trastevere, though the funeral service itself took place in Santa Maria in Vallicella. He left his considerable wealth to be divided out among his two brothers and two nephews.

Paul Cullen

Ireland is commonly regarded as being one of the foremost Catholic countries in Europe, perhaps in the world. It is odd, therefore, that it was not until 1866 in the person of Paul Cullen, that Ireland had its first resident cardinal. He was born in Prospect, near Ballintore in County Kildare on 29 April 1803, the third son in a family of fifteen children, eight of them boys. His father Hugh was a prosperous farmer – though a tenant farmer – who had married Mary Maher, also from a relatively well-off farming family. The local school in Ballintore, which he attended from the age of ten, was a Quaker one, but at fourteen he entered the junior seminary at Carlow. He was diligent and scholarly, and was offered a place at the Irish national seminary at Maynooth, but his father thought he ought to go to Rome. This he did at the age of seventeen, entering the Collegium Urbanianum, the college run by the Congregatio de Propaganda Fide, the Congregation in charge of all missionary territories – which Britain then was, Ireland at the time being subject to the Westminster government.

Though at first he had doubts about the education offered at the Urbanianum, he excelled as a student, especially of ancient languages, and was selected to defend his doctorate before Pope Leo XII during the pontiff's visit to the college. He was ordained priest on 19 April 1829. His bishop in Ireland wanted him to return to take up a post at Carlow, but he was kept in Rome by Cardinal Cappellari who headed Propaganda, and was made professor of Scripture. In 1831 his patron Cappellari became Pope Gregory XVI, and when in 1831 the post of rector of the Irish College became vacant, Cullen was appointed to it. Shortly afterwards became agent in Rome for the Irish bishops, a position which brought him not only a reasonable salary but also a good deal of influence.

Under Cullen the Irish College flourished, and had to move to larger premises, to a convent attached to the church of Santa Agata dei Goti on the Quirinal hill, given to the College by Pope Gregory. He also maintained links with Propaganda. He had been head of its publishing arm, and he edited the *Acta* of the Congregation as well as other learned works. He was several times approached to accept a bishopric in the United States, but always refused. As agent of the Irish bishops he had problems: they were bitterly divided over the issue of primary education. The Archbishop of Tuam, John MacHale, believed that the British-funded system was meant to wean the Irish away from their Catholicism. In this view he was supported by nine of the other twenty-five bishops. MacHale was therefore bitterly at odds with the Archbishop of Dublin, Daniel Murray, who did not suspect the British of attempting to subvert the faith. Cullen sympathized with MacHale until he visited Ireland in 1841. During his visit he came to the conclusion that the bishops had nothing to fear, and told the Roman authorities so. Sometime later, however, he again sided with MacHale over a couple of issues, one being the possibility that the Holy See would establish diplomatic relations with Britain, which the fiercely nationalistic MacHale was against. Cullen gave credence to the rumour of a concordat with Britain and was severely reprimanded by Pope Gregory, upon which he had a nervous breakdown. In 1845 had again to return to Ireland to recover his composure.

Despite his unhappy experience in backing MacHale he did so again when the British government proposed establishing 'Queen's Colleges' to provide university education for Catholics and Presbyterians. MacHale was against them, Murray in favour. This time Cullen managed to persuade the new Pope Pius IX that the former was right, the latter wrong, and the Pope condemned the idea. It should be remembered that at this period English Catholics were forbidden to attend Oxford and Cambridge, though some did so, and this ban was therefore not out of keeping with Catholic policy in general. The Pope at this time, of course, had troubles of his own, and had to flee Rome (pp. 186f.). During the Roman Republic Cullen earned the Pope's gratitude by taking over the Collegium Urbanianum as rector, and placing it under the protection of the United States, thus saving it from destruction.

The division between Murray and MacHale was a bitter one, and when Murray died in April 1849 it was difficult to find a replacement. Pius IX eventually decided on Cullen, who was consecrated bishop in the church of Santa Maria dei Goti on 24 February 1850. Cullen returned to Ireland in May of that year not only as Archbishop of Armagh, but as Apostolic Delegate. His first task was to hold a synod – at Thurles – which managed to reconcile most of the bishops to each other, at least for a time, and to find a way to resolve the dispute over education. MacHale was not, however, reconciled to Cullen, and especially not after Cullen was transferred in May 1852 to the Archbishopric of Dublin. MacHale resented Cullen arriving from Rome and emerging as the de facto leader of Irish Catholics. He set about attempting to undermine him.

This he did in a number of different ways, but nowhere perhaps more obviously than in his support for the Tenants' League. The situation in the Ireland to which Cullen returned after three decades in Rome was dire. In the famine of 1845–47 a million people perished while another million sought a better life abroad. In 1850 there were well over a hundred thousand evictions of tenant farmers. The Tenants' League was established to fight for their rights. Cullen was well aware of the plight of the poor – he had written a pastoral letter about it even before he had left Rome. The problem for Cullen was that the clergy were active supporters of the League, and playing an increasingly political role. In June 1853 he held a provincial synod in Dublin which banned the holding of political meetings in churches, forbade clergy denouncing individuals of whose political views they disapproved, and called upon them not to discuss politics or attend political meetings. These provisions might hold fast in the Dublin province, but elsewhere they had little or no impact, except in allowing MacHale and his supporters to present Cullen as being sympathetic to the British administration. That was unfair to Cullen, but he saw no reason not to collaborate with the government unless there were some issue of principle, and to make use of the administration's Catholic members. He thought there ought to be more Irish in the administration, on the ground that they were more intelligent than the English. MacHale's campaign against him, however, seriously affected his health, and he had another breakdown. This time he retreated to Rome.

In the 1860s he was confronted with a revolutionary movement in Ireland which had grown out of the Irish Republican Brotherhood, founded in Dublin on St Patrick's Day 1858. The Brotherhood's American supporters called themselves Fenians, and it was as Fenians that those engaged in efforts to overthrown British rule in Ireland came to be known. Cullen was completely opposed to the Fenian movement, despite the widespread support it enjoyed among the clergy and some of the bishops. For him it was a secret society plotting against both Church and State. The fact that police raids on Fenian offices found weapons, and several of those arrested confessed themselves to be antipathetic to the Church, provided evidence for his convictions that the Fenian movement ought to be suppressed. When he approached the Vatican for a condemnation, all Rome did was to restate the principles governing secret societies without explicitly condemning Fenianism. An explicit condemnation only came in June 1870, which was after the abortive uprising of 1867. Some of those arrested after the earlier police action had been given long prison sentences – too long, thought Cullen – but they were released after only a couple of years. After the uprising some were condemned to death but were reprieved, in one instance clearly through Cullen's intervention. He did not, however, intervene when three men were executed for killing a policeman in Manchester in a successful attempt to free a Fenian prisoner.

Cullen possibly thought, probably quite rightly, that his intervention would have been useless, but his inaction was taken as further evidence of his hostility to Irish nationalism. This was unfair. He was very much a nationalist, but was concerned to avoid violence. But he was also convinced that it was essential to move forward slowly, and as far as possible to cooperate with the government in Westminster. He urged Irish members of parliament to accept offices in government, a stance which again brought hostility from some of the bishops, many of the clergy, and of course from Fenians themselves. The Irish bishops, like bishops from around the world, attended the Vatican Council, which met in Rome from the end of 1869 to mid 1870. Cullen was very much in favour of the definition of papal infallibility, and is credited with the formulation which was eventually passed. MacHale opposed it. When MacHale returned to Ireland he was given an enthusiastic welcome. Cullen was not.

By this time he was a cardinal. He was created Cardinal Priest of San Pietro in Montorio in June 1866. It was not so much a reward for his political stance, though Rome approved of it, as for his largely successful efforts in making the Irish Church much more Rome-oriented. The religious change which created Catholic Ireland, as it came to be known down to recent times, happened while Cullen was the leading force – far more priests, far more convents, many more confraternities pursuing an active devotional life in the parishes.

Yet all this was, in people's minds, overshadowed by his political position. He was frequently denounced as being too sympathetic to the Westminster government. He was sympathetic to Gladstone in the disestablishment of the Church of Ireland and in the passing of the 1870 Land Act, but although he personally backed Gladstone's Irish University Bill of 1873 he failed to carry the majority of the Irish bishops with him and they withdrew support, bringing down Gladstone's government. It was a great embarrassment to Archbishop Manning in Westminster, who had assured his old friend Gladstone that through Cullen he could deliver the Irish vote.

Paul Cullen died on 24 October 1878. His death was unexpected. He was in the midst of a discussion with the Conservative government of Disraeli over a new university bill. His funeral was celebrated with great pomp, and he was buried at Holy Cross church, Clonliffe. The church had been built on the model of Rome's Santa Maria dei Goti – only bigger.

Secretaries of State

There is a touch of confusion about the title of Secretary of State. The best-known politician to hold such a title is that member of the administration of the United States who deals with foreign affairs, the equivalent of the British Foreign Secretary. It is a common misunderstanding to transfer that meaning of the term to the papal administration. The Cardinal Secretary of State holds a rather different office in the Vatican from that of Secretary of State in Washington.

Naturally enough, for as long as any structures are discernible in the way the bishops of Rome ran their Church, popes have always had secretaries. Because the papacy dealt with many different nationalities, there had to be, at least from the beginning of the fifteenth century, secretaries who were able to deal with different geographical regions. As papal documents were commonly in Latin, the skills required by the secretaries were not so much linguistic as political. In 1487 there were twenty-four such secretaries, organized into a formal 'college' by Pope Innocent VIII. But he added to them a 'domestic secretary', who, in modern parlance, seems to have been a cross between a personal private secretary and a personal assistant. But by this time there had also come into existence the role of Cardinal Nephew. This office first appeared under Pope Sixtus IV (1471–84), who perhaps more than any pontiff developed nepotism into a fine art. It has already been remarked (see above, p. 14f.) that there was good reason for the pope of the day to trust his close relatives rather than the other cardinals from among whose number he had been elected. The role of the Cardinal Nephew grew in significance as a formal post in the papal curia during the sixteenth century until it eclipsed the office of domestic secretary, and the latter was abolished in 1586. As can be seen in the life of the indolent Innocenzo Ciocchi del Monte (see p. 211), the papal nephew himself needed staff, someone to deal with papal correspondence. The first time a cardinal was appointed to this post, and given the express title 'Cardinal Secretary of State', was in 1644, and the office of Cardinal Nephew disappeared, the last one being appointed under Alexander VIII (1689–91).

Under Alexander's successor, Pope Innocent XII, the Cardinal Secretary of State came to be a diplomatic one, dealing with foreign states: the internal affairs of the Papal States were handled by another department of the Vatican. With the election of Pius IX in 1846, however, there came to be one Secretariat of State with two departments, one for the Papal States and the other for foreign affairs, the Cardinal Secretary of State presiding over both, making him therefore much more of a Prime Minister in the British model than a Secretary of State in the US one. Though popes have tinkered with the structure ever since, that is basically what survives today: one Secretariat of State with two sections, the first dealing with issues internal to the Catholic Church, the second concerned with the Church's enormous web of diplomatic relations: at the beginning of January 2010 the Holy See had diplomatic relations with one hundred and seventy-eight countries around the world as well as with other institutions, such as the European Union.

To date, some fifty individuals have held the title of Cardinal Secretary of State. Sometimes the prelate appointed is not yet a cardinal. His elevation to the Sacred College usually soon follows, but in the meantime he is the pro-Secretary: Giacomo Antonelli whose life is recorded below began as pro-Secretary. A few, including Ercole Consalvi, who is also one of the cardinals discussed, held the office more than once. None of those mentioned below have been ineffectual, and at least one, Consalvi, was quite outstanding in his post: he would have made a more than adequate foreign minister in any of the European states of the day. Antonelli, on the other hand, although highly competent, was not popular within the papal curia, partly because of his reclusiveness. Nor was he popular among the governments of Europe because of his apparent inflexibility. It could be said in his defence that he was only carrying out his master's wishes. The most controversial of those included below was without doubt Rafael Merry del Val.

Ercole Consalvi

At the end of the eighteenth century it must have seemed as if the papacy as an institution was at an end. France had declared itself an atheist state. Napoleon had overrun Italy and Rome itself had been occupied. Pope Pius VI had been exiled, first to Florence and then, eventually, to Valence, held as a prisoner there until his death in August 1799. That the papacy did not disappear but emerged from the confusion of the Napoleonic wars both renewed and admired was largely the result of the diplomatic skill of Ercole Consalvi, one of the two cardinals to be created, on 11 August 1800, in the first consistory of the pontificate of Pius VII. By that time he had already had a substantial and distinguished career in papal service.

Ercole, born in Rome on 8 June 1757,was the eldest of four brothers and a sister, though only three brothers survived infancy. The family was wealthy and noble: after the death of his grandfather (his father having died earlier) he inherited the title of Marchese, which he passed on to his brother Andrea, with whom he was particularly close, when he entered the service of the papacy. The three brothers were sent to a school run by the Piarist fathers in Urbino, which they hated, and then to a seminary in Frascati, which they loved.

Frascati was chosen for them by their guardian, Cardinal Andrea Negroni. Negroni was a close friend of Henry Stuart, the Cardinal Duke of York (see p. 222), who was Bishop of Frascati and who had just started a seminary in his city. The brothers went there in 1770, a year after it had opened. Part of the attraction of Frascati was the Cardinal Duke himself, who took a strong liking to the young Marchese, and became something of a patron. Ercole repaid the interest Henry Stuart took in him by learning English and developing a particular fondness for England and its people: there came to be a good many English among his closest friends.

In 1776 he left the seminary for Rome, where he attended the Academy for Noble Ecclesiastics, and then the University of Rome, La Sapienza, where in 1784 he became a doctor in canon and civil law. He had decided upon a career in the administration of the Papal States, which at that time (he was to change the rules) required him to be a cleric. He entered the service of Pope Pius VI in the lowly office of a supernumerary chamberlain in 1783, but just over a year later he formally entered paid employment as a domestic prelate, which entitled him to the rank of Monsignor. He was clearly a competent administrator, for various offices were heaped upon him, but John Martin Robinson, his biographer, suggests that it was his good looks which most attracted Pius VI – who in turn considered himself to be rather handsome. But as far as good looks were concerned, Consalvi had a rival in the slightly younger Annibale Della Genga, whose rise was somewhat swifter than Consalvi's. Shortly after Della Genga's ordination as a priest – while still below the canonical age – he became private secretary to the Pope. The competition between Consalvi and Della Genga, remarks Robinson, made the former ill.

The advance of the French through Italy gave rise to revolutionary movements within the Papal States. The papacy needed to reform the army, and Pius VI created a military commission for the purpose, putting Consalvi in charge. When a French general was accidentally shot in Rome the French seized upon the excuse they had anyway been looking for, and on 10 February 1798 occupied the city. The Pope was bundled out of Rome and Consalvi was imprisoned in Castel Sant'Angelo, where he whiled away the time by playing cards with his captors. He was a personable young man, cultured and fluent in French, who was easy to like. His charm was unfeigned, and throughout his life it won him a wide variety of friends – among them several crowned heads, including the King of England.

After a relatively brief imprisonment he was threatened with deportation to the French penal colony in Cayenne, but instead was exiled to Naples, where he found his old patron the Cardinal Duke of York also languishing. From Naples he went to Certosa to see the Pope, and eventually made his way to Venice, which was in Austrian territory. The Cardinal Duke was there also. Having lost all his wealth in the occupation of Rome he was now – despite being a Catholic and a Stuart – in receipt of a pension from the Protestant Hanoverian King George III of England.

After the death of Pius VI there was much discussion among the cardinals now gathered in Venice about where the conclave should be held. Consalvi, not a cardinal himself, was chosen as secretary to the conclave when it was finally decided that the election should be held in Venice. Cardinal Chiaramonti was elected on 14 March 1800: four days later he declared that Consalvi would be pro-Secretary of State. He could not yet be fully Secretary of State because not yet a cardinal: this was rectified on 11 August when he was created cardinal deacon (he was ordained deacon for the occasion, but never became a priest) of Santa Maria dei Martiri: this, his titular church, is also known by its ancient name, the Pantheon.

He was just 43, remarkably young for one of Europe's most influential statesmen. He had a two-fold role: he had to govern the Papal States, and to deal with the Great Powers, especially with France. The first task for his energies was the reform of the administration in the Papal States. He attempted to free up commerce by the abolition of customs and tariff barriers between the different entities which made up the States. He allowed the lay nobility of the States to become involved in their governance, a role hitherto limited to clerics. He also created a new army from the ranks of the aristocracy by establishing the Noble Guard: it gave young aristocrats something to do, and was relatively inexpensive because aristocrats did not need to be paid. One of his most pressing tasks was to bring papal expenditure under control. More money was needed, which might come in part from tourism. He set about the restoration of classical Rome, and forbade the exporting of ancient artefacts.

But his main concern was Napoleon. Bonaparte had changed his mind about the Church. Far from suppressing Christianity, he now wanted to harness its moral authority to that of the State, and a new concordat, or treaty, between the Vatican and Paris was proposed. Consalvi went to Paris to negotiate. Negotiation, however, was not what Napoleon had in mind. He kept demanding conditions to which Pius VII could not possibly agree. After lengthy talks Napoleon had it announced that agreement had been reached when it had not, though this tactic helpfully put pressure on both sides to reach an accord.

When eventually an agreement was reached Consalvi returned to Rome. The text as published by the French in April 1802 was not what had been agreed. It had appended to it what were known as the 'Organic Articles', provisions which the Secretary of State had explicitly struck out. Nonetheless the concordat had one significant feature helpful to the papacy: it swept away the various jurisdictions which had impinged upon the appointment of bishops, and left the Pope effectively in sole charge of this crucial function within France.

Napoleon now decided that he would declare himself an Emperor. Traditionally emperors had been crowned by popes, and in 1804 Pius VII was summoned to Paris for the purpose. Pius did not want to go, but Consalvi persuaded him on the ground that he might have the opportunity of getting the Emperor to repeal the offending Organic Articles. This did not happen, nor in the end did Pius crown Napoleon (he crowned himself), but at least he enjoyed the visit to the imperial court.

Relations with France might have seemed to be improving, but they took a dramatic turn for the worse when in 1805 the French seized the papal port of Ancona in order to deny it to the English fleet. Consalvi protested that this action compromised papal neutrality. Napoleon rejected the papal complaints, blaming Consalvi for Pius's intransigence, and went on to occupy another papal port, that of Civitavecchia. On 17 June 1808 Consalvi resigned as Secretary of State, hoping that removing himself would dissipate Napoleon's anger with the Pope. It did nothing of the sort. The French occupied Rome and in May 1809 declared the Papal States to be part of the French Empire. Pius VII was carried off to France, but his presence on French soil being something of an embarrassment, he was sent back to Savona. A few months later Consalvi was also seized – after being refused permission to leave Rome – and was also sent to France. He arrived in Paris in late February 1810, where he steadfastly refused to fraternize with his captors despite pressing invitations.

The next crisis came over the proposed marriage of Napoleon to the Archduchess Marie Louise of Austria. Emperors need heirs, and the Empress Josephine had failed to provide any. The Archduchess might do so, and marrying into the ruling house of Austria would give the Emperor the royal legitimacy for which he craved. The obvious problem was that he was already married to Josephine, and the Pope would not – could not – agree to annul his marriage. The wedding to the Archduchess went ahead anyway, leaving the cardinals gathered at Paris in a quandary. Napoleon had made it clear their presence was expected at the events surrounding the nuptials. Consalvi and a group of similarly minded cardinals refused to attend anything that passed for a wedding, civil or ecclesiastical. Other cardinals decided to go. Those who did not attend were forbidden from wearing their red cardinatial robes, and Consalvi himself, seen as the ringleader, was banished to Rheims.

The situation changed after Napoleon's Russian campaign, and the destruction of the *Grande Armée*. When the Emperor returned from Moscow he decided he ought to make his peace with the Pope, who had in the meantime been brought to Fontainebleau. Under pressure the weary Pope, eager to return to Rome, at last agreed to a concordat with France on Napoleon's terms: the fact was announced with great jubilation and the singing of a *Te Deum* at the beginning of February 1813. But then Napoleon made the mistake of allowing Consalvi to join Pope Pius, and the former Secretary of State persuaded Pius to retract. By this time, in any case, Napoleon was effectively finished. He had made his brother-in-law, Joachim Murat, King of Naples and the Two Sicilies – though Murat had managed only to take possession of Naples. Now he turned on Napoleon and drove the French from Rome. Pius was allowed to set out for Rome and on the way, at Cesena, he was joined by Consalvi, who was reinstated as Secretary of State on 17 May 1814.

The peace conference was being held in London. Instead of returning to Rome with the Pope, Consalvi set out for England, and wearing full cardinatial rig he was received by the Prince Regent on 1 July 1814. He greatly enjoyed London, especially the music, and stayed just under a month. He was, however, unable to dissuade the Allies from giving the former papal territory of Avignon to France. He got on particularly well with the English Foreign Secretary, Lord Castlereagh, agreeing with him on most matters except the freedom of the press (on that he later conceded that England was a special case). He undertook to ally the papacy to the campaign to abolish the slave trade.

From London he went on to Vienna. For a time it looked as if some at least of the Papal States would be lost, but the Austrian Chancellor, Prince Metternich, decided that the survival of the States was more in Austria's interest than a possibly united Italy, and most of the papal territories except Avignon were returned to the papacy. In the end it was probably Napoleon's return from Elba – which led to Murat, who again changed sides, driving Pope Pius out of Rome to Genoa – that saved the States for the papacy. The Congress of Vienna even ordered the restoration to Rome of all the treasures and documents that had been taken by the French.

It was not until June 1815, after an absence of five years, that Consalvi returned to Rome. To his annoyance, in his absence there had been a restoration of the *ancien régime* in the Papal States. Not only did this alienate Consalvi's friends among European statesmen, who regarded the system of government operated by the Vatican before the Napoleonic Wars as corrupt and archaic, it alienated the populations of the States who had enjoyed a greater measure of freedom during the French occupation.

His attempts at reform were blocked by conservative cardinals, and he thought of once again resigning. But he had the backing of Pope Pius, and by dint of getting most of the reins of power into his own hands he bit by bit began to improve conditions in the States and in Rome itself. As (almost) always the papal treasury was empty, but he improved the system of tax collection, and by encouraging agriculture – he set up an agricultural college in Rome – he also bettered the lot of the citizens of the States. He created a new army and the Carabinieri to keep the peace, and ruthlessly had bandits put to death. Once again he encouraged visitors to come to Rome, especially to see the Roman ruins, which he had excavated by galley slaves. The arch of Titus was restored, the Piazza del Popolo remodelled, the area around the Pantheon, his titular church, cleared. He employed Antonio Canova, a much-admired sculptor but also good friend, first to recover the works of art from Paris and then to renovate the Vatican museum. Still an ardent Anglophile (the Dowager Duchess of Devonshire, resident in Rome, was a particularly close friend), he even took over the management of the English seminary in Rome, the Venerable English College.

Only a very tiny number of Vatican offices survive the death of a pope. Pius VII died on 20 August 1823, and Consalvi resigned as Secretary of State the following day. His former rival, Annibale Della Genga, was elected as Pope Leo XII a month later: the vote in the conclave was at least as much an anti-Consalvi vote by the conservatives among the cardinals as it was a vote for the new pontiff personally. Consalvi decided to leave Rome, though not before commissioning a tomb in St Peter's for Pope Pius. Canova had died, so Consalvi gave the task to another sculptor he greatly admired, the Dane Bertel Thorvaldsen. The monument, for which Consalvi paid personally, is the only one in St Peter's by a Protestant.

Della Genga did not appoint Consalvi to his old post, but nor did he prove as hostile as perhaps Consalvi had feared. He brought him back to Rome, and often consulted him. He even gave him the important office of Prefect of Propaganda Fide, the office of the Vatican with responsibility for the Church's missionary activity – and, at the time, for the Catholic Church in England. The Dowager Duchess looked forward to Consalvi returning to his place in Roman society. It was not to be. He died, only six months after the Pope he had served so well, on 24 January 1824. Someone has said he was the best pope the Church never had – except that he never became a priest.

Giacomo Antonelli

It is easy to be wise after the event. The papacy has existed quite satisfactorily within the confines of the Vatican, transformed by the Lateran Treaty of 1929 into the world's smallest state (see p. 197), but when in 1870 Rome fell to the troops of the Kingdom of Italy, there were many who feared for the pope's independence. The Papal States had survived for more than a thousand years, providing the Pope's income and – up to a point – freedom from interference from the other European powers. The task of attempting, ultimately unsuccessfully, to ensure its continued existence in the crucial third quarter of the nineteenth century fell to Pope Pius IX's Secretary of State, Cardinal Giacomo Antonelli.

He had been born on 2 April 1806 at Sonnino in the southern Papal States, on the border with the Kingdom of the Two Sicilies (though, with its capital in Naples, this largest of the states of nineteenth-century Italy was commonly known as the Kingdom of Naples). Giacomo's father was Casimiro Tommaso Maria Domenico, and it was by the last of these Christian names he was generally known. He was married to Loreta Mancini, who bore him four sons and three daughters. He was an agent for Cardinal Albani in nearby Terracina, and a dealer in agricultural products of all kinds. He was highly successful. In 1813 the family moved to Terracina, but Domenico eventually acquired property in various parts of the Papal States, including in Rome itself. It was not surprising that he should want one of his sons to enter the civil service of the papacy.

Giacomo was sent to Rome to study. He was at the Collegio Romano from 1816 to 1823, and then moved on the University of Rome, where he graduated in 1830 with a doctorate in canon and civil law. In the same year he took the examination for admission to the papal civil service. He was appointed to a number of minor posts, thanks in part to the patronage of Cardinal Dandini, to whom he was related through his eldest brother's, Filippo's, marriage. He had wanted to join the diplomatic service, but although his family was by now wealthy, it was not noble, and such posts tended to be reserved for members of the nobility. His rise was remarkably swift. His first major appointment was as Apostolic Delegate in Orvieto. This was a recently created office, devised by Cardinal Consalvi (see p. 179) as a means of updating the administration of the papal territories. It was a prestigious posting for one so young, but he was not at ease, not least because he had to use his family's money to meet some of his expenses. He did, however, manage to get his family recognized as being among the nobility of Orvieto. In 1836 he was transferred to Viterbo and in 1839 to Macerata, the largest of the papal provinces.

He was brought back to Rome in 1841 to a senior post in the Ministry of Internal Affairs, internal, that is, to the Papal States, and was rewarded with a canonry of St Peter's. He chose this moment to become a deacon. It is sometimes said that Antonelli was the last 'lay cardinal', but he was not a layman. He had received minor orders in 1829, thereby acquiring the status of a cleric. It was easy to dispense someone from minor orders, but the diaconate is a major order, requiring a person to live a celibate life. The fact that he never went on to receive ordination to the priesthood, clearly a conscious decision, does not imply that he was a lay cardinal.

In June 1846 Cardinal Mastai-Ferretti emerged from the conclave as Pope Pius IX. He had a largely undeserved reputation as a liberal, and his pontificate opened with great hopes for reform in the Papal States. Antonelli, who a couple of years before had been made assistant minister of finance in the papal government, was conservative by inclination, but a technocrat and a pragmatist. He decided to support the early reforms, and Pius IX, Pio Nono, was suitably grateful. In the consistory of 11 June 1847, the second of a total of twenty-three consistories in this long pontificate, he was created a cardinal deacon, and given the title of Santa Agata alla Subarra. (In March 1868 he received the title of Santa Maria in Via Lata, though he also retained that of Santa Agata.)

Part of the reforms instituted by Pio Nono was the establishment of a 'Consulta', an advisory panel, of which Antonelli was president. Its remit took in every aspect of the government of the Papal States. Some members regarded it as, or hoped that it would become, a legislative body in a quasi democratic sense, but that had never been Pius's intention. Antonelli persuaded the Pope that further reform was needed, if only to mollify the more radical tendencies among the Pope's citizens. When on 10 March 1848 he was appointed Secretary of State, he was also made president of a new constitutional Council of Ministers. Four days later a new fundamental law was promulgated which turned the College of Cardinals into a senate for the Papal States.

There was from the start, however, a divergence of views between the Pope and his chief minister. The Council of Ministers was hamstrung by what Pio Nono regarded as religious considerations. One of the reforms the Council wanted was the abolition of the Roman ghetto, but the Pope would not agree. The people of Rome wanted the Jesuits expelled, something the Pope thought shameful, though Antonelli got the Jesuits to withdraw of their own accord. Antonelli wanted the papal army to go to the assistance of Milan in its war on Austria: Pio Nono agreed that the army might go, but required it to act only defensively. He steadfastly refused to declare war on Austria, a Catholic power, and said publicly he would not do so. His Council of Ministers had wanted the war. They promptly resigned – including Antonelli, though he did not himself sign the letter of resignation which some thought a touch duplicitous. He continued to advise the Pope, and was the instigator of a letter to the Austrian Emperor effectively asking him to leave Italy to the Italians, though to no avail.

There were disturbances in Rome. On 15 November the Pope's Prime Minister, Pellegrino Rossi, was assassinated on the steps of the Palazzo della Cancelleria. An angry mob marched on the Quirinal Palace, where the Pope was barricaded in. Two days later, to Antonelli's considerable relief, Pope Pius agreed to leave Rome, and on the 24th escaped to Gaeta dressed as a simple priest. He stayed there, in the Kingdom of the Two Sicilies, until April 1850, accompanied by Antonelli, who ran the Papal States from this place of exile while the French put down the rebellion in Rome. On returning, Pio Nono took up residence not in the Quirinal Palace but at the Vatican.

Antonelli, who became Secretary of State once again on 18 March 1852, had a complex balancing act to undertake. The King of Naples, who had given the Pope shelter, wanted him to pursue a conservative policy; the French, who had pacified his capital city, wanted to see more reform. Some modest reforms were undertaken. Antonelli extended the railways, introduced tariff reform, printed postage stamps, and set up municipal councils with elected members. But Pius was adamant that officials of the Papal States should remain clerics, against the wishes of the French monarch, Emperor Napoleon III. Napoleon, whose troops remained guarding Rome, was meanwhile stirring up trouble for the Pope by allying himself with the Piedmontese, the major threat to the integrity of the Papal States, against Austria. The war which followed was brief, the treaty which ended it (Villafranca, 11 November 1859) ineffectual, but it was a spur to the establishment of civil, in place of clerical, government across Italy. Villafranca had proposed an Italian confederation with the Pope at its head; Napoleon himself, on the other hand, favoured a much more restricted Papal State consisting of little more than Rome and its environs.

In the on-going threat to the existence of the Papal States, Antonelli favoured a softly-softly approach. Mgr François-Xavier de Merode, on the other hand, was much more bellicose and urged on the Pope a universal crusade against encroachment on his territory. Pio Nono agreed with Merode, and made him Minister for War. He recruited an army that was enthusiastically joined by many Frenchmen hostile to Napoleon, and sent it off to defend the States from the Piedmontese, with no success whatsoever. As Garibaldi and his army marched northwards from Sicily, overthrowing the Kingdom of the Two Sicilies, Umbria and the Marches fell to the Piedmontese government of Turin, reducing papal territory by three-quarters. De Merode was still not disheartened and set about recruiting a new army. Antonelli by this time felt he had suffered enough, and offered his resignation, but Pope Pius refused it. One thing the Pope and his Secretary of State agreed upon: there was to be no negotiation if the condition of negotiations was that Pius accepted the loss of his territory. The Piedmontese King Victor Emmanuel was proclaimed King of Italy on 17 March 1861. The following day Pius publicly rejected any offer of negotiation. He went further, and in 1864 in the *Syllabus of Errors* anathematized the ideologies which underlay, as he believed, the politics of the new Kingdom of Italy. It was, however, conceived in such broad terms that

Antonelli, who had not been in favour of publishing the *Syllabus*, was able to assure governments that it dealt only with abstract principles and not with currently existing political institutions.

Meanwhile he had to get on with governing what little remained of the Pope's territories. He was faced with a financial crisis, as the source of the Pope's income had been drastically reduced. Like a true technocrat he set about reorganizing and fostering the payment of Peter's Pence, the tribute to Rome with its origins in Anglo-Saxon England. It had largely fallen out of use; now it underwent a more or less spontaneous revival. Antonelli, with the assistance of his brother Filippo at the head of the Banca Romana, succeeded in putting the much-diminished state back on a sound financial footing. Ever the pragmatist, the cardinal also negotiated on matters of common interest, such as the suppression of brigands, with the Turin government. But once again his efforts at compromise were frustrated by events beyond his control. The Kingdom of Italy had allied itself with Protestant Prussia against Austria in an effort to drive the Austrians out of Italy for good. Though in the war between Prussia and Austria the Prussians had quickly gained the upper hand, in Italy itself the Italian army had been defeated by the Austrians. The Turin government attempted to distract attention from this humiliation by launching another attack on the rump of the Papal States. It was not at this point successful. The French sent back their troops, who had been withdrawn, and on 7 November 1867 a papal army of vastly superior numbers defeated Garibaldi and his men at Mentana just outside Rome.

Napoleon proposed an international conference on the 'Roman Question'. Antonelli was deeply opposed to the idea that non-Catholic powers might be making decisions about the papacy, but thought it politic not to reject the idea outright. He would attend, he indicated, so long as all the lost papal provinces were returned. But he recognized the dangerous situation in which the papacy found itself. It was defended by a French army. Napoleon had maintained the army in Rome because he had believed it would preserve the loyalty to him of French Catholics. But now he had other priorities, such as opposing the unification of Germany, that were at conflict with his support for the Pope. The Pope himself made matters worse by calling the bishops of the world to what became the First Vatican Council. On the agenda was the definition of papal infallibility, a doctrine highly unpopular with governments who had Catholic citizens.

The crisis came, however, not with the question of infallibility – a doctrine with which Antonelli concurred even if, like so many others, he thought the definition inopportune – but with the outbreak of the Franco-Prussian war. It started on 18 July 1870; the definition of infallibility occurred on 19 July. On 20 July the Council Fathers were sent home. Antonelli was informed before the end of the month that French troops were being withdrawn: they left Rome on 5 August. The way was now open for the government of Italy to seize the city. Antonelli advised Pio Nono to talk to the Italian government, and Victor Emmanuel sent a representative to talk to him, but the Pope would not meet him, though Antonelli did. When presented with the draft proposals for guaranteeing the safety of the Pope, the Cardinal Secretary of State responded that because the Italian government was a constitutional one, it could change, and it could not oblige its successor governments. Therefore the guarantees being offered were worthless.

On 20th September 1870 the Italian army entered Rome. Antonelli had advised the Pope that there should be no attempt to defend the city as it was doomed to fall, and any loss of life would only make the situation worse. Pope Pius, however, insisted on token resistance so that it would be clear to other governments who was the aggressor. At the fall of Rome – Pope Pius's military commander signed the capitulation in the afternoon of the 20th – Antonelli once again offered his resignation, and once again it was refused.

The capitulation agreement left the Leonine City, the area around St Peter's, under papal control, though the papal army having been disbanded, Italian troops had to be called in when it was feared that unruly citizens might invade the Vatican. There were practical matters to be addressed. Vatican money lay in banks now under Italian control: the Italian government gave it back. The government wanted the papal palace of the Quirinal as the residence for the King. Antonelli objected, but it went anyway. There were even matters beyond the borders of Italy claiming his attention. Bismarck, the German Chancellor, wanted the Pope to advise the Catholic Centre Party to moderate its opposition to his policies. Antonelli rather suggested that something might be done, but because Pope Pius was a firm supporter of the Centre Party, Antonelli had to be one likewise.

The Cardinal Secretary of State had always displayed immense loyalty to the Pope even though Pius had sometimes, and disastrously, rejected his advice. The service of the papacy was the only life he ever had. He never left Italy, and rarely travelled outside Rome. Even in Rome he seems almost to have had no social life. After his death a young woman, Countess Loreta Lambertini, claimed to be his daughter with a right to his estate, but not even the Italian courts upheld the suit. He left quite a deal of money, but his family had been wealthy almost before he set out on his clerical career. He had amassed a collection of precious stones: those he bequeathed to the Vatican museum.

After suffering from gout for some years, he died on 6 November 1876. Two days later he was buried, almost secretly, in his family's tomb in Rome's Campo Verano cemetery.

Rafael Merry del Val

Rafael Maria José Pedro Francisco Borja Domingo Gerardo de la Santísima Trinidada Merry del Val had an ancestry even more complicated than his name. He was born at 33 Portman Square, London, on 10 October 1865, the son of the secretary to the Spanish legation in London; his father was also called Rafael. His mother, Sofia, was the daughter of Pedro de Zulueta, a banker, and Sophia, née Wilcox, who was part Scottish, part Dutch. Despite his grandfather's Spanish background (Pedro's father was a political refugee), Pedro and Sophia were both converts to Catholicism under the influence of the Oxford Movement. The 'Merry' of Merry del Val was a faint reminder of distant Irish roots.

At the age of nine Rafael was sent to Bayliss House school in Slough, and then to Remington's, a school in Brighton which was run by a convert Anglican clergyman. When he was twelve his father was appointed Spanish minister to Belgium so the family moved to Brussels. There he attended first Notre Dame de Namur, and then the Jesuit St Michael's College. He thus effortlessly became trilingual, with English and Spanish at home, and French at school in Brussels. Later in Rome he was to become fluent in Italian, and he made an effort to learn German. He was formally Spanish by nationality but, apart from Italy, he seems to have felt himself most at home in England: he once told an inquisitive questioner that he dreamt in English. He may perhaps have chosen to say so because it was what his interrogator wanted to hear – that he was unfailingly courteous was one of his characteristics regularly remarked upon.

He returned to England after deciding to become a priest and entered the seminary at Ushaw, near Durham, where he was a popular pupil. He was bright, but he was also a sportsman, keen on riding, shooting and swimming. He enjoyed his time at Ushaw, and carried away fond memories of it, but he did not stay long. His father had become Spanish ambassador to Vienna and he decided his son ought to go to Rome for his priestly education. The Scots College was chosen, but before he could take up residence his father arranged an audience with Pope Leo XIII. The Pope, on discovering that he was destined for the Scots College, insisted that he instead attend the Academy for Noble Ecclesiastics, the training school for papal diplomats. He did so, attending lectures at the Jesuit-run Gregorian University, but it must have been an awkward position for him to be in: he was the only non-priest among the alumni.

Further potential embarrassment was to follow. In 1887 he was sent to London in the entourage of the papal emissary to offer Queen Victoria the Pope's congratulations on her golden jubilee. For the occasion he was made a papal privy chamberlain, which entitled him to be called Monsignor, though he was still only in minor orders. He was ordained priest at the end of December

1888, and chose to celebrate his first mass in the rooms of the founder of the Jesuits, Ignatius Loyola, in the Jesuits' main church in Rome, the Gesù. In the meantime he had been a member of papal delegations to the funeral of the German Emperor and the coronation of his successor, and to the court of Franz Joseph in Vienna. He no doubt owed his meteoric rise through the ranks to his facility with languages, but the fact that he was extremely good-looking may also have helped.

He continued his studies at the Gregorian and at the Academy, eventually graduating with doctorates in philosophy and theology, and also in canon law. The energy he had once devoted to sport he now spent in Trastevere, where he founded an association for poor boys of the area to whom he taught soccer, and failed to teach cricket. He said constantly that it was his dearest wish to undertake pastoral work in England. This may have simply been the pious remark which is expected of clergy, but among the poor of Trastevere he found an outlet for his pastoral zeal. It was to last all his life, and when he was in Rome he rarely failed visit Trastevere each day.

At the very end of 1891 he became an active member of the papal court. His role was a modest one as privy chamberlain: he had to greet visiting dignitaries, chat to them while they were awaiting an audience with the Pope, and then lead them into the papal presence. It gave him, however, constant access to Leo XIII, who came to rely upon him for intelligence on the affairs of England. It was a time when England was high on the papal agenda. Lord Halifax, through a chance meeting with the Abbé Portal in Madeira, had conceived a plan for the reunion of the Catholic and Anglican Churches. No sooner had Merry del Val heard of the project than he was campaigning against it, accusing the Church of England of ignorance of sixteenth-century history. When the Pope set up a commission to investigate the question of the validity of Anglican Orders Merry del Val was made its secretary, though it was no secret he was very far from neutral on the issue. When the Commission had reported unfavourably on Anglican Orders, Merry del Val, along with his friend, the Benedictine Aidan Gasquet, were charged with drafting the papal encyclical *Apostolicae Curae* of 1896, which declared the Orders of the Church of England to be invalid. He then composed a prayer for the conversion of England which was used in English Catholic churches for over half a century.

In March 1897 he was given his first major task. The Canadian federal government had requested a French-speaking Apostolic Delegate with knowledge of British institutions to help resolve a crisis over schools in Manitoba. Merry del Val was sent and was received with considerable pomp in Canada, where he helped to settle the dispute. On his return to Rome he was asked by the Pope to become president of the Academy for Noble Ecclesiastics of which he had only recently ceased being a student. He held the post from 1899 to 1903.

Meanwhile he also been made a consultor to the Congregation of the Index.

Ecclesiastical preferment was now inevitable. On 6 May 1900 he was conse-crated Archbishop of Nicaea by the then Secretary of State, Cardinal Rampolla, after the ceremony giving a dinner for two hundred residents of Trastevere. In 1903, after the death of Cardinal Vaughan, his ally in the battle over Anglican Orders, his name was promoted as a possible replacement at Westminster. Also in 1903 died his great patron Pope Leo XIII. He was elected as secretary to the conclave, in which role he refused to communicate to the cardinals the veto of the Austrian Emperor against the election of Rampolla to succeed Leo. It was left to the embarrassed Cardinal Archbishop of Kraków, whom the Emperor had charged with the task, to himself announce the veto.

The cardinals elected Giuseppe Sarto to the papacy: he took the name Pius X. Sarto was the son of a postman and a seamstress from a remote part of Italy. He needed someone with the urbane flair and language skills of Merry del Val. On 12 November he was created cardinal priest of Santa Prassede, and imme-diately named Secretary of State. It was not just the former Secretary of State, Rampolla, who was, as it were, reduced to the ranks: Rampolla's number two, Giacomo della Chiesa, was despatched to Bologna without the customary red hat. There was to be a new regime in the Vatican.

The major crisis facing the new Secretary of State was France, where rela-tions between Church and State were increasingly fraught. When in 1904 the President of France visited Italy he naturally paid a call upon the King of Italy, who was residing in the former papal palace of the Quirinal. Merry del Val protested in the strongest, and undiplomatic, terms at the recognition of the Kingdom of Italy by France, which he regarded as an insult to the Pope. When the protest was published in France, the French government withdrew its ambassador and moved to revoke the concordat between the Holy See and France which had been drawn up under Napoleon. This meant that all fund-ing for the Church ceased and Church property became the property of the State. The government proposed setting up *associations culturelles* (= associa-tions for worship) to administer the property, but Merry del Val was adamantly opposed, though most of the French bishops were in favour of this solution. The problem of the *associations* was that they would have been lay-controlled, and neither the Pope nor his Secretary of State approved of that: Merry del Val composed the intransigent encyclical which rejected this solution. The Law of Separation was finally passed in February 1911, leaving the French bishops entirely dependent on the papacy.

There were a number of other initiatives from the Vatican which also increased its control over the Church. The encyclical of 1905, *In fermo pro-posito*, brought all lay organizations firmly under the control of the bishops, though the Vatican allowed a relaxation of the decree *Non expedit* which had forbidden Catholics to become involved in Italian politics. The main campaign of the pontificate was against the Modernists, those who, especially in Scripture studies, were using modern techniques to interpret the Bible. There was a philosophical and theological underpinning to the movement, and one of its leading exponents was the English Jesuit George Tyrrell. Even before he had become a cardinal Merry del Val had conspired with Cardinal Vaughan of Westminster against Tyrrell, who was eventually driven out of the Church. It seems, however, that in the general attack on Modernism, though he helped compose the papal encyclical on the subject, Merry del Val was rather more cautious than others in the Vatican. But there was no doubt about his innate conservatism. He was a supporter of *Action Française* which Pius X's successor-but-one, Pius XI, condemned (see the life of Cardinal Billot, p. 220). There was one final gaffe on Merry del Val's part when, in 1914, he appeared to signal to the Austrian ambassador that the Vatican would support Austria's assault on Serbia: his father, after all, had been Spanish ambassador to the court in Vienna, a court which the cardinal knew well: in 1907 he had been awarded the Austrian Grand Cross of St Stephen.

At the conclave following the death of Pius X in 1914, Giacomo della Chiesa, only recently elevated to the purple, became Pope Benedict XV, and he promoted Pietro Gasparri (see p. 194) to the office of Secretary of State in place of Merry del Val. Merry del Val was given the Holy Office to run, but the campaign against Modernism was wound down by the new pope, leaving him rather less to do. In the conclave of 1922 he was a possible candidate, but when his own votes fell away he tried to strike a bargain with Achille Ratti, who was about to be elected Pope Pius XI, to keep Gasparri out of the Secretariat of State. Ratti refused to bargain, which in any case was against the rules of the conclave: Merry del Val should have suffered automatic excommunication for his interference (see the life of Gasparri, p. 194).

Pius XI appointed him papal delegate in 1926 for the celebrations in Assisi to mark the seven hundredth anniversary of the death of St Francis. It was a particularly splendid occasion which Merry del Val relished, made remarkable by the fact that the papal train was used to convey him, the first time it had left the Vatican station since 1870. It was the first time that Italian Church and State had collaborated since the fall of the Papal States. The cardinal accepted the greetings offered him by Mussolini's representative, and returned them.

At this same period he was again concerned with the affairs of England. The conversations which Lord Halifax and the Abbé Portal had initiated between Anglicans and Catholics were reopened at Malines. The cardinal was as antipathetic now as he had been back in the 1890s, and unfortunately for the conversations he managed to persuade the Pope that his was the voice to be listened to. A papal encyclical, *Mortalium animos* of 1928, appeared to rule out any future improvement in ecumenical relations.

In addition to the Holy Office, in 1914 he had been made archpriest of the Vatican basilica. With his love of ceremony, this was an office which suited him well, and he was punctilious in fulfilling his duties. Although he had a taste for pomp, he had not lost his schoolboy delight in practical jokes. He often went about (relatively) incognito, and enjoyed the confusion upon sundry nuns and local clergy when his true status was revealed. He also kept up his links with the association for boys in Trastevere. It was a group of these boys who carried his coffin to its final resting place, near the tomb of Pope Pius X in the Vatican. He had died on 26 February 1930 while being operated upon for appendicitis.

Pietro Gasparri

In any political history of Europe during the twentieth century the names of popes would inevitably be mentioned, those of cardinals, on the other hand, would occur rarely if at all. One notable exception, however, would almost certainly be Pietro Gasparri, Cardinal Secretary of State during two pontificates. That is a fairly uncommon achievement. A newly elected pope may for a while retain the officials of his predecessor, but it is usually the case that he wants to bring in his own team. Gasparri had served Benedict XV as Secretary of State. He continued to serve Pope Pius XI from Pius's election until the cardinal's retirement in 1930. It was an unusually eventful career.

He was born at Capovallazza in the diocese of Nocera in Umbria on 15 May 1852, the youngest of nine children. His parents were sheep farmers, but his mother had a brother who was archpriest of the cathedral at Nepi, and vicar general of the diocese. He personally undertook Pietro's early education, then sent him to the seminary at Nepi. The seminary closed, and on 18 September 1870, already in minor orders, he entered the Roman seminary of Sant' Apollinare. He was a diligent student, and graduated with a doctorate – for a time he also taught at the seminary, as well as at the missionary college of Propaganda Fide, the Urbanianum. He was ordained priest in the Lateran basilica at the end of March 1877, and became chaplain and secretary to Cardinal Teodolfo Mertel, an Italian cardinal of Germany ancestry. Mertel was one of the last cardinals who was never ordained priest, and consequently it was his custom to attend the mass of his chaplain.

Thanks to Mertel's patronage he was offered a post at the recently founded Institut Catholique in Paris. He was there from 1880 to 1898, largely engaged in the teaching of canon law. Church law was then a jumble of sometimes contradictory texts, known as the *Corpus Iuris Canonici*, and it was Gasparri's particular skill to reorganize these texts for teaching purposes into a coherent pattern. In the course of it he also produced a number of books, important in their day, on marriage, the Eucharist and the sacrament of ordination.

The last was perhaps particularly significant. Drawing on this work he also produced *De valeur des ordinations anglicanes*. In it he showed himself hostile to the idea that the sacrament of orders conveyed in the Anglican ordination ceremony was a valid one. Possibly it was this stance that led to his being appointed to a committee established by Pope Leo XIII in 1896 to study the question of Anglican ordinations. In September of the same year the Pope issued a bull, *Apostolicae curae*, which declared such orders 'absolutely null and utterly void'. By that time, however, Gasparri had studied the question further and had changed his mind, though he could not change the Pope's. He contributed to an ecumenical journal, and in the 1920s was a supporter of the Malines conversations which attempted, in vain, to settle the differences between Canterbury and Rome.

Gasparri would have preferred to continue his academic career, but the Vatican had other plans. In the summer of 1894 he was sent to work in the Apostolic Delegacy in Washington, and in the summer of 1897 he was sent to Latin America to help prepare a plenary conference of Latin American hierarchies. He returned to Paris, but there received news that he was to be made a bishop, with the title of Caesarea in Palestine. He was consecrated in Paris in 1898. This was a prelude to the role of Apostolic Delegate extraordinary in Ecuador, Peru and Bolivia. He spent most of his time in Lima, but it was Ecuador, where the government was actively hostile to the Church, that chiefly concerned the Holy See. Gasparri managed, however, to agree a revision of the concordat – the treaty – between the Holy See and Ecuador, which was something of a minor triumph.

He returned to Rome as a permanent member of the Congregation for Extraordinary Affairs, the Holy See's office of foreign affairs. He almost immediately ran into problems with Pope Pius X's Secretary of State, Rafael Cardinal Merry del Val (see p. 190), and with the Pope himself. The issue was France. Its anticlerical government repudiated the concordat which, in 1801, the Holy See had concluded with Napoleon. Pope Pius, abetted by Merry del Val, fired off an angry (it was entitled *Vehementer*) encyclical condemning the action of the French but without directly rejecting the proposals on Church–State relations which the government was enacting. But this failed to move the government, while the French right wing wanted sterner action. Pius obliged with another encyclical, *Gravissimo*, six months after *Vehementer*, rejecting outright the government's plans and thereby leaving the bishops, who had been reluctantly prepared to cooperate, with no official structures by which to run the Church. *Gravissimo* was published without any reference to the Congregation for Extraordinary Affairs, whose business it was to conduct relations with states. Gasparri, it was known, had been ready to be much more accommodating, far less intransigent.

The confrontation with Merry del Val was, however, postponed. Apart from a brief mission to Syria and Palestine in 1907 Gasparri found himself otherwise engaged. In April 1904 he was appointed as secretary of the commission to codify the Church's law. It was to occupy him for the remainder of Pius X's controversial pontificate. To some on the right wing the idea of a 'Code' of Church law sounded too much like the Napoleonic Code, the introduction of French Revolutionary ideas into the heart of Catholicism. To those on the left the Code seemed to be yet another way of centralizing papal authority. The latter were, of course, correct. The Code assigned to the Pope the right to nominate bishops throughout the world, a right which had not been his during the history of the Church, and certainly was not when the Code was drawn up. It has, of course, become so since. But compared to the *Corpus Iuris Canonici* which it finally replaced in 1917, the Code was a model of clarity and ease of use. Late in life Gasparri claimed that he had been the one to think up the idea.

In December 1907 Pietro Gasparri was made a cardinal priest, with the title of S. Bernardo alle Terme. When the conclave came in August 1914 Gasparri was the Camerlengo, the cardinal in charge of summoning the cardinals and arranging for their meetings before the conclave started. In the first ballot he received one vote, but his own preference was for the man who became Pope Benedict XV, Giacomo della Chiesa. Benedict promptly appointed him Secretary of State in place of Merry del Val.

By this time Europe was at war. Gasparri was closely involved with all Benedict's efforts to bring about peace among the warring powers. However the suggestion that, despite Gasparri's long association with France, the Holy See tended to favour the Austro–German Axis is not perhaps without substance. As may be seen in the life of Cardinal La Fontaine (p. 50), after Italy joined the alliance of France and Great Britain, Austria emerged as the greatest threat to the country, and the Vatican was concerned about the balance of power in Europe after the war was over, proposing at one point that Catholic Bavaria might unite with Catholic Austria to create thereby a buffer zone between Italy and a largely Protestant Germany. It was also upset by the fact that Britain seemed to be conceding too much to Orthodox Russia in the Middle East, and by the Pact of London, which laid down that the Vatican would be left out of any peace conference. Gasparri judged that the Treaty of Versailles was far too harsh on Germany and tried to moderate the demands for reparation, which were of a scale the Vatican considered to be unjust. France remained unmoved.

After the war Gasparri made strenuous efforts to repair relations with France, aided by the canonization of the French hero Joan of Arc. He also moved to improve relations with the Kingdom of Italy. Clandestine talks had begun in 1919, and when Benedict XV died in January 1922 Gasparri included Italy among the states which he formally notified. Merry del Val was incensed, arguing that Gasparri, still Camerlengo, had exceeded his authority and was therefore excommunicate. It was, however, Merry del Val himself who was the more likely candidate for excommunication. In the conclave which elected Achille Ratti as Pius XI Gasparri polled a dozen or so votes in the first ballots, but then his support dropped away, as had those of his opponents, the intransigent cardinals. The intransigents hatched a plan, not so much to prevent the election of Ratti, as to ensure that Gasparri would not be reappointed as Secretary of State. Merry del Val and Cardinal de Lai approached Ratti and offered to put their votes behind him if he were to undertake not to have Gasparri as his Secretary of State. It would be a mistake, de Lai is supposed to have told him. Ratti responded that, were he elected, he would undoubtedly make many mistakes during his pontificate, and the reappointment of Gasparri would be the first of them. But trying to strike this sort of pact, as Gasparri himself pointed out, was flatly contrary to Pius X's regulations of the conclave, and should have incurred excommunication.

What most upset the intransigents was Gasparri's readiness to agree to treaties between the Holy See and nation states which recognized the separation of Church and State, a situation which many in the Vatican were forced to accept in practice but which they rejected in theory. The test case was the Kingdom of Italy itself, which in 1870 had seized Rome, the last remaining territory of the Papal States. There had since been a stand-off, with Catholics forbidden to involve themselves in Italian politics. This policy had been weakened gradually, and the Vatican did not disown the Catholic Partito Populare, led by the priest Luigi Sturzo, when it was established.

But the overriding consideration of the Vatican was the solution of the 'Roman Question', safeguarding the position of the Holy See within the territory of the Kingdom of Italy. The rise of Benito Mussolini, to whom Gasparri was sympathetic, seemed to hold out hope. Under Gasparri as Secretary of State the Vatican had agreed a string of concordats: why not one with Italy? But Italy wanted to keep the Church out of politics. That meant the Partito Populare had to go: it was dissolved, and Sturzo exiled to London. In 1929 the Lateran Pacts were agreed with Italy, establishing the independent Vatican City State and, in a concordat, regulating relations between the Vatican and the Italian government.

Cardinal Gasparri does not seem to have been a major figure in the final rounds of negotiations on the Lateran Pacts. He resigned from the post of Secretary of State on 7 February 1930, to be replaced by Eugenio Pacelli. He spent his final years once again at work on canon law, this time preparing the way for the codification of the law of those Eastern-rite Churches in communion with Rome.

He died in Rome on 18 November 1934. Shortly before his death he gave all he had to the Congregatio de Propaganda Fide, the Congregation which oversees the work of the Catholic missions.

Agostino Casaroli

In modern times it has been the popes who have made history rather than their cardinals. But in histories of East–West relations during the period of the Cold War the name of Agostino Casaroli is as likely to be found as those of the popes he served – John XXIII, Paul VI and John Paul II.

He was born at Castel San Giovanni, near Piacenza, on 14 November 1914. His biographies usually state that his family was of 'modest means' – in fact his father was the local tailor. He attended school in Piacenza, then entered the episcopal seminary of Bedonia. He was ordained priest in Piacenza in May 1937, and travelled to Rome to undertake further studies in canon law at the Lateran Pontifical Athenaeum, where he received a doctorate, and then at the Academy for Noble Ecclesiastics, which trains Vatican diplomats. He taught there from 1958 to 1961. In 1940 he began his Vatican career in the Secretariat of State in the section for Extraordinary Affairs, as the department was called which handled the Holy See's relations with other sovereign states. It was a humble beginning, working as a secretary and in the archives. After the war he undertook a course of professional development provided by the Italian Society for International Organizations. He had slowly risen through the ranks, and in 1945 was made a privy chamberlain, which meant he was entitled to be called Monsignor. In 1950 he was transferred to the Latin American desk and began to travel on Vatican business, to Rio de Janeiro for a conference of Latin American bishops in 1955, to Spain in 1958 to deliver the red biretta to a newly created Spanish cardinal, in 1961 to Vienna for a UN conference on diplomatic relations, followed by one on consular relations. To these last he went as head of the delegation, for he had been promoted to Undersecretary of State.

This trip to Vienna was a turning point in his career. For the first time he met officials from the Soviet states. The Pope was now John XXIII, whose attitude to the communist regimes of the Eastern bloc was much less confrontational than that of his predecessor, Pope Pius XII. Casaroli now began to make regular trips to Eastern Europe, Prague and Budapest being the first destinations a few weeks after the Vienna meeting, using a passport made out in his mother's maiden name so that he could travel incognito. In Prague in May 1963 he negotiated the release of Cardinal Josef Beran, who was persuaded to leave for Rome. Beran expected to return to Czechoslovakia. The Prague government and Casaroli knew otherwise. The first written agreement with a communist state was that with Hungary, signed in Budapest in September 1964 after negotiations, alternately in Rome and Budapest, which had gone on for a year and a half. It was, said Casaroli, a practical agreement. By that he meant it was not all-encompassing, or what in a perfect world the Vatican might hope for, but it was a start. There had been no new bishops for fourteen years, now there could be five more, chosen from a list of names acceptable to both the Vatican and the government but ideal for neither. There was also an agreement that, although they were to take an oath of loyalty to the State, they were to be obliged by it only insofar as it was compatible with their status as clergy. Casaroli hoped that this agreement might serve as a basis for a further softening of the communist government's hostility to the Church, but that was not to happen for some time.

The communist bloc was not Casaroli's only concern. Just before the signing in Budapest he had been in Tunisia agreeing with the Tunisian government a protocol on the status of the Catholic Church in that country. But Eastern Europe was his main focus. He more than anyone was the architect of what became known as the Vatican's 'Ostpolitik'. His technique was not to push hostile governments too far, to recognize the limits of what was possible, and to persuade such regimes that it was in their own best interests to cooperate with an understanding Vatican rather than to run the risk of international condemnation by persecuting the Catholic Church. His aims, therefore, were limited, and he himself risked being misunderstood by some of his more gung-ho coreligionists. After his elevation on 30 June 1979 with the title of cardinal priest of Sancti XII Apostoli, he was occasionally called the 'red cardinal' by people who took his careful diplomacy to reflect sympathy for the communist regimes with which he had to deal. As his autobiographical jottings, published after his death, clearly reveal, it was nothing of the sort.

It is possibly true that, during the era of the Ostpolitik, the communist bloc gained rather more from the negotiations than the Church. When in 1970 the USSR's foreign minister proposed what became the Conference on Security and Cooperation in Europe of 1975 (it was preceded by a meeting of foreign ministers in 1973 which Casaroli attended), Pope Paul and Casaroli were ready to agree. Their justification was that the Helsinki Agreement, as it became in 1975, could guarantee freedom of religion. In practice the situation of the Church in Eastern Europe after Helsinki was little better than it had been before, while the USSR got what it wanted, an endorsement of the prevailing political boundaries. It may be that the Vatican diplomat in Casaroli got the better of the pastor: this was the first occasion in modern times that the Holy See had been formally a part of an international treaty.

There were certainly those within the Church in countries with communist regimes who were less than happy at the Vatican's intervention in what they considered to be their affairs. The most obvious example is Poland, where a powerful Church had been battling a hostile government for over two decades, and the bishops thought they could handle the situation on their own. They did not want to be sidelined in any discussions between the regime and the Holy See. The Polish Primate Cardinal Wyszynski made that clear both before Casaroli visited the country in 1975, and again during his stay – most remarkably when in Warsaw cathedral he preached before the Vatican's foreign minister in Italian, so that he would not miss the point. Casaroli was not put off. He established permanent relations with the Warsaw government, promising that the bishops of Poland would be kept up to date with what was being discussed.

Wyszynski could lecture him the way he did perhaps because Casaroli at this point was still only an Archbishop: he had been consecrated in St Peter's on 16 July 1967. Pope John Paul II who, as a Polish bishop, had been involved in the debates about Vatican intervention (he was thought less confrontational than Wyszynski), created him pro-Secretary of State in April 1979. He was 'pro' because not yet a cardinal. The red hat followed in June, as has been remarked. In May 1985 he became a cardinal bishop, with the title of Porto e Santa Rufina. He had now full charge, under the Pope, of the Vatican's foreign relations, but the tensions were by now much less. In 1988, when the Russian Orthodox celebrated the millennium of the arrival of Christianity in their lands, he was in Moscow as a guest – though he took the opportunity to address Mikhail Gorbachov on the subject of Catholics in the USSR.

But he also had other problems to address which were closer to home. Pope John Paul made him not only Secretary of State but also President of the Commission for the Vatican City State. He had to deal with the murky finances of the Vatican in the aftermath of the collapse of the Banco Ambrosiano, and the role of American Archbishop Paul Marcinckus in the affair. He resigned the latter office in 1984, and from the Secretariat of State on 1 December 1990. Despite his official duties he had, throughout his life, maintained a pastoral role in Rome. After his retirement he devoted his time to young people in the city who had been sent to gaol. He died in Rome on 9 June 1998, and was buried under the high altar of his titular church, the basilica of the Twelve Apostles.

The Exes

Thanks to the indefatigable Salvador Miranda we have on his website 'The Cardinals of the Holy Roman Church' a list of all those who resigned the office of cardinal from the mid fifteenth century down to Cardinal Billot in the twentieth (see below, p. 220). There are twenty-two of them. In the Catholic Church the Pope can grant a dispensation for practically anything except sin, and that, of course, can be forgiven. But there is no great problem of dispensing someone from holding the rank of cardinal. Although as has been seen in the Introduction (p. 9) cardinals in the middle ages made extravagant claims for their office – they were to the pope as the apostles were to Christ – no one is 'ordained' with a cardinal's hat. It is a service to the Church which can be terminated, either by the Pope of the day or by the individual cardinal involved. If the cardinal in question is not in sacred orders, so much the easier.

At the beginning of the fifteenth century when there were two, and then three, rival claimants for the title of Pope, popes of each of the three 'obediences', Rome, Avignon and Pisa, had their own College of Cardinals, but when the three were united in one again in 1417 all the cardinals were recognized as such and even the egregious Pope John XXIII (see p. 40) was able peacefully to return from papal to cardinatial status. The same was not true of the creations of the antipope Felix V (1439–49). After his abdication they were all demoted, though the former Felix, who had been Duke of Savoy and a devout layman before his irregular election, became a cardinal.

There were a couple of ex-cardinals who had simply not wanted to be cardinals, and were therefore allowed to decline the office, but mainly they wished to withdraw because they wanted to get married. In several cases marriage had become something of an obligation: the cardinal's elder brother having died without issue, the cardinal had to take a wife to preserve the family lineage. Sometimes it was simply a desire to abandon the celibate life which was an obligation (though often not observed) of the status of cleric. As Camillo Pamphilj is reported to have said, quoted below, 'Much as I admire the virtue of chastity, I find myself unable to practise it without a wife.' Similarly one cannot but have sympathy for Luis Antonio Jaime de Borbón y Farnesio (1727–85), the younger son of King Philip V of Spain, who had the rank of cardinal foisted on him at the age of eight. He bore it for twenty years, but then, as Salvador Miranda puts it, 'Conscious of his lack of religious vocation and his strong sexual drive' he asked to be released.

There were of course some of those who resigned who did so out of piety. One of those who did not want it, but nearly had it imposed by the will of the King of Spain, simply wanted to spend his life preaching, hearing confessions and caring for the poor. Ardicino della Porta wanted to retire to a monastery to live a life of solitude. He was allowed to do so, though some among the remaining cardinals demurred, and they required his presence in the conclave of 1492, so although he abandoned the life of a cardinal he had not, it seems, been allowed totally to abandon the office. In the nineteenth century Carlo Odelscalchi – a member of one of the 'dynastic' families – resigned so as to become a Jesuit.

A handful of cardinals have been dismissed from office. The story of Odet de Coligny is told below. His fate was similar to that of Étienne-Charles de Loménie de Brienne who, contrary to the instructions of the Pope accepted a bishopric under the French Revolutionary government. Later, when in prison and under threat of death, he apostatized. He died suddenly the following day, still in his prison cell. Rome itself was not free from the turmoil of the Revolution. Feeling himself harassed by the Roman Republic, Tommaso Antici resigned his office in search of a quiet life, though he gave old age as his excuse. For seemingly similar reasons Vincenzo Altieri resigned in 1798, and his resignation was accepted, but after the death of Pius VI he changed his mind and handed over a retraction to the dean of the Sacred College. But he was too late. He died before the matter could be dealt with.

Some cardinals were dismissed for dishonest or other forms of scandalous behaviour. Adriano Castellesi, mentioned immediately below, was one such, and Niccolò Coscia another, though in Coscia's case he was allowed back into the Sacred College after expressing his contrition. Innocenzo Ciocchi del Monte has been included even though he was not strictly speaking ever dismissed from the College. He was, however, held in prison for a long period of time and, when released and permitted to return to Rome, was ostracized by the other cardinals. As will be seen, he had led a particularly colourful life.

Adriano Castellesi

Very little indeed is known about Adriano Castellesi before in 1488 he was sent to Scotland to intervene in the civil war there. He was born in Corneto, now Tarquinia. His date of birth is uncertain but, as he was senior enough in the papal service to be sent on the mission to Scotland, he was probably born about the year 1460. The mission was a complete failure because before his arrival King James III had been either killed in battle, or assassinated soon afterwards. He returned to Rome, but on his passage through England met King Henry VII. It is not surprising that there should have been an encounter between the monarch and a papal emissary, all the more so because the papal interest and the English interest coincided: James III had espoused the policy, unpopular in Scotland, of an alliance with England. Henry seems to have been charmed by the vivacious Italian, as many were, and it was no doubt the King's influence that gained him the highly profitable office of collector of papal taxes in England. And to the money to be made through his role of collector, Castellesi could soon add the income from a prebendary in St Paul's Cathedral and the rectory of the church of St Dunstan's-in-the-East. These were granted in 1492, two years after his return, and in the same year he was granted English nationality. He was also, it seems, provided with a juridical role in the Canterbury diocese.

In 1494 Henry VII sent him back to Rome as his representative. He retained his role as papal collector, indeed being confirmed in it by the Borgia Pope Alexander VI, who also appears to have given him a somewhat ill-defined role to reform the clergy. The duties of collector were undertaken by others on his behalf, one of his proxies being Polydore Vergil, author of the massive *Historia Anglica*, an important, if not always reliable, source for the history of the early Tudor period. Castellesi's role was now to speak for the English King, and he was much involved in the negotiations for the dispensation to permit Prince Henry, later Henry VIII, to marry the widow of his elder brother: a later Pope's refusal to overturn this dispensation was the catalyst for England's break with Rome.

Meanwhile he was making his way in the papal service, becoming clerk of the papal treasury in December 1494 and in 1497 a protonotary apostolic, one of those permitted to engage in the lucrative trade of drawing up ecclesiastical documents. The following year he attempted to purchase the rank of cardinal, but failed. Presumably the offer of twenty thousand ducats was not considered, by the venal Borgias, as being enough. He was however sent that year, 1498, as part of the embassy to congratulate the new King of France on acceding to the throne. Neither King Henry nor the Borgias forgot him. In February 1502 both collaborated in creating him Bishop of Hereford. He was still in Rome: Polydore Vergil was installed at Hereford serving once again as his proxy. He was now much more wealthy. In the consistory of 3 May 1503 he was created a cardinal priest, and later given the title of San Crisogono.

Castellesi, for some years Alexander Borgia's personal secretary, was one of only three Italians in a papal curia otherwise composed of Catalans. Obviously he was close to the pontiff, certainly close enough to throw on 5 August 1503 a farewell party at his palace for Cesare Borgia (see p. 206), who was about to leave Rome. A week after the dinner Alexander fell ill, and died on 18 August. There has been much speculation that Castellesi had poisoned the Pope and his son, or that Cesare had poisoned his father, or that Alexander and Cesare had both attempted to poison Castellesi, but ended up poisoning themselves. Cesare and Castellesi were themselves taken ill after the meal, Castellesi particularly so, but there is no reason to think that anyone had been trying to kill anyone else: it was a very humid month, and malaria and other diseases were rife.

Castellesi was sufficiently recovered to take part in the conclave which elected the short-lived Pius III, during whose pontificate he maintained his status as England's representative at the papal court. And he was flattered by the attention paid to him by Alexander VI's great adversary, Cardinal Giuliano della Rovere, who was swiftly elected to replace Pope Pius, taking the name Julius II. Two days after the election Castellesi was back pressing the royal request that Prince Henry might have a dispensation to marry Catherine of Aragón. But he was feeling less sure of the King's favour. Henry VII may well have wondered how someone would fare who had been so close to Alexander under the pontificate of Alexander's arch enemy. There were others – or, specifically one other, a former friend called Silvestro Gigli – who may have been agitating to replace him. To ensure Henry's favour Castellesi made over in a formal deed his palace, now the Palazzo Torlonia on the Via della Conciliazione, to the English monarch as the residence for English ambassadors to the Pope. This, he no doubt hoped, would identify himself as the permanent English representative. He continued to live in the palace.

The ploy did not work. Julius, who had confirmed Castellesi in his office as papal collector, with the apparent connivance of the King, now made his nephew the English representative. Henry it seems had a degree of sympathy for Castellesi because he now gave him the see of Bath and Wells, a diocese with revenues well in excess of those of Hereford. Castellesi had his detractors at Rome, but Julius appeared to be on his side. Suddenly, however, the cardinal felt threatened. On 1 September 1507 he fled Rome without receiving the requisite papal permission. He was tempted back, but then fled again on 5 October. Julius lost patience. He instructed Polydore Vergil to send no more of the funds he had collected to Castellesi, and await the arrival of a new collector. No one was appointed.

He stayed away from Rome until Julius had died, spending some of his time in Venice, then taking refuge with the Emperor. He wrote to congratulate Henry VIII on his accession in 1509, and received a kindly reply: neither had Henry tried to deprive the cardinal of his income from his English diocese, though Henry VII had requisitioned the Bishop of Bath and Wells's London residence. Castellesi was back in Rome for the election of Cardinal Giovanni de'Medici, for whom he voted, as Leo X on 11 March 1513.

But by now his career was on a downward spiral despite at first having Leo's support. In England there were plans to deprive him of his post as papal collector, an office he had continued to hold, though he had not been in the country for two decades. He managed to retain it, though Polydore Vergil was replaced as his deputy and briefly imprisoned. Castellesi was desperately trying to maintain a semblance of friendship with Thomas Wolsey, who himself became a cardinal at this time, but both in Rome and in England there were people sowing seeds of suspicion about him. When in 1517 there was a plot by some of the cardinals to poison Leo X, Castellesi was implicated. Afraid for his life – one of the cardinals was executed – he fled once again to Venice even though Leo had only put him under house arrest, and imposed a fine. Wolsey was a much more implacable foe: he did not allow the fact that Castellesi had assisted him in his campaign to become a cardinal interfere with his desire to lay hands on his English revenues. The fact that Castellesi was given succour by the Emperor and the Venetians only increased Wolsey's antipathy.

The English agent in Rome, now Silvestro Gigli, was instructed to claim on the King's behalf the palace which Castellesi had made over to him. He also tried to have him deprived of the see of Bath and Wells on the grounds that he had been an absentee bishop. Castellesi offered to resign the bishopric in return for a pension, but Wolsey had already effectively taken it over. But he was also agitating for Castellesi to be deprived of his rank as cardinal, and would not allow Cardinal Campeggi, who had been sent to England as a papal legate, to cross the Channel until this had been done. At the consistory of 5 July 1518 Castellesi was demoted from his cardinatial state on the grounds of disobedience to Leo X: he had fled from the city without papal permission, and then failed to return when ordered to do so. Wolsey got the see of Bath and Wells, and Campeggi got to stay in the Bishop of Bath and Wells' London house.

The now ex-cardinal remained on in Venice, living beside the Grand Canal in the palace of a friend. When he received news that Leo X had died on 1 December 1521, Castellesi hoped to be able to take part in the conclave to elect his successor, his doubtful status notwithstanding. He determined to set out for Rome, but either just before he started, or somewhere on the way, he was murdered, apparently by a servant. The exact date and place of his death, the name of the assassin, and the location of his grave, all remain unknown.

Given all the intrigue in his turbulent career, it is perhaps surprising to discover that Castellesi was also a considerable scholar. He was a more than competent classicist, and wrote a treatise on the correct use of Latin, and another work entitled *On the true philosophy, drawn from four fathers of the*

Church which displayed a considerable knowledge of Scripture, and of Greek and Hebrew as well as Latin. Published in 1507, it was dedicated to King Henry VII.

Cesare Borgia

Of all the very many dubious cardinals of the Roman Church, none is more notorious than Cesare Borgia, not least because he is a major character in Niccolò Machiavelli's *The Prince*, the treatise on how a ruler can gain, and maintain, power. In late 1502 Machiavelli came to spend some months in the court of Cesare's father, the Borgia Pope Alexander VI.

Cesare was the eldest of the four children born to Vannozza Catanei while she was the mistress of Rodrigo Borgia. The exact date of Cesare's birth is unknown, but it was probably in September 1475. The relationship between Vannozza and Rodrigo seems to have ended sometime in the 1480s, and although Vannozza kept close links with her children, they were handed over to someone else for their upbringing. There were three boys, Cesare, Juan and Joffre, and one daughter, Lucrezia Borgia. They were not Rodrigo's only children, however. Three before Cesare had been born to an unknown woman – though some suspect it was also Vannozza. Of these there were two girls and a boy, Pedro Luis, who was therefore Rodrigo's eldest son. (There were, it ought to be said for completeness, more children of Rodrigo who were born while he was Pope, certainly one and just possibly two others.)

It was the fact that he was only the second son of Rodrigo that launched him on an ecclesiastical career for which, even by the standards of the day, he was thoroughly unsuited. He began early to collect benefices, all of them in Spain whence the Borgia, or more correctly Borja, family came. They originated in the province of Valencia, more particularly in Jativa, and Cesare became a canon of Valencia cathedral and archdeacon of Jativa. In 1491 he was named Bishop of Pamplona.

He began his clerical education in Perugia, but in 1491 moved to the University of Pisa where one of his fellow students was Giovanni de'Medici, born the same year but already from the age of just over thirteen a cardinal: he was to become Pope Leo X. After Pisa he moved to Spoleto, and then eventually to Rome. His father did not want him at the coronation, but it was fairly shortly afterwards that he nominated him as Archbishop of Valencia. When he finally took up residence in Rome it was in a palace in Trastevere, where he maintained a princely court. His father wanted to make him a cardinal. In order to do so he decided he had to declare that Cesare was the legitimate offspring of Vannozza and her husband. This he did by means of a papal bull, while issuing another for Cesare personally, assuring that he was the illegitimate offspring of Vannozza and the Pope himself. In September 1493 he created him cardinal deacon of Santa Maria Nuova.

He now began to play a large part in his father's schemes for enriching his family. He married Joffre to the granddaughter of the King of Naples, and when Charles VIII of France invaded Italy on his way to attack Naples, Cesare went with him, ostensibly as a papal legate, in reality as a hostage for his father's good behaviour. But no sooner had Charles left Rome on his way south than Cesare fled. In the conflict with Charles, the French King had been helped by the Orsini family, and Alexander now decided to launch a campaign against them. For that he called back to Italy from Spain his eldest son, Pedro Luis, now Duke of Gandia, whom he invested with further Italian territories.

Although the campaign against the Orsinis went well, it ended with the death of Pedro Luis in mysterious circumstances. He and Cesare had both been visiting their mother Vannozza on 16 June 1497 and had left her house together. The following day Pedro's body was dragged from the Tiber: he had been stabbed nine times. Suspicion fell on Cesare. He had reason to be hostile to his brother, who was clearly Alexander's favourite son. But there were other suspects, not least an assassin in the pay of the Orsinis, and it was evident that Alexander did not suspect his second son because he immediately sent him off to Naples as papal legate – it had been the imminent departure of Cesare on this mission that had been the occasion for the dinner with Vannozza. In Naples for the coronation of King Frederick he performed his duties as a papal legate punctiliously, and contracted syphilis.

Cesare returned to Rome from Naples and attended a gathering of cardinals, but it was already being rumoured that he was finding his ecclesiastical role irksome, and wanted to get rid of it. Alexander fostered the notion of an alliance with the King of Naples through the marriage of Cesare to the King's daughter Carlotta, but neither Frederick nor Carlotta thought much of the idea, especially Carlotta. Alexander's ambitions for his dynasty required a prestigious marriage for Cardinal Cesare, but that was impossible while he was a cleric. On 18 August 1498 he resigned the cardinalate on the grounds that he was endangering his soul by remaining in it. He also resigned his many and profitable ecclesiastical benefices. His fond father promptly made him captain general of the papal armies.

If plans for an alliance with Naples had collapsed, the ever resourceful Pope turned to France, where the new King, Louis XII, also had designs on Naples. But Louis also needed to marry his predecessor's widow, Anne of Brittany, to retain Brittany as part of his kingdom. Inconveniently he was already married. The Church, therefore, had to provide a dispensation. A small commission of cardinals gave their authorization, and Cesare set off for France with the Pope's approval for Louis's marriage, and a red hat for the King's closest advisor. He left with a new title, the Duke of Valence, rather appropriately bestowed by Louis on a former Archbishop of Valencia (he was nicknamed Valentino by the Italians), and in May 1499 an alliance with France was cemented by Cesare's marriage to Charlotte d'Albret, sister of the King of Navarre.

By the end of the year, with the assistance of a largely French army, Cesare was back in Italy overthrowing the semi-independent vicars in the Romagna, reducing the territory to obedience to the papacy, and in the process carving out for himself a duchy. On 25 February 1500 Cesare entered Rome in triumph. The French alliance had been a success, but it had its casualties. When an alliance with Naples seemed attractive, Lucrezia had been married to Alfonso, the illegitimate son of the deceased King of Naples. He had already fled Rome once, fearful of his safety, but was persuaded to return. On 15 July 1500 he was attacked and left for dead on the steps of St Peter's. He did not die, but was nursed back to health by Lucrezia, only to be strangled on 18 August by one of Cesare's men. Whether it was Cesare who had ordered the assassination is not known, but it suited him. And people thought he was to blame, which further damaged an already doubtful reputation.

He did not let this trouble him unduly. In October 1500 the former cardinal marched out of Rome to complete his subjugation of the Romagna, this time at the head of a largely Spanish force, though with French assistance. He was swiftly successful, but then was tempted to turn against Florence, which would have put at risk his French alliance. He and the Florentines reached an understanding without a battle. He then turned south to aid the French in their, again swiftly successful, assault on Naples. His next objective, carefully concealed, was Urbino which, taken by surprise, surrendered without a shot being fired. 'He arrives in one place before it is known he has left another', wrote Machiavelli to his masters in Florence, who were seriously alarmed. So were the French, and rather than risk the alliance Cesare decided to visit the French King in Milan. He went in disguise. His father the Pope was worried he was putting himself in danger, but Louis XII was flattered, and for a month entertained him splendidly, until Cesare decided to rejoin his army.

One reason why he needed to strengthen his links to the French was because he feared a rebellion among the commanders of his mercenaries, the *condottieri*. Once he was back with his troops he set out to invest Senigallia. Just after they had arrived, on 31 December 1502, he summoned the *condottieri* to meet him and enter the city with him. They did so. The city's gates were closed behind them, they were seized and some were put to death. The Orsinis had been part of the conspiracy against Cesare, and when news reached Rome Alexander had Cardinal Orsini imprisoned in Castel Sant'Angelo, where he soon died. But one of the Orsinis escaped capture and threatened war on the

Borgias. Cesare was summoned back to Rome, to which he returned with reluctance, pausing on the way to overcome the most troublesome member of the Orsini family.

Then, just as the Borgia family seemed at the height of its power, Alexander VI died (see p. 203f. for the circumstances). Himself ill, Cesare tried to make a deal with the cardinals gathering for the conclave, and they confirmed him in his office as captain general of the Church, but they also ordered out of Rome all armies and private militias. Nonetheless he still felt powerful enough during the very short pontificate of Pius III, and then threw his weight behind Giuliano della Rovere in the second papal election of 1503, in the hope of currying favour. He had the Spanish cardinals to count on, as well as his possession of Castel Sant'Angelo. When della Rovere was elected as Julius II he was at first uncertain what to do with Cesare, but eventually he demanded the surrender of Borgia strongholds in the Romagna. Cesare refused, and was arrested and confined to the Torre Borgia. He was given his liberty on condition that his castles all surrendered to the papacy which, after some hesitation, they did. Cesare made his way to Naples, but there he was arrested again and sent to Spain.

In Spain he found himself imprisoned near Valencia, thus paying his first ever visit to his former diocese. He was later moved to Medina del Campo, still a prisoner, but he escaped on 25 October 1506 and made his way to the court of his brother-in-law, Jean d'Albret, the King of Navarre. It was a curious move. He had spent only a few weeks with Charlotte d'Albret in the summer of 1499, and after he returned to Italy she never saw him again though he had fathered a daughter by her. Cesare was, however, received into the Navarrese court and not long after his arrival, on 12 March 1507, he died in battle at Viana fighting for the King, and was buried in the church of Santa Maria de Viana. Charlotte spent the rest of her life in mourning for the husband she hardly knew.

Odet de Coligny de Châtillon

The family of Coligny was one of the most distinguished in sixteenth-century France. His father Gaspard was Marshal of France, one of his brothers, also named Gaspard, Admiral of France. As a second son, Odet chose an ecclesiastical career. It seems, however, he was never ordained to any office in the Church, though in his time he held many.

He was born in the castle of Châtillon on 10 July 1517, his mother being Louise de Montmorency, who converted to Calvinism before she died in 1547. Nothing is known of Odet's early life or education until at the age of sixteen he was made a cardinal deacon in the consistory of 7 November 1533 by Pope Clement VII, with the title of SS Sergio e Bacco. Rome had not long before (1527) been devastated by imperial troops and the Pope, who had been forced to live for some time outside the city, was eager to strengthen ties with Francis I of France to counterbalance the power of the Emperor Charles V. Shortly before the consistory he had been in Marseilles to marry his grandniece to the King of France's second son: elevating to the cardinalate a scion of one of France's most noble houses was a further step to cement the relationship. Pope Clement went on to endow him with the valuable Archbishopric of Toulouse, though technically he remained its administrator, not being in episcopal (or any other) orders. He took part in the conclave that elected Clement's successor, Paul III, in October 1534, and was subsequently endowed with a number of abbacies. He also added to Toulouse the administration of the diocese of Beauvais, which he retained until deprived of his cardinalate, though he resigned from Toulouse in 1550.

As a cardinal he voted in successive conclaves, including that of 1559 which elected Pope Pius IV who, the following year, appointed him Grand Inquisitor for France, an odd choice as he had defended Rabelais in 1550: Rabelais dedicated to him one of his books. The Parlement of Paris forbade him from taking up the post. Coligny nonetheless continued to amass benefices almost up to the moment, in April 1561, that, under the influence of his family, he announced that he too had converted to Calvinism. He then served the Protestant cause, particularly as an intermediary between the Huguenots and Queen Regent Catherine de' Medici. In 1562 the Inquisition determined he was a heretic, at which point he abandoned his cardinatial title and the bishopric of Beauvais, subsequently calling himself the Count of Beauvais. Then in December 1564 he married Isabel de Hauteville wearing, it was reported, his full cardinal's robes. But by that time he had been stripped of his rank and all his benefices. In a consistory of 31 March 1563, Pius IV deprived him of all his offices and declared him a heretic.

The wars of religion in France turned against the Huguenots, and on 10 November 1567 he took part in the battle of Saint Denis, when they were defeated by an army under the command of a relative, Anne de Montmorency. In 1568 Odet de Coligny took refuge in London, and attended the court of Elizabeth I in the hope of raising troops, or at least money, to finance his coreligionists: at court his wife was addressed as Mme la Cardinale. In April 1571 he decided to join his brother in the Huguenot stronghold of La Rochelle. He never made it. Possibly at the orders of Queen Catherine de' Medici he was poisoned while in a pilgrim's hostel in Canterbury. One of his servants was suspected, but no assassin was ever prosecuted.

He died on 17 April 1571 and was buried in a tomb, still to be seen, in the

Trinity chapel of Canterbury cathedral. It was meant to be a temporary resting place, but the opportunity of returning his body to France never arose.

Innocenzo Ciocchi del Monte

The town of Fidenza in northern Italy used to be called Borgo San Donnino after its saint, Donninus, who was martyred in 304 and to whom the local cathedral is dedicated. Up to 1927 it had been known as Borgo San Donnino: the name-change recalled its original Latin name, Fidentia Iulia. Innocenzo was born there in 1532. His mother was a beggar; his absent father was quite possibly a mercenary soldier: the boy was undoubtedly illegitimate. He was also bright if never, as it transpired, academically gifted, and with, by all accounts, a sharp wit. He could be uncouth, he was also often quite charming. Relying upon such natural talents as he had, at the age of fourteen or so he left his mother's hovel to seek his fortune – or at the very least a more comfortable existence. He found his way to Piacenza, no great distance away.

At the time the city of Piacenza had as its governor Cardinal Giovanni Maria Ciocchi del Monte, and he managed to enter the cardinal's service as some kind of footman. The cardinal took a liking to him. Given how much he was detested by others later in life, this is surprising, but del Monte took him under his wing, and even provided him with a tutor in an effort to inculcate a semblance of civility and make him more socially acceptable. One task that was given to him was to take care of the cardinal's pet monkey. It attacked him, he broke free and then battled with it. It was no doubt a small incident, but it was remembered. In later life he was nicknamed 'Cardinal Monkey'. After a time Giovanni Maria asked his brother Baldovino to take him on, and Baldovino adopted him: thus he came by the name Innocenzo Ciocchi del Monte and abandoned his original surname, if he had ever had one. The cardinal also provided Innocenzo with an income: he was made provost of the diocese of Arezzo at the age of seventeen.

In February 1550 the fortunes of both Giovanni del Monte and his protégé Innocenzo changed dramatically when the cardinal was elected Pope at the age of 67. On 30 May 1550, in the first consistory of his pontificate the new Pope Julius III made Innocenzo a cardinal deacon against the protests of other members of the Sacred College – the English cardinal Reginald Pole (see p. 43) was particularly outraged. Innocenzo was given the title – and the income – of San Onofrio. Julius was to elevate other members of his family, but in the May consistory only Innocenzo was so honoured, and further honours came when Julius named him Cardinal Nephew. The promotion of 'nephews', real or, as in Innocenzo's case, adoptive was a feature of the way in which popes operated from the fifteenth through to the seventeenth centuries. Though nepotism is now a pejorative term, for renaissance popes it served an essential purpose, and few minded, though there was an occasional pontiff who refused to benefit his relatives. Popes needed assistance and advice and, like the renaissance princes they so closely resembled, they believed that they could rely upon their family as upon no one else.

In Innocenzo's case, however, Pope Julius had got it wrong. Opposition to Innocenzo continued, partly on the grounds that he was illegitimate. Julius resolved that problem with a papal bull, but he could not make his Cardinal Nephew a polished prince of the Church, or cure by a directive his innate indolence. To force him to work, Julius had even insisted that all letters were to be addressed to Innocenzo, but that stratagem failed to make any difference. The work of the Cardinal Nephew went undone, but rather than sack him in favour of one of his other nephews he had created cardinal, Julius simply instituted a new post, that of Cardinal Secretary of State, which survives down to the present day. It was officially part of the office of the Cardinal Nephew, but all Innocenzo had to do was to turn up and sign papers put before him.

It has been suggested that the relationship between Julius and Innocenzo was a homosexual one. There is no evidence of this, and Innocenzo, at least, was aggressively heterosexual. A cardinal at seventeen, he was still an attractive young man. He promptly had an affair with the woman who was afterwards to marry Julius's brother. The Pope protested, but to little avail. Despite his protests, he continued to endow the young man with benefices, including that of the abbey Mont Saint Michel off the coast of Normandy. He became Rome's wealthiest prelate, with an income in the region of 36,000 scudi a year. Yet Julius wanted to lavish more riches on him, perhaps as compensation for the disdain with which he was treated within the Sacred College. He made him administrator of the see of Mirepoix, and would have made him its bishop but for the opposition of King Henry III of France, who was minded to bestow it on someone else.

In the first conclave of 1555 to elect a successor to Julius III, the cardinals chose the reform-minded Marcello Cervini. As Pope Marcellus II he reigned only three weeks, though long enough to rebuke Innocenzo for his licentious behaviour. Marcellus II's successor, Paul IV, was, surprisingly, a touch more sympathetic: he reserved 1,500 scudi from the revenues of Mirepoix for Innocenzo. Just possibly he was angered by the King getting his own way.

Pope Paul died in August 1559. Innocenzo was in the north of Italy, and hurried back to take part in the conclave. As he passed through Nocera there was an altercation between him and an ostler who had, in Innocenzo's view, failed to show him the proper respect due to a cardinal. In a fury he drew a sword and killed the man. The ostler's son rushed to his father's defence, and Innocenzo killed him too. The cardinal then rode calmly on to Rome.

The conclave which elected Pius IV lasted from mid September to Christmas Day 1559. Six months later, at the end of May 1560, the Pope ordered the arrest of Innocenzo, who was charged with the murders in Nocera and other crimes. He was imprisoned in Castel Sant'Angelo and held there (with three other cardinals) for sixteen months before being sent into solitary confinement at the monastery of Montecassino. From Montecassino he was released on the petition of Cosimo II de'Medici, Duke of Tuscany, but was fined 100,000 scudi and stripped of his benefices, being left only with an income of a thousand scudi a year. He was also banished, under supervision, to Tivoli.

He was back to take part in the conclave over the New year, 1565–66, which elected Pope Pius V. In the course of it he committed some misdemeanour – a forbidden note was found on his person, though what it was about and why it was forbidden remains a mystery. He was put under close supervision, and his servants banned from leaving the conclave. Despite that he came to play a major role in the coronation service for the new Pope.

Two years later, however, his crimes again caught up with him. In December 1567 he was charged with what sounds like the rape of two poor women near Siena: a Spanish Jesuit was appointed to investigate the offence. Again Cosimo de'Medici came to his aid, and at the Duke's request he was not this time imprisoned but put in the charge of two Theatines, members of an austere religious order. Two Jesuits were later added to his custodians. The Cardinal Deacon of Santa Maria in Via Lata, as he had become in December 1568, was found guilty of fornication, but his crimes, a tribunal decided, were not enough to have him executed. Instead he was once again sent off to Montecassino.

He stayed in isolation at Montecassino for two years, and then was permitted to move to a monastery in Bergamo, where he stayed for another three years. He was not allowed to attend the conclave of 1572 which elected Pope Gregory XIII, but the new Pope gave him permission to return to Rome. And it was in Rome that he died, on 2 November 1577. In a Church now determined on reform, Innocenzo had become an embarrassment. No one attended the funeral which followed swiftly on his demise. He was buried in the Del Monte church of San Pietro in Montorio, but unlike the other members of his adopted family who lie there, no marble slab marks his grave.

John Casimir

In Robert Bolt's script for *A Man for All Seasons* he has his hero Thomas More rebuke his interrogator Richard Rich, then attorney-general for Wales, for putting his soul at risk for the sake of his office. 'But for Wales?' asks More. At least among English audiences the remark always raises a laugh in what is, for the most part, a sombre play. John Casimir, Jan II Kazimir Vasa, surrendered his cardinal's hat for a rather grander principality, the kingdom of Poland.

He was born in Kraków, then the Polish capital, on 22 May 1609, the son of King Sigismund II of Poland, and his second wife Constance of Habsburg, Archduchess of Austria; he had a younger brother, Jan Olbracht Vasa (1612–34) who also became a cardinal. Both were educated by the Society of Jesus, and both entered the Jesuits though, as will be seen, John Casimir's Jesuit career was extremely short. Sigismund, a generous patron of the arts (he was himself an accomplished painter) and an enthusiastic protagonist of the Counter-Reformation, died in Warsaw in 1632, to be succeeded by his son, and John Casimir's half-brother, Władysław IV Vasa. It was an event which blighted the early years of John Casimir, though not because the two were particularly at odds. Władysław tried to arrange a suitable marriage for John, but without success. The Prince's problems were compounded by the refusal of the Sejm, the Polish parliament of nobles, to approve any allowance. He was not popular, despite his proven skill and valour as a military commander. He was morose, and regarded as overly religious. He was not particularly enamoured of Polish culture, making no secret of his preference for the Austria of his mother. He was therefore made ambassador to the Austrian court at Vienna, but abandoned his office and joined the Austrian imperial army to fight against the French. His regiment was defeated, but he nonetheless returned to Vienna to live for a while at court.

In 1636 he was captured by the French while on his way to Portugal, and spent some time in a French prison. After a couple of years he was permitted to return to Poland, but did not stay there long, setting off again, this time for Germany. In 1643, against his half-brother's vociferous protests, he entered the Society of Jesus in Rome. A Jesuit Prince living in Rome with a claim to inherit not only the crown of Poland but the Grand Duchy of Lithuania, then united to Poland, must have been something of an embarrassment, which Innocent X tried to resolve by creating him a cardinal in the consistory of 28 May 1646. Before he could receive his red hat, however, the restless Prince set off again for Poland. The red hat followed him, but on 9 November 1647 he wrote to the Pope from Poland resigning his cardinatial office. Six months later his half-brother Władysław died, and the following November John Casimir was elected to succeed him: he was crowned on 19 January 1649. At the end of May that year he married Władysław's widow, Marie Louise, daughter of the Duke of Mantua but born and brought up in France, whom he had first met in Paris in 1640. It was the second time he had married her. Her marriage to Władysław had taken place in November 1645: it was done by proxy, John Casimir representing Władysław.

John Casimir had a relatively successful reign in difficult circumstances. He settled the long-drawn-out conflict with the Cossacks, parting them from their erstwhile Tatar allies, and was able to avoid war with Muscovy by threatening to unleash the Cossacks upon it. Peace with the Cossacks proved illusory, and much of John Casimir's reign was engaged in battle with them, as well as with Charles X of Sweden, and with Muscovy, which allied itself with the Swedish King. The invasion of the Swedish armies with Russian support overthrew John Casimir, and in 1655 he and his wife, together with some of the most loyal of the Polish nobility, fled to Silesia. On his return the following year the King placed Poland under the patronage of the Virgin Mary, and pledged not only to recover Polish territory but to reform the constitution to produce a more stable society. He set about the necessary reforms, including the establishment of an hereditary, in place of an elective, monarchy, but was frustrated by both internal politics and external interference. After his wife, who had given him energetic and politically astute support, died on 10 May 1667, he gave up his efforts. He abdicated on 16 September 1668, blaming his failure on the lawlessness of his subjects.

He then retired to France, where the King bestowed on the former Jesuit the abbacy of St Martin in Nevers. He died there on 16 December 1672, and was buried in the abbey of Saint-Germain-des-Prés in Paris. On 31 January 1676, however, he was reinterred in Kraków, in the royal basilica attached to Wawel Castle.

Camillo Pamphilj

There is a problem with recounting the brief life as a cardinal deacon of Camillo Pamphilj: his story inevitably becomes dominated by that of his mother, the redoubtable Olimpia Maidalchini (1594–1657). Olimpia came from Orvieto, and when only eighteen married a merchant of that city who died three years later leaving her extremely wealthy – there was a son of the marriage but he also died. She promptly remarried, by chance meeting the Roman aristocrat Pamphilio Pamphilj in an inn as she made her way on pilgrimage to the shrine of the Virgin at Loreto. The Pamphiljs might have had a palace on the Piazza Navona, but they were short of cash, which is what Olimpia provided. A major beneficiary of her largesse was Pamphilio's brother Giambattista, a prelate in papal service who became nuncio in Naples. Olimpia followed him there, and it was in Naples, on 21 February 1622, that Camillo was born.

Aided by Olimpia's money Giambattista's career took off. He went to France and Spain in the entourage of Urban VIII's nephew, Francesco Barberini. He must have made a good impression because, in 1626, he became papal nuncio in Spain and a cardinal in 1627, though his elevation was not announced for another couple of years. He was elected Pope, as Innocent X, in September 1644. Olimpia's expenditure on him – though he had himself come back from Spain a wealthy man – appeared to have paid off. Immediately after the election she was rewarded with her son Camillo's promotion to the role of captain of the papal armies. In November, he was created a cardinal deacon with the title of Santa Maria in Dominica. He never received any of the clerical orders, and was granted a dispensation to act in his official roles as if he had, including being granted a vote in any conclave. He never participated in any papal election, however, because much to his mother's irritation he resigned the cardinatial rank on 21 January 1647, and less than three weeks later he married Olimpia Aldobrandini, Princess of Rossano, the immensely wealthy widow of Prince Borghese. 'Much as I admire the virtue of chastity,' he is reported to have said, 'I find myself unable to practise it without a wife.'

Camillo may have married for love, he certainly married for money, but he may also have married to escape his mother. She had set herself up in the papal court as the only means of access to her brother-in-law (her own husband, the Pope's brother, had died long before). Innocent was besotted, and did not take any significant decisions without consulting her. Her ambition for her family, and her rapacity for riches, had been observed by the people of Rome long before the election of Innocent, and she was heartily disliked, a dislike which expressed itself in pasquinades. Innocent occasionally made feeble efforts to break free by banishing Olimpia, but she always found her way back. When in 1655 the Pope lay dying after a long illness at the age of 80, she was seen going through his papers and collecting what valuables she could find. Then, however, she refused to pay his funeral expenses, even for a coffin – she was, she said, only a poor widow. His body was placed in a storeroom in St Peter's used by builders, and one of Innocent's former staff – a man he had dismissed – paid for a simple burial in St Peter's. In 1730, however, the tomb was moved to the family church of Sant'Agnese in the Piazza Navona, beside the Palazzo Pamphilj, where a monument was erected. Olimpia herself was exiled from Rome by Innocent's successor, Alexander VII, and in 1657 she died at San Martino al Cimino alone, of the plague, after suddenly having an apparent change of heart and distributing much of her worldly goods on charitable causes. She died before the many lawsuits threatened against her could be brought to court.

Although by the time of her exile Camillo had asserted his independence of his mother, the ex-cardinal and his wife, it is safe to say, must have been vastly relieved by her removal from Rome. So hostile was his mother to his bride that Camillo was ordered by Pope Innocent to leave Rome for Frascati. When they returned to Rome Camillo set about renovating the Villa Doria-

Pamphilj on the Janiculum, and his wife's family's palace, the Palazzo Doria Pamphilj, on corner of the Via del Plebiscito and the Corso. It now houses a gallery displaying many of the pictures which Olimpia Aldobrandini brought with her on her marriage. Camillo was himself a considerable patron of the arts, but, rather like his mother, was far from generous, and some of the artists he employed had to sue for payment of bills. He died in Rome on 26 July 1666 in the Palazzo Doria Pamphilj, which he and Olimpia had made their home after their return from exile in Frascati.

Niccolò Coscia

Niccolò Coscia was born in the small town of Pietradefusi in the Italian province of Avellino, and – crucially for Niccolò's story – in the archdiocese of Benevento. He was born on 25 January 1681 to Vincenzo and Gerolama, but beyond that little or nothing is known of his background. What changed the young boy's life for good was the pastoral visit of a zealous Archbishop, the Dominican Pietro Francesco (Vincenzo Maria in religion) Orsini, who somehow came to encounter him, and took him into his household at Benevento. He was thus started on a clerical career, and though without any obvious sacerdotal training he became a priest on 28 March 1705. Under the patronage of the Archbishop, a cardinal from 1672, he held ever more significant posts in the archiepiscopal household, and in the administration of the cathedral and of the archdiocese. Along the way he somehow acquired a doctorate in civil and ecclesiastical law from La Sapienza, Rome's university, the degree being conferred in 1715.

In the conclave of 1721, which lasted throughout the whole of April and the first week of May, he assisted Cardinal Orsini as his 'conclavist' – the secretary cum manservant who accompanied a cardinal into a papal election. He was also at Orsini's side in the even longer election of 1724, from 20 March to 29 May, which elected his Archbishop as Pope Benedict XIII (Orsini had originally chosen Benedict XIV before learning that the previous Benedict XIII had been an antipope). Orsini was a holy man, who never forgot that he was a friar, and treated the Master General of the Dominicans as his superior. He was horrified at the thought of living in the papal apartments and built himself a hermitage in the Vatican grounds. He was more interested in being Bishop of Rome than occupying the office of Pope, and set off on a round of pastoral visits of his new diocese: he therefore needed someone to look after the affairs of the wider Church – and he alighted upon Coscia, creating him cardinal priest with the title of Santa Maria in Dominica on 11 June 1725. He had already benefited from his patron's elevation, having earlier been made an Archbishop in June 1724 and an assistant at the papal throne in January 1725.

Benedict had imported a whole retinue of Beneventans from his beloved diocese to help him run the Church, something which enormously irritated the entrenched Roman bureaucracy. Though they had put up with that, the cardinals revolted at the proposal to make Coscia one of their number. Several expressed their hostility to Coscia in the consistory, nine voted against the appointment, but his promotion went ahead nonetheless: he was in any case already the most significant person at the papal court, with instant access to Pope Benedict. He was far more influential than any of the other cardinals which, not unnaturally, they resented. They presented a whole host of accusations against Coscia arising from his administration of Benevento, but the Pope was deaf to their complaints. He was not only deaf to them but he made Coscia coadjutor Bishop of Benevento (Benedict had remained Archbishop despite his removal to Rome) with right of succession to the see.

Coscia set about making money, almost immediately amassing great wealth through the sale of offices and benefices. He stripped other apartments in the Vatican to enrich his own so as to live in great style. He also managed to impoverish the Papal States. Victor Amadeus II of Savoy won recognition of his royal title, assumed despite papal disapproval in 1713, and an extremely favourable concordat with the Vatican giving him control over the Church. The Emperor Charles VI was similarly granted a favourable bull concerning relations between Church and State in the Kingdom of Sicily. Both these agreements were to the detriment of the Church; both were achieved by passing substantial sums of money to Coscia and his henchmen.

In the summer of 1729 Benedict, who was approaching seventy, began to ail. Much agitated at the thought of losing his patron, Coscia started to move his ill-gotten wealth back to Benevento. When the Pope eventually died the following February, all Beneventans were promptly banned from the papal palace, and such was the hostility expressed by a mob in the piazza in front of St Peter's that Coscia had to be smuggled out to the house of a friend on a stretcher. That house, too, was attacked, and he had to be smuggled out of Rome itself. When the conclave to elect a successor to Benedict XIII opened on 5 March, Coscia was not present but nonetheless claimed the right to be there, insisting that without his vote the election would be invalid. The cardinals relented, and he was allowed back into Rome and entered the conclave on 4 April: it lasted until 12 July, electing a seventy-nine-year-old with the title of Clement XII. In the meantime, however, the cardinals had sent an emissary to Benevento to investigate the complaints which they had received about Coscia's behaviour. The report arrived just before Coscia entered the conclave. It was not quite as clear-cut as had been expected: the charges proved difficult to substantiate. However, the cardinals persuaded Coscia that it would be better if he surrendered the governorship of Avignon which the late pontiff had bestowed on him, and this he agreed to do.

Immediately after Clement's election the new Pope set up a number of Congregations to investigate and put right some of the abuses which had been rife in the Papal States while they were being administered by Coscia. One of them, the Congregation 'de Nonnullis' ('about not a few things'), was directed against the Beneventans who had so dominated the previous pontificate, chief among them being Coscia himself. He tried to appeal to the Emperor for assistance, requesting permission to leave Rome with the intention of taking refuge in the Kingdom of Sicily. He was allowed only to move to a locality in the Papal States, but not beyond its borders. The Congregation then stripped him of the archdiocese of Benevento, which had become his by right of succession on the death of Benedict. The news was greeted by everyone in that city with considerable delight, and the authorities sealed up his residence and other property in the region. He now took fright, fearing he was going to be arrested, and fled Rome, without papal permission, for the Kingdom of Sicily. Clement reacted immediately. Coscia, he said, by leaving Rome without his approval, had incurred excommunication and the sequestration of his possessions. He was told to come back to the city. He prevaricated, claiming, with the backing of sundry doctors, that he needed his native air for the good of his health. But eventually he returned, taking up residence in the convent of Santa Prassede.

There was a whole string of charges against him, basically of fraud and general evil-doing, but also of disobeying the orders of the Pope. He was sentenced on 9 May 1733 to ten years of strict imprisonment – he was allowed the use of three rooms – in Castel Sant'Angelo, a heavy fine of 100,000 ducats, an order to repay a further 39,000 scudi fraudulently obtained, suspension from his offices, of the right to active and passive vote in any conclave – though he was not stripped of the cardinalate itself. After an attempt to get Charles VI to plead for him, Coscia finally expressed his contrition, as a result of which the excommunication was lifted, and the right to vote in a conclave was restored. He was also allowed out of Castel Sant'Angelo to visit spas for the good of his health.

After the death of Pope Clement, Coscia was one of the electors in the conclave which chose Pope Benedict XIV, from 18 February to 17 August 1740, the longest of modern times. In January 1742 the new Pope decided to remove all disabilities from Coscia, though he was not to become Archbishop of Benevento and was required, before his status was restored, to write a letter of resignation from his see. With Benedict's permission he was allowed to leave Rome for Naples, where he lived the remainder of his life in almost complete retirement, emerging only once to attend the royal court for celebrations to mark the birth of a prince. He died, still in Naples, on 8 February 1755 and was buried in the Jesuit church in that city.

Louis Billot

In the twentieth century only one cardinal has resigned his rank. Louis Billot went from being the mainstay of the papacy to being out of step with Vatican policy, and ended his days, as wayward members of religious orders are wont to, back in the obscurity of the noviceship.

He was born in Sierck-les-Bains, in the diocese of Metz, then part of France, on 12 January 1846. A pious youth, he studied for the priesthood at the seminary in Blois, and was ordained in Blois on 22 May 1869. He then decided to join the Society of Jesus, entering the noviceship at Angers soon after his ordination. He was sent to do pastoral work in Paris and in Laval, in January 1883, he took his final vows as a Jesuit. His brilliance as a theologian had already been recognized. By the time he took his final vows he had been teaching dogmatic theology in the Catholic University of Angers, and he was then sent to teach Jesuit students then in exile in Jersey. In 1885, however, he was called to Rome to teach theology at the Jesuit flagship university, the Gregorian.

It was a critical time for the teaching of theology in the Catholic Church. Cardinal Gioacchino Pecci had been elected as Pope Leo XIII in February 1878. Eighteen months later, on 4 August 1879, he had issued his encyclical, *Aeterni Patris*, commending the study of St Thomas Aquinas, and insisting on the importance of the study of philosophy as a preparation to the study of theology. As someone who was an expert in speculative (i.e. arising from philosophical reflection) theology grounded in the writings of Thomas Aquinas, Father Billot was exactly the man who was needed to forward Leo's campaign to reinstate Thomas. Leo not only reorganized the Academy of St Thomas, of which Billot was a leading member, but commissioned a definitive edition of Thomas's works, the Leonine Edition, which is still being published, and promoted a journal, *Divus Thomas*, dedicated to interpreting Thomism. Billot had something of a battle before him. There were several competing schools of theology in Rome. The Franciscans were promoting their own scholars Duns Scotus and St Bonaventure, while the common theological approach in Jesuit houses of study such as the Gregorian was based upon Thomas, but Thomas as understood by their own sixteenth-century theologian Francisco Suarez.

From 1892 through to 1912 Billot produced a whole range of books tackling, from the perspective of his speculative Thomism, every one of the major themes in theology, on Christ, on sin, on the Trinity, on the Church, on grace. They were, as was the custom of the day, all written in Latin, and only one was ever translated into English: *Liberalism: A Criticism of its Basic Principles and Diverse Forms*, which appeared in 1922. The title gives a clue to Billot's stance both theologically and, as will be seen, politically. Towards the end of the nineteenth century there developed an approach, at first especially to biblical studies, based on historical criticism. Billot took little or no account of historical studies, neither did he make much use of the Bible or of the Fathers of the Church in his own research: 'dogmas have no history', he declared. He was allied with Pope Leo's successor, Pius X, in his opposition to the movement which encapsulated the historical approach (though it was not limited to that) known as Modernism. He collaborated with Pope Pius on the preparation of his 1907 encyclical, *Pascendi Dominici Gregis*, which condemned Modernism, and the decree *Lamentabile* of the Holy Office, published the same year, which spelled out the propositions being condemned: it is often said that *Lamentabile* itself created Modernism as a heresy. He became a Consultor of the Holy Office in 1909. In November 1911 he was created cardinal deacon with the title of Santa Maria in Via Lata.

Pope Benedict XV was elected to succeed Pius X in September 1914. Though Benedict did not repudiate his predecessor's anti-Modernism, he put an end to the virulent campaign against those judged to be tainted with Modernism.

Meanwhile Billot had allied himself with the traditionalist movement, *Action Française*. This had been founded at the end of the nineteenth century. It had begun as a campaign to restore the French monarchy – a campaign with which many French Catholics sympathized – but after the 1905 law separating Church and State in France it also stood for the restoration of Catholicism as an integral part of the French State. Its chief ideologue was Charles Maurras (1868–1952), a professed agnostic (though he returned to Catholicism shortly before his death) who regarded the Church as an essential element in the social cohesion of the nation. Pope Benedict's successor, Pius XI, regarded Maurras's ideology as unacceptable, and in 1926 banned Catholics from membership of *Action Française*. He also put Maurras's writings on the *Index*. Billot, who had already criticized the Jesuit periodical *Action Populaire* for leaning too far, as he saw it, towards socialism, was committed to *Action Française*, and the condemnation came as a bitter blow. In September 1927 he wrote a letter to the Pope resigning from the College of Cardinals: Pius XI read it out in the consistory of December that year.

Louis Billot retired to the noviceship house of the Jesuit Roman province, then near Arriccia, and he died there on 18 December 1931.

Family Men

It has been one of the recurring themes of this book that most cardinals were 'family men'. They often achieved their rank in the Church because of family connections, whether to other cardinals or to the Pope of the day. Once ensconced in their position they commonly used their status to acquire wealth both for themselves and for their relatives. There were of course some exceptions. Jacopo Sadoleto, for example (see p. 78), was not a wealthy man and indeed seemed relatively unconcerned about his own lack of fortune so long as he had his books, but nonetheless he felt obliged to support numerous relatives who were a drain upon his resources. Certainly until the reforms introduced by the Council of Trent (which met spasmodically from 1545 to 1563) and for some time afterwards, the rank of cardinal was a sure way of amassing wealth through the accumulation of benefices. It was no wonder that the noble families of Italy were eager see their second sons, who would inherit neither the title nor the estates, be raised to the purple.

The two men whose lives are outlined below, however, were rather different. Both, as it happens, were English – at least, Henry Stuart was English by heritage – and both were already relatively wealthy before their elevation to the Sacred College, which was, in both cases, something of a surprise. In their respective biographies both men come across as rather attractive characters, and both men were deeply devoted to their families. While it is not impossible that someone with a substantial close family will ever again become a cardinal as did Thomas Weld, it is extremely unlikely. It is even more unlikely that the Sacred College will ever again have a would-be crowned head, such as Henry Stuart, among its members. As something of an afterword to this book, both deserve a mention.

Henry Stuart, Cardinal Duke of York

In 1719 Pope Clement XI, at the papacy's expense, took out a lease on the Palazzo Muti at the end of the Piazza of the Holy Apostles. Not greatly distinguished architecturally, it had been built for the Muti family in 1644, but later became the residence of the Balestra family. The Balestras left their name inscribed above the door, with the result that the building is more commonly known as the Palazzo Balestra. The Pope needed the Palazzo as a residence for James Stuart, the Old Pretender, and his wife of a few weeks Maria Clementina Sobieska. James was the son of James II of England, and claimant to the English throne. Since James II's overthrow the family had been living in France, but had become an embarrassment to the French monarch, especially after the abortive Stuart uprising of 1715. It was the Pope who took in James, gave him sanctuary in Rome, and a pension. It was in the Palazzo Muti that the would-be King's two sons were born, Charles Edward Stuart, the Young Pretender, better known as Bonnie Prince Charlie, on 31 December 1720, and Henry Stuart, on 6 March 1725. Clementina, the granddaughter of John III Sobieski, the Polish saviour of Vienna from the Turks, died a decade later. In her last years she had become extremely devout, with a future saint, the Franciscan Leonard of Port Maurice, as her spiritual guide. Her funeral was attended by almost three dozen cardinals, and she was buried in the habit of a Dominican.

Perhaps some of her religiosity conveyed itself to her younger son. Henry, who had been baptized by Pope Benedict XIII and had Benedict as his second name (followed by Thomas Edward Maria Clement Francis Xavier), was a lively child, rather more popular, and said to be far better-looking, than his elder brother. In his teenage years, however, he became somewhat withdrawn and pious. Despite that, the two brothers were very close, and when Charles set off for Scotland in an attempt to rally the Scots to the Stuart cause, Henry was eager to follow. He reached the Channel coast, nominally in command of a French fleet, but when the news of the devastating defeat of the 1745 uprising at Culloden reached him, he turned back to Paris, where he was given a residence by the French King. Still wanting to prove his military prowess, in 1746 he joined the French army besieging Antwerp, and acquitted himself well.

Charles also returned to Paris. He never recovered from the humiliation of the defeat in Scotland, and took to womanizing and to drink. He became an embarrassment in the French court and an embarrassment to his brother, whom he seems to have blamed for not having supported him. Relations between the two deteriorated. Henry appeared to be making an effort at reconciliation when he invited the Young Pretender to dinner. Charles arrived, and was greeted by Henry's servants in the manner befitting his rank as a Prince. The dinner was prepared – but Henry was not there. He had gone to Rome, where he was named a cardinal by Pope Benedict XIV, on 3 June 1747, receiving the tonsure in the Sistine Chapel, the first symbol of his new clerical status, from the hands of the Pope himself. Charles was furious, and was estranged from Henry for nearly two decades. He believed that his family's association with the Catholic Church, made even more evident by the cardinal's hat, was a major hindrance in the way of him ever succeeding to the throne of England. A clandestine visit to London in 1750 convinced him of the fact, and much to the distress of his family he became a member of the Church of England.

It is perhaps a puzzle why Henry took such a step. He had the backing of his father at least to the extent of the cardinalate. He was the younger son, and a clerical career was deemed appropriate for younger sons. It was also likely to make him wealthy – which indeed it did, much wealthier than his father, who eventually came to resent the fact. While his new rank made it unlikely that he would ever succeed to the title his father claimed, it seemed very likely that Charles would marry (which he did) and have legitimate heirs (he had a son who died in infancy). But there was always the possibility that Charles would die without issue. In that case Henry would become the Stuart claimant to the throne of England. It was not impossible to resign the rank of cardinal and, provided no priestly ordination had taken place, then marry. Perhaps that was what James Stuart had in mind for his son.

But Henry, ever pious, was ready to commit himself to the clerical state. He was appointed Cardinal Deacon of Santa Maria in Campitelli while still a layman, but a year later, on 1 September 1748, he was ordained priest without, apparently, having had any education in theology. He became archpriest of the Vatican basilica, and in April 1758 Camerlengo of the College of Cardinals, a role which gave him charge of the conclave later that year which elected Pope Clement XIII. He had not voted for the pro-Jesuit Clement, but the new Pope bore him no ill-will. Shortly afterwards, on 19 November 1758, he was consecrated bishop, with the title of Archbishop of Corinth, by the Pope himself in the basilica of the Twelve Apostles, just across the road from the Palazzo Muti where he had continued to live with his father despite being by now the most wealthy member of the College of Cardinals.

In 1761 he was appointed Bishop of Frascati, just south of Rome. He was enthroned in the cathedral there on 13 July. He had never hitherto held any pastoral role, but he entered into the role of a bishop with remarkable vigour – he was still only 36 when appointed – and success. He used his wealth to build orphanages and schools, and to distribute medicine and alms to the poor of his city. When the Jesuits were suppressed he was able to take over their seminary at Frascati, and turn it into a beacon of learning, donating his own collection of books to its library, thereby making it one of the best in Italy and an attraction for scholars. Among its first pupils was the future Cardinal Ercole Consalvi (see p. 179), who not only benefited from the education he received but became a good friend of Henry Stuart, perhaps drawn to him by their common love for music. Henry Stuart was not himself a particularly learned man, but he valued scholarship and the arts.

Above all, perhaps, he loved pomp. His father had appointed him the

Stuart Duke of York, and he was known throughout his life as the Cardinal of York. He insisted on retaining his title as Royal Highness, which was added to the cardinatial title of Eminence – and woe betide anyone who forgot it. He was much attached to his family, nursing his father at the Palazzo Muti through his last days. After James's death on 1 January 1766, Henry began to lobby hard for the recognition of his brother Charles as the rightful King of England. Successive popes had accorded James III royal honours, but Clement XIII was not prepared to extend recognition to Charles III, though he called a consistory of cardinals to discuss the issue. With the papacy at odds with the Catholic Bourbon powers over the future of the Jesuits, Clement was not about to alienate Protestant England. Nonetheless Charles came to Rome, where he was reconciled with Henry, and where, against the Pope's wishes, the rectors of the English and Scots Colleges acknowledged him as King. They were promptly removed from their posts and so were any of the clergy who did likewise. Even Henry was rebuked when he sat Charles beside him in his carriage, giving him precedence as if he were a crowned head. Clement was driven to issue an instruction that Charles was not to be given royal status, and even though Clement eventually agreed to receive Charles, he did not receive him as a monarch.

In 1772 Charles married Louisa, Princess of Stolberg-Gedern, and two years later the couple moved from Rome to Florence, where they used the names of the Count and Countess of Albany. The marriage, however, did not last. Louisa, a feisty young woman, would not put up, she said, with his drunken behaviour and brutality towards her. She abandoned Charles for a convent in Florence, and then for one in Rome. Henry, who was at first outraged by Louisa's conduct, was won over by her charm and readily believed her stories of Charles's brutality. He allowed her to settle in his grand apartment in the Cancelleria, the palazzo he occupied as Vice-Chancellor of the Roman Church, a post to which he had been appointed in 1763. Louisa, however, had been followed to Rome by the romantic poet Count Vittorio Alfieri who was her lover and the real reason she had left Charles, and the cardinatial apartment proved a suitable place for their encounters.

Although all Rome knew of the relationship, Henry only discovered it from his brother when he journeyed to Florence in the mistaken belief that Charles was dying. He now turned his anger against Louisa, threw her out of the apartment in the Cancelleria, and Alfieri out of Rome. When Charles and Louisa were formally separated Charlotte, Charles's daughter by an earlier liaison, moved into Charles's residence in Florence. Her father bestowed on her the title of Duchess of Albany – Henry protested when he tried to claim for her the title of Royal Highness – and she was declared legitimate. The pair moved back to Rome at the end of 1785. The Palazzo Muti was prepared to receive them and Henry rode out to Viterbo to greet them. Charles did not long survive. He died on 31 January 1788, and was buried by his grieving brother in Frascati: Charlotte died just under two years later.

Except for Louisa, who kept popping up but generally at a distance, the cardinal was now free of all family encumbrances. In his own eyes, moreover, he was now King Henry IX, though was astute enough not to attempt to insist upon 'His Majesty the Cardinal' as a form of address. But he no longer thought of himself as Duke of York. He insisted that when people addressed him they should use the form 'the Cardinal known as Duke of York'. He was quite put out when, in 1792, Pope Pius VI formally recognized George III as King of England. Despite this apparent pomposity he remained immensely affable, especially to English people on the Grand Tour. Such encounters might have had their difficulties because it is not clear whether he spoke English well, although he certainly wrote it elegantly. He was visited almost as if he were one of the historic sites of Rome – and in a way he was indeed a relic. One of those who came to know and like the cardinal was Sir John Hippersley, whose appointment as an unofficial English representative to the Papal States was the occasion for the recognition of King George. The cardinal did not bear him a grudge which, as matters turned out, was all to the good.

As a monarch, at least in his own eyes, Henry was shaken by the French Revolution and the execution of Louis XVI, and celebrated a solemn requiem for King Louis at Frascati. His income was dramatically reduced when his French benefices were sequestered, and he could no longer trust to payments from his Spanish benefices. When the French ravaged Italy and demanded tribute from the Pope, Henry loyally surrendered his wealth. When the Roman Republic was proclaimed, and Pius VI taken off to France, he fled to the Kingdom of Naples where, through a chance meeting with an English diplomat, he learned of Nelson's victory over Napoleon at the battle of the Nile. He asked that his delight at the outcome be communicated to King George.

When he had to leave Naples he made his way to Messina, where he shared lodgings with three other refugee cardinals. It had been agreed that, in the inevitable event of the Pope's death, the conclave to elect a successor would be held in Venice, and the four members of the College of Cardinals made their way there. It was in Venice, in the middle of the conclave, that he learned that through the good offices of Sir John Hippersley, abetted by the very favourable impression which his old friend Ercole Consalvi had made at the English court, King George III had awarded him an annual pension of £4,000.

As soon as it was feasible the new Pope and his cardinals returned to Rome. After calling in at the Cancelleria, Henry hurried on to Frascati, where he was greeted with great enthusiasm. Fortified by his handsome English pension – and other income, which began once again to build up – he set about restoring the Cancelleria and La Rocca, his palace at Frascati, to something like their former splendour. In 1802 Pius VII, accompanied by the King of Sardinia, who was just about to resign his throne to become a priest, came out to Frascati to pay a visit to the aged cardinal. Henry met the pair outside Frascati, and was invited by Pius to ride back to the city sitting next to him in the papal coach, a singular honour.

Much as he loved titles and pomp there was one honour which he did not particularly appreciate. In 1803 Cardinal Albani died, making Henry the longest serving member of the College of Cardinals, and therefore its dean. But with the rank of dean went the bishopric of Ostia-Velletri. He succeeded to the bishopric, which he visited for a few days in November 1803, but begged to be allowed to remain in Frascati. Which is where he died, on 13 July 1807. His funeral was held in Rome, in the church of San Andrea della Valle. There was no sign of his royal status except for the arms of England propped up against the catafalque. He was buried in the same tomb in St Peter's as his father, the Old Pretender. The Young Pretender's body was later brought from Frascati and laid to rest beside his father and brother. Pope Pius VII in 1819 commissioned a monument to the three of them from Antonio Canova, which still stands over the spot where they are buried. The Prince Regent, the future King George IV, contributed £50 to the cost.

Thomas Weld

It is commonly said of Thomas Weld that he was – albeit briefly – educated by the English Jesuits at their college-in-exile at Liège. That cannot be true because, a few months after his birth in London on 22 January 1773, the Jesuits ceased to exist: the order was suppressed, under pressure from the Bourbon courts, by Pope Clement XIV. It is rather a pedantic point because the former Jesuit community continued their communal existence at Liège until, in 1794, the wars of the French Revolution drove them back to England. Then they travelled with their pupils to northern Lancashire, where they settled at Stoneyhurst, a house given them by Thomas's father, who had acquired it through marriage. It was surplus to his requirements. So if Thomas was ever at Liège, and it is not certain, then he was taught by former Jesuits who, by the papal decree, had become ordinary diocesan clergy – though they did not have a diocese.

It is also commonly said that he came of noble birth, which again is not quite true. The family, of Lulworth Castle in Dorset, was an ancient one, and owned the greater part of their county. And despite being stubbornly Catholic, it was on good terms with the Protestant monarch: King George III came to visit four times, and gave permission for a Catholic chapel to be built at Lulworth. (One Jesuit of the former English province, John Carroll, was consecrated bishop in the chapel in August 1790 and then crossed the Atlantic to become the bishop of Baltimore and the first native-born bishop in the United States.) But for all that the family was not noble. It was a particularly wealthy part of the English gentry, or squirearchy.

Before going, if he ever did so, to Liège, Thomas was educated at home by Charles Plowden, a leading member of the former Jesuits, who was eventually to become provincial when the province was restored, and rector of Stoneyhurst. The world of these Old Catholic families was a small one. On 14 June 1796 Thomas married Lucy Clifford, and their daughter, also named Lucy, married the seventh Lord Clifford. But on 1 June 1815 Thomas's wife died, and in 1818 he decided to become a priest. He settled the estate on his younger brother – it turned out to be a complicated process and the arrangement was not sorted out for a decade – and went over to Paris for his theological education, studying under the learned and holy Abbé Carron. Carron had spent many years in England, a refugee from the French Revolution: he had established a parish in London which still survives. The Welds had been close to the French émigré clergy, and also to the nuns who fled the persecution across the Channel, providing them with support and accommodation though not, it has to be said, without incurring from time to time considerable problems.

Thomas was ordained priest on 7 April 1821 and was sent as an assistant priest to Chelsea, to St Mary's, Cadogan Street, and subsequently became chaplain to a convent of Benedictine nuns in Hammersmith. In 1826 he was appointed assistant bishop to the Bishop of Kingston in Upper Canada, and was consecrated at St Edmund's, Ware, on 6 August. But he never went. There were a number of difficulties. The matter of his estate had not yet been finally settled. A more pressing concern, however, was the health of his daughter Lucy, and it was for the health of Lucy that, in the winter of 1829–30, shortly after the passing of the Catholic Emancipation Act (13 April) which removed most of the remaining hindrances to Catholics joining fully in the political life of the nation, he went off to Rome. He had not been long in Rome when Pope Pius VIII announced that he was going to create him a cardinal – at which point he resigned from the post in Canada he had never been able to take up. He was created cardinal priest in the consistory of 15 March 1830, and was later given the title of S. Marcello al Corso. The appointment may well have been a gesture of thanks to the British government, reflecting the Vatican's pleasure at the removal of the last of the penal laws against Catholics.

Cardinal Weld lived in some style in Rome, where he spent the rest of his life. He rented an apartment in the Palazzo Odescalchi opposite the basilica of the Twelve Apostles, and therefore very close to the palazzo in which Henry

Stuart had spent his childhood. His daughter and her husband and their six children lived with him, though Lucy died in May 1831. He took an active part in the affairs of the Vatican, but failed to learn adequate Italian, which must have limited his usefulness. He was thought by Vatican officials to be competent in the ecclesiastical affairs of England and America, but in reality knew very little about either. He became protector of the English College in Rome, but not without controversy. Until the suppression of the Society of Jesus the College had been run by Jesuits, but was now under the control of the secular clergy. There were opponents of the Society in England who feared that Weld, known to be close to the Jesuits, who had been brought back into being by Pope Pius VII, might contrive their return.

His apartments in the Palazzo Odescalchi were the centre of English life in Rome, and visitors to the city from England were always welcome. He became one of the more curious sights of Rome, driving about the city in his cardinatial carriage accompanied by his grandchildren. He died unexpectedly, though with his grandchildren around his bedside, on 19 April 1837. Having been married as well as ordained he had been known as 'the cardinal of seven sacraments', though the last of the seven was administered only as he lay dying. He was buried next to his daughter and son-in-law in his titular church. Of his grandchildren one became a nun, two became priests – one of them later a bishop in England. Another grandchild won the Victoria Cross during the Crimean War.

Bibliography

Allen, John L., *Conclave* (New York: Doubleday, 2002).

Andrieu, Michel, 'L'origine du titre de cardinal dans l'église romaine', in *Miscellanea Giovanni Mercati* V (Città de Vaticano, 1946), pp. 113–41.

Aubert, Roger, *et al.*, *The Church in a Secularised Society* (London: Darton, Longman and Todd, 1978).

Ballerini, Luigi (ed.), *The Art of Cooking ... by Maestro Martino* (Berkeley CA: University of California Press, 2004).

Baumgartner, Frederic J., *Behind Closed Doors* (New York: Palgrave Macmillan, 2003).

Bellenger, Dominic Aidan and Fletcher, Stella, *Princes of the Church* (Stroud: Sutton Publishing, 2001).

Biographisch-Bibliographisches Kirchenlexikon (consulted online at www.bautz. de).

Buehrle, Marie Cecilia, *Rafael Cardinal Merry del Val* (London: Sands, 1957).

Burkle-Young, Francis A., *Papal Elections in the Age of Transition, 1878–1922* (Lanham MD: Lexington Books, 2000).

Burke, Peter, *The Historical Anthropology of Early Modern Italy* (Cambridge: Cambridge University Press, 1987).

Burkle-Young, Francis A., *Passing the Keys*, 2nd edition (Lanham MD: Madison Books, 2001).

Burkle-Young, Francis A. and Doerrer, Michael Leopoldo, *The Life of Cardinal Innocenzo del Monte* (Lewiston MD: The Edwin Mellen Press, 1997).

Chadwick, Owen, *A History of the Popes 1830–1914* (Oxford: Oxford University Press, 1998).

Chadwick, Owen, *The Popes and European Revolution* (Oxford: Clarendon Press, 1981).

Chambers, D. S., *A Renaissance Cardinal and his Worldly Goods* (London: Warburg Institute, 1992).

Chambers, D. S., *Renaissance Cardinals and their Worldly Problems* (Aldershot: Variorum, 1997).

Chambers, D. S., *Popes, Cardinals and War* (London: I. B. Tauris, 2006).

Coppa, Frank J., *Cardinal Giacomo Antonelli* (Albany NT: State University of New York Press, 1990).

Courtney, F., *Cardinal Robert Pullen: An English Theologian of the Twelfth Century* (Rome: Gregorian University, 1954).

D'Amico, John F., *Renaissance Humanism in Papal Rome* (Baltimore MD: The Johns Hopkins University Press, 1983).

Davis, Raymond, *The Book of Pontiffs* (Liverpool: Liverpool University Press, 2000).

Davis, Raymond, *The Lives of the Eighth-Century Popes (Liber Pontificalis)*, 2nd edition (Liverpool: Liverpool University Press, 2007).

Dahm, Charles, *Power and Authority in the Catholic Church* (Notre Dame IN: University of Notre Dame Press, 1981).

Dick, J., *The Malines Conversations Revisited* (Louvain: Leuven University Press, 1989).

Dizionario bigrafico degli Italiani (Rome: Istituto della Enciclopedia Italiana, 1960–).

Douglas, Richard M., *Jacopo Sadoleto, 1477–1547: Humanist and Reformer* (Cambridge MA: Harvard University Press, 1959).

Dupré, Louis and Saliers, Don E. (eds), *Christian Spirituality Post-Reformation and Modern* (London: SCM Press, 1990).

Fitzgerald, Billy, *Father Tom* (London: Fount, 1990).

Fogarty, Gerald P., *The Vatican and the American Hierarchy from 1870 to 1965* (Stuttgart: Anton Hiersemann, 1982).

Fothergill, Brian, *The Cardinal King* (London: Faber and Faber, 1968).

Hallman, B. C., *Italian Cardinals, Reform, and the Church as Property* (Los Angeles: Center for Medieval and Renaissance Studies, 1985).

Harcourt-Smith, Simon, *Cardinal of Spain: The Life and Strange Career of Alberoni* (New York: Alfred A. Knopf, 1944).

Harvey, Margaret, *The English in Rome 1362–1420* (Cambridge: Cambridge University Press, 1999).

Hollingsworth, Mary, *The Cardinal's Hat* (London: Profile Books, 2004).

Izbicki, Thomas M., *Protector of the Faith: Cardinal Johannes de Turrecremata* (Washington DC: Catholic University of America Press, 1981).

Kelly, J. N. D. and Walsh, Michael J., *Oxford Dictionary of Popes*, 2nd edition (Oxford: Oxford University Press, 2010).

Kidwell, Carol: *Pietro Bembo: Lover, Linguist, Cardinal* (Montreal: McGill-Queen's University Press, 2004).

Kittler, Glenn D., *Papal Princes* (New York: Dell Publishing, 1961).

Kuttner, Stephan, 'Cardinalis: The history of a canonical concept', *Traditio* 3 (1945), pp. 129–214.

Lampe, Peter, *From Paul to Valentinus* (Minneapolis: Fortress Press, 2003).

Larson, Roy, 'In the 1980's, a Chicago Newspaper Investigated Cardinal Cody' (Nieman Reports, accessed 8 December 2009: www.nieman.harvard.edu/reportsitem.aspx?id=101190).

Lee, Andrew, *The Most Ungrateful Englishman: The Life and Times of Adam Easton* (Gloucester: Corpus Publishing, 2006).

Levi, Anthony, *Cardinal Richelieu and the Making of France* (New York: Carroll and Graf, 2000).

Levillain, Philippe (ed.), *The Papacy: An Encyclopedia* (New York: Routledge, 1994).

Luxmore, Jonathan and Babiuch, Jolanta, *The Vatican and the Red Flag* (London: Geoffrey Chapman, 1999).

Majanlahti, Anthony, *The Families who Made Rome* (London: Chatto and Windus, 2005).

Mallet, Michael, *The Borgias* (London: The Bodley Head, 1969).

Masson, Georgina and Jepson, Tim, *The Companion Guide to Rome* (Woodbridge: Companion Guides, 1998).

Mayer, Thomas F., *Reginald Pole, Prince and Prophet* (Cambridge: Cambridge University Press, 2000).

Mayeur, Jean-Marie *et al.* (eds.), *Histoire du Christianisme* (Paris: Desclée, 1993–).

Misner, Paul, *Social Catholicism in Europe* (London: Darton, Longman and Todd, 1991).

Morris, Colin, *The Papal Monarchy* (Oxford: Clarendon Press, 1989).

O'Carroll, Ciarán, *Paul Cardinal Cullen* (Dublin: Veritas, 2008).

Oxford Dictionary of National Biography (consulted online at www.oxforddnb.com).

Paravicino-Bagliani, A., *The Pope's Body* (Chicago: University of Chicago Press, 2000).

Paravicino-Bagliani, A., *Cardinali di Curia e 'Familiae' Cardinalizie* (Padua: Antenore, 1972).

Partner, Peter, *The Lands of St Peter* (London: Eyre Methuen, 1972).

Pasztor, Lajos, *La Segreteria di Stato e il suo archivio, 1814–1833* (Stuttgart: A. Hiersemann, 1984–85).

Pollard, John F., *Money and the Rise of the Modern Papacy* (Cambridge: Cambridge University Press, 2005).

Richardson, Carol M., *Reclaiming Rome* (Leyden: Brill, 2009).

Robinson, John Martin, *Cardinal Consalvi, 1757–1824* (London: The Bodley Head, 1987).

Rowland, Ingrid D., *The Culture of the High Renaissance* (Cambridge: Cambridge University Press, 1998).

Sanderson, Margaret H. B., *Cardinal of Scotland* (Edinburgh: John Donald, 1986).

Saunders, Frances Stonor, *Hawkswood: Diabolical Englishman* (London: Faber and Faber, 2004).

Schofield, Nicholas and Skinner, Gerard, *The English Cardinals* (Oxford: Family Publications, 2007).

Schultenover, David, *A View from Rome* (New York: Fordham University Press, 1993).

Sobel, Dava, *Galileo's Daughter* (London: Fourth Estate, 1999).

Spalding, Thomas W., *The Premier See: a History of the Archdiocese of Baltimore, 1789–1989* (Baltimore MD: The Johns Hopkins University Press, 1989).

Stehle, Hansjakob, *Eastern Politics of the Vatican 1917–1979* (Athens OH: Ohio University Press, 1981).

Stinger, Charles L., *The Renaissance in Rome* (Bloomington IN: Indiana University Press, 1998).

Strathern, Paul, *The Medici: Godfathers of the Renaissance* (London: Jonathan Cape, 2003).

Tanner, Norman P. (ed.), *Decrees of the Ecumenical Councils* (London: Sheed and Ward; Washington DC: Georgetown University Press, 1990).

Treasure, Geoffrey, *Richelieu and Mazarin* (London: Routledge, 1998)

Vanysacker, D., *Cardinal Giuseppe Garampi (1725–1792): An Enlightened Ultramontane* (Brussels: Institut Historique Belge de Rome, 1995).

Walsh, Michael J., *The Conclave: A Sometimes Secret and Occasionally Bloody History* (London: Canterbury Press, 2003).

Wilkie, William E., *The Cardinal Protectors of England* (Cambridge: Cambridge University Press, 1974).

Willie, David, *God's Politician* (London: Faber and Faber, 1992).

Wood, Diana, *Clement VI* (Cambridge: Cambridge University Press, 1989).

Zizola, Giancarlo, *Il Conclave: Storia e Segreti* (Rome: Newton Compton, 1993).

Index

Note: Rome itself has not been indexed: it occurs *passim*. Some locations in Rome, however, especially churches and palaces, have been included.